The Principal's Guide to
Time Management

The Principal's Guide to Time Management

Instructional Leadership in the Digital Age

Richard D. Sorenson

Lloyd M. Goldsmith

David E. DeMatthews

CORWIN
A SAGE Publishing Company

FOR INFORMATION:

Corwin

A SAGE Company

2455 Teller Road

Thousand Oaks, California 91320

(800) 233-9936

www.corwin.com

SAGE Publications Ltd.

1 Oliver's Yard

55 City Road

London EC1Y 1SP

United Kingdom

SAGE Publications India Pvt. Ltd.

B 1/I 1 Mohan Cooperative Industrial Area

Mathura Road, New Delhi 110 044

India

SAGE Publications Asia-Pacific Pte. Ltd.

3 Church Street

#10-04 Samsung Hub

Singapore 049483

Executive Editor: Arnis Burvikovs

Senior Associate Editor: Desirée A. Bartlett

Senior Editorial Assistant: Andrew Olson

Production Editor: Melanie Birdsall

Copy Editor: Cate Huisman

Typesetter: C&M Digitals (P) Ltd.

Proofreader: Annie Lubinsky

Indexer: Wendy Allex

Cover Designer: Michael Dubowe

Marketing Manager: Anna Mesick

Library of Congress Cataloging-in-Publication Data

Names: Sorenson, Richard D., author. | Goldsmith, Lloyd Milton, author. | DeMatthews, David, author.

Title: The principal's guide to time management: instructional leadership in the digital age / Richard D. Sorenson, Lloyd M. Goldsmith, David E. DeMatthews.

Description: Thousand Oaks, California : Corwin, A SAGE Company, 2016. | Includes bibliographical references and index.

Identifiers: LCCN 2015042328 | ISBN 9781506323107 (pbk. : alk. paper)

Subjects: LCSH: Teachers—Time management. | School principals—Time management. | School administrators—Time management. | Educational leadership. | Educational technology.

Classification: LCC LB2838.8 .S67 2016 | DDC 371.102—dc23 LC record available at http://lccn.loc.gov/2015042328

This book is printed on acid-free paper.

16 17 18 19 20 10 9 8 7 6 5 4 3 2 1

Contents

List of Figures

Preface

A classic, high-powered muscle car came to a screeching halt at a country crossroad. The driver shouted to an old fellow sitting on the front porch of a run-down house: "Can you direct me to Falls City, sir? I'm lost and I don't have much time." "No I can't," the elderly man replied. "Then which road to Karnes City; can't you tell I'm losing precious time?" the driver asked. "Can't rightly say," answered the old timer. "You don't know much, do you?" asked the young man sarcastically. "No, I don't know much," replied the old man. "But I'm not the one who's lost and wasting valuable time!"

Sometimes it seems school principals are lost when it comes to finding time to properly administer the instructional program in ever-changing schools where technology is continuously advancing and the digital age seems to surpass everyone with each ticking second. Principals ask for directions but all too frequently find themselves bewildered, overwhelmed by the daunting task of playing catch-up, and out of time in a world where keeping all the plates spinning, lest they topple, leaves a campus leader with nothing more than an afterthought—"I guess I'd better pick up the shattered pieces."

You think to yourself, "Life as a school leader has to be more than picking up the shattered pieces." Then you reflect, "I don't have time, and even if I did, I don't know where I'm going!" If you find yourself lost as an instructional leader in this digital age, and you can't seem to manage the time you have, and you are unable to find the time you've either lost or wasted, then *The Principal's Guide to Time Management: Instructional Leadership in the Digital Age* can help. Consider the adage "You'll never leave where you are until you decide where you'd rather be!" Where would you rather be, where would you rather lead? How about starting from where you are, but with the right tools to best manage valuable but ever-escaping time? This book has been purposefully written to provide school principals with the right tools to manage time—tools such as instructional leadership expertise and technological skills essential in this digital age. Both are critical to effective and efficient time management.

Principal leadership has changed dramatically in recent decades. Reasons for changes in principal roles and responsibilities vary, but most are attributed to the accountability movement, requirements to improve instruction and increase student achievement, the extensive expertise demanded as a technological leader, and of course, the continued need to serve as the campus manager, maintaining facilities, managing student conduct, supervising personnel, administering budgets, and playing politics with district administration, policy makers, parents, business leaders, and community members.

Recall the vintage Oldsmobile commercial (check the YouTube site: www.youtube.com/watch?v=1TFRxwmMwg4) with former Beatle Ringo Starr saying to his daughter, Lee, "This is not your father's Oldsmobile"! Well, this is not your father's principalship. More than ever before, effective time management, enhanced instructional capacity, and increased digital proficiency dictate the principal's role.

When it comes to time and the act of managing time for self and the benefit of others, *The Principal's Guide to Time Management: Instructional Leadership in the Digital Age* prompts an epiphany: "Sometimes I have to forget the time lost, appreciate the time that remains, and look forward to making the best of the time that is coming." In reality, isn't that what every principal desires? Take this challenge: Use your time efficiently and read this book. Learn how to become a stronger instructional leader, a better technological expert, and an exceptional manager of increasingly valuable, but fleeting, time!

To enhance this book's usefulness as a desk resource, it has been purposely organized into topic-focused chapters. Each chapter begins with an appropriate quote and general overview, and includes numerous visuals, tables, and relevant segments such as *Pause and Reflect* scenarios, brief vignettes, the *Silent Time Thief* segments, *Ralph and Alice* cartoons, and chapter-concluding *Self-Reflection* activities as well as other relevant and timely examinations and discussions.

Chapter 1, "Time Management and Your Leadership," serves as an introduction to the text, reflecting on effectively and efficiently managing time through lenses incorporating the new Professional Standards for Education a Leaders. The standards fall into the six categories, or lenses, of Vision, Mission, and Time; Leading, Teaching, Learning, and Time; the Learning Organization and Time; Collaboration and Time; Ethics, Integrity, and Time; and the 21st Century Education System and Time. The chapter concludes with a case study application and a self-reflection on your time management, and it introduces our *Time Management Self-Assessment Instrument* (TMSI).

Chapter 2, "Vision, Mission, and Time," reviews the heart of student academic success and explores the connection and influence of time upon an organization's vision and mission. The first of the new Professional Standards for Educational Leaders and its accompanying elements provide the framework for examining vision and mission. Theory connects with practice as this chapter presents *A Voice From the Field* (a conversation with a school superintendent) along with sections covering the development and writing of SMART goals and how time management and campus planning go hand in hand. Vision and mission are examined from a digital-age perspective, as the chapter incorporates seven habits for tech-savvy leaders. This chapter includes an examination of personal time management tips and their use and effectiveness. It concludes with a case study application: *The Madge Simon School.*

Chapter 3, "Leading, Teaching, Learning, and Time," examines methods by which a principal can best manage time as the campus instructional leader. The chapter investigates principles of instructional capacity and how to maximize student learning by presenting research-based instructional designs, enhancements, and time-oriented interventions. The chapter concludes with a process for saving time when time counts, followed by a case study application, *Death by Meeting!*

Chapter 4, "The Learning Organization: Culture, Climate, Technology, Safety, and Time," showcases methods by which a principal can create a positive climate and an open, time-efficient culture. This chapter provides step-by-step, how-to time-saving examples. A means for creating effective and efficient campus operations and management is revealed, and a section is devoted to school safety and technology and how each can save time and lives. The chapter concludes with a case study application, *As the Sun Sets Slowly in the West, or How to Develop a Learning Community.*

Chapter 5, "Collaboration and Time: Two Keys to Instructional Success," reflects upon a 21st century expectation of principals—collaboration with all stakeholders. Numerous collaborative and time management techniques are examined, and the chapter concludes with the case study application, *If All the Feedback Is So Positive . . . ?*

Chapter 6, "Ethics, Integrity, and Time," discloses the strong existing and interwoven relationships among ethics, integrity, moral character, and the 2015 Professional Standards for Educational Leaders, which create expectations that all principals must follow. The chapter begins with an examination of the Professional Standards for Educational Leaders using the Sorenson-Goldsmith Integrated Budget Model. Readers will recognize the essential connection between ethics, integrity, and time, on the one hand, and their campus budgeting process, on the other. Additionally, the chapter provides a school leader's thoughts on integrity, ethics, and time in another *A Voice From the Field* segment. Professional behavior, personal integrity, and appropriate ethical and moral conduct must be defining qualities of all principals. These leaders show respect, exhibit honesty, resist temptations, and provide service. Nothing less will do! The chapter includes a vignette, *The Concerned Parents Meeting,* and concludes with a case study application, *The Texting Coach.*

Chapter 7, "The 21st Century Education System: Improvement, Time, and Technology," explores the role of public education today with a serious emphasis on continuous school improvement, initiating systemwide change, and preparing exceptional lessons—a time-saving means of promoting mutual accountability. Time is showcased as it relates to instructional leadership and teaching and learning, including the need for principals to provide the right professional development at the right time. Additionally, time-saving technological applications are evoked throughout the chapter, which concludes with a case study application, *Has Our School eVolved?*

Chapter 8, "Technology: Staying a Step Ahead of the *Silent Time Thief*," investigates the process of adopting new technologies and the associated time requirements, and provides an examination of the critical implementation curve. Additionally, the chapter proposes recommendations school principals must consider regarding potential technological and digital adoptions. The reader is provided a crash course in time management relative to digital organization, which details five time management tips integrated with technology. The reader also gains essential information about working with digital tools that allow school principals to "save time and make hay!" Numerous screenshots of digital applications aid the reader in avoiding the *Silent Time Thief*. The chapter reveals how technology can improve instruction and leadership capacity and concludes with a case study application, *A New Leader, an Old Problem: How to Integrate Technology Into a School's Culture.*

Important elements of the book include

- The *Time Management Self-Assessment Instrument* (see Chapter 1),
- Discussion questions,
- Case study applications and questions,
- Technological and digital applications, and
- References.

Managing time can be a daunting task. A study by the Society for Human Resource Management (2009) revealed that 70% of Americans fail to effectively and efficiently manage time.

Principals are no different. Finding time, making time, and using time—all are issues that campus leaders can relate to. Time is a precious commodity. However, *The Principal's Guide to Time Management: Instructional Leadership in the Digital Age* proves time can be captured by principals and used most efficiently and effectively.

The authors of this text certainly understand the issue of time and are sensitive to its many constraints. The authors have "been there and done that," as they are former school administrators with a combined 93 years of experience in the public school and higher education arenas, and they have extensive practical experience managing time in service as instructional leaders in the digital age. This experience has enabled them to create a text that provides the necessary skills, relevant information, and functional tools needed to promote and incorporate time management, instructional leadership, and technological ideals into real school applications.

SPECIAL FEATURES OF THE BOOK

Three special features are interwoven throughout the book:

1. The Professional Standards for Educational Leaders (PSEL) 2015;
2. *The Silent Time Thief* series; and
3. The *Ralph and Alice* cartoon sequences.

The newly adopted PSEL 2015, previously the Interstate School Leaders Licensure Consortium (ISLLC) Standards, were approved and adopted by the National Policy Board for Education Administration on October 22, 2015, and the full standards and elements were published in November 2015. These ten standards and their accompanying 83 elements are possibly first introduced in book format in *The Principal's Guide to Time Management: Instructional Leadership in the Digital Age*. This is an important distinction, as these new standards are cutting-edge criteria and models for practicing educational leaders.

The standards are designed to ensure that district and campus leaders, as well as university principal preparation programs, are able to improve student achievement; meet new, higher expectations; and receive essential support. The new 2015 Professional Standards for Educational Leaders were developed to guide preparation, practice, support, and evaluation for school leaders.

While adopting the standards is voluntary, most states adopt them to fit their educational leadership needs. Additionally, these new standards and elements will replace or enhance state principal preparation program standards. For example, the state of Texas has formed a Preparation Standards Committee that will develop a set of standards, based on the national standards, to guide the preparation of building-level leaders. One of the coauthors of this book, Dr. David DeMatthews, serves as a core member of this committee.

The Silent Time Thief series has been purposefully incorporated into each chapter as a means of revealing how essential time is to all school administrators and how time can be "stolen" by multiple means and parties. This particular series provides the reader with methods of preventing the theft of time.

The *Ralph and Alice* cartoon sequences are designed to add a unique learning perspective to the chapters. Two cartoon characters, Ralph and Alice, present the reader with a different or unique spin on chapter-related material. Ralph and Alice, like most married couples or working colleagues, find moments of personal and collective reflection. In *The Principal's Guide to Time Management: Instructional Leadership in the Digital Age*, the reflections of these cartoon characters are frequently related to a school leadership issue or problem. Enjoy the camaraderie and humor displayed by our own Ralph and Alice!

Finally, as you take time to journey through *The Principal's Guide to Time Management: Instructional Leadership in the Digital Age*, think back to the opening paragraph of this preface. Then reflect upon these words of Frank A. Clark, American writer, cartoonist, and creator of *The Country Parson* newspaper vignettes: "If you find a path with no obstacles, it probably doesn't lead anywhere" (n.d.). Excellent words of wisdom. Know where you are going, and know how to get there in a timely fashion. *The Principal's Guide to Time Management: Instructional Leadership in the Digital Age* is the next best thing to a leadership GPS. Enjoy the trip!

A Note to the Reader

R ecognize that technology is an integral part of *The Principal's Guide to Time Management: Instructional Leadership in the Digital Age*. Schools, like society, cannot function without recognizing the importance of technology and adopting it for instructional uses. We do live in a digital age. As a result, principals must lead the technological and digital charge. To best meet this expectation, principals need a tool kit that contains specialized equipment for bringing the most up-to-date digital measures into their schools. The first item or instrument that a principal must grab from this tool kit is a list of questions to be considered before moving further into technological enhancements. Listed below are fifteen essential, if not critical, questions for examination and contemplation.

15 QUESTIONS PRINCIPALS MUST ASK ABOUT TECHNOLOGY

The authors of this text strongly believe in the use of technology in schools. Each chapter within this book exemplifies this. However, the authors never purposefully pursue technological utilization in schools and classrooms, nor do they advise others to do so, without addressing serious research, analysis, and "students-first" considerations. Further, while the authors believe it is imperative that technology be incorporated into all aspects of schooling, they strongly recommend that principals first ask fifteen important questions.

1. Does the school culture emphasize students first?

2. Does the culture of the school emphasize caring about students?

3. Do the principal and faculty acknowledge the problems that confront effective instruction in classrooms?

4. Does the existing school culture allow for new, technological methods (changes) to solve time-sensitive instructional problems?

5. Does the principal offer technological innovative solutions that motivate students to explore, love learning, and incrementally improve by examining mistakes made?

6. Are the digital delivery processes accessible, inexpensive, time saving, and easy to use?

7. Do the principal and team focus on high-quality technological content that is incorporated appropriately, efficiently, and effectively by experienced teachers who use the technology to promote deep-learning strategies and critical thinking?

Does the technology:

8. Save time, improve instruction, and increase student achievement?

9. Make it easier for faculty to focus on what they do best?

10. Motivate students to be proactive and complete their assignments?

11. Deliver customized content based on detailed individual feedback as related to the performance of each student?

12. Provide fun and/or interesting learning tools, games, and/or relevant experiences that engage and motivate students and manage instruction in a timely manner?

13. Extend beyond the textbooks, providing searchable, accessible, and more extensive content?

14. Allow for time-saving interactive user experiences that encourage students to think critically?

15. Generate and integrate time-saving instructional content prepared for and by teachers?

Comment: The authors have made every effort to provide accurate and up-to-date Internet, technological, and digital information throughout the text. However, technology, the Internet, and digitally posted information are continuously changing. Therefore, it is inevitable that certain websites and other technology-oriented sources, resources, and materials listed within this text will change or become obsolete.

Acknowledgments

First, I would like to acknowledge Daniel Correa, who served as a student worker in the Educational Leadership and Foundations Department at The University of Texas at El Paso. Daniel in many respects was my personal research assistant, not only as I wrote this book, but for so much more. His untiring diligence with respect to all tasks, his exceptional work ethic, and his digital expertise were always apparent. He always had a smile, and he never failed to lend a helping hand—which I frequently needed.

Whenever there was a technical glitch (and there always was), Daniel was there to move behind my desk, into my chair, to take over and get it right. For all you did for me, Daniel, I am most grateful and genuinely appreciative. I wish you Godspeed as you work to finish your degree and as you proceed into life and career. You are an exceptional young man and your research for this book proved invaluable. You're my superhero, Batman!

Second, I must acknowledge the expertise, competence, and assistance of Rita Monsivais, El Paso, Texas, school administrator. Rita has a keen understanding of technology-oriented educational programs, and she was instrumental in providing essential information and guidance regarding the case study, Has Our School eVolved? in Chapter 7. I have been privileged to serve as a professor to Rita in her master's degree and principal preparation and certification program, and as her doctoral program advisor. Rita exemplifies the traits and characteristics of those exceptional principals described within this text. She is a strong moral and ethical person and a tremendous asset to our profession! Most important, she is dedicated to the students she serves! Rita, you are the best!

Finally, in memoriam: Dr. Lalo Garza—good friend, Cohort IV member, and wonderful educator. Your life was cut too short. I miss you.

—RDS

I want to thank Mary, my patient wife and confidant, for having patience with me through this process. I want to thank Dr. Karen Maxwell and

Dr. Bruce Scott for their invaluable support and advice. I greatly appreciate them as professional colleagues, confidants, and friends.

I would also like to recognize Alex Carruth, a graphic artist and student at Abilene Christian University. Alex is responsible for the *Ralph and Alice* cartoon series in the book. He grew up in Brazil and enjoys illustrating and playing keyboard.

—LMG

I am appreciative to my family, friends, and colleagues for their unwavering support and love. In particular, I am thankful for my doctoral advisor, Dr. Hanne Mawhinney, and her love, dedication, support, encouragement, and mentoring. I remain grateful for the gifts she imparted to me as a scholar and person, and I hope to live up to her expectations and example.

—DED

PUBLISHER'S ACKNOWLEDGMENTS

Corwin gratefully acknowledges the contributions of the following reviewers:

John Carver
Superintendent
Howard-Winneshiek
    Community Schools
Cresco, IA

Chris Hubbuch
Principal
Excelsior Springs Middle School
Excelsior Springs, MO

Neil MacNeill
Head Master
Ellenbrook Independent
    Primary School
Ellenbrook, Western Australia

Alan Penrose
Assistant Principal, Adjunct
Professor of Education
North Kansas City School District,
    Rockhurst University
Kansas City, MO

Tricia Peña
Professor, Consultant
Northern Arizona University
Vail, AZ

Lena Marie Rockwood
Middle School Assistant Principal
Revere Public Schools
Revere, MA

Susan Soderlind
Coordinator, Student
    Information Services
Escambia County School District
Pensacola, FL

About the Authors

Richard D. Sorenson, professor emeritus, is the former department chairperson of the Educational Leadership and Foundations Department at The University of Texas at El Paso (UTEP). He also served as the director of the Principal Preparation Program. He earned his doctorate from Texas A&M University at Corpus Christi in educational leadership. Dr. Sorenson served public schools for 25 years as a social studies teacher, principal, and associate superintendent for human resources.

Dr. Sorenson continues to work with graduate students at UTEP, teaching school-based budgeting and school personnel management. He was named The University of Texas at El Paso College of Education Professor of the Year in 2005, and he remains an active writer with numerous professional journal publications. Dr. Sorenson has authored textbooks, teacher resource guides, and workbooks related to elementary and secondary social studies curricula. He conducts workshops at the state and national levels, and he has been actively involved in numerous professional organizations, including the Texas Elementary Principals and Supervisors Association (TEPSA) and the Texas Association of Secondary School Principals (TASSP), for which he conducted annual new-principal academy workshops for 12 years.

Dr. Sorenson continues his research agenda in the area of the school principalship, specifically the examination of conditions and factors that inhibit and discourage lead teachers from entering school administration. He makes time each day to exercise, walking 4 to 10 miles, depending on how industrious he feels!

Dr. Sorenson has been married to his wife, Donna, the love of his life, for the past 40 years, and they have two adult children, Lisa (a second-grade teacher with Cypress-Fairbanks ISD in Houston, Texas) and Ryan (an exercise physiologist in El Paso, Texas), a wonderful son-in-law, Sam (a petroleum engineer in Houston, Texas), and two grandchildren, Savannah Grace and Nehemiah Timothy—all of whom are the pride and joy of his life. Rick and Donna reside in El Paso, Texas, on the U.S./Mexico border, with their home facing the majestic Franklin Mountains. The Sorenson family is a lover of pugs, most notably Little Bit (wanna go?) and Olive (wanna snack?).

Lloyd M. Goldsmith is the director of the Principal Preparation Program and former chairperson for the Graduate Studies in Education Department at Abilene Christian University. He earned his EdD from Baylor University in the area of educational leadership. Dr. Goldsmith served public schools for 29 years as an elementary school teacher, junior high school assistant principal, and elementary school principal.

Dr. Goldsmith led the migration of the graduate education program to an online format. He is currently involved in developing an online EdD in educational leadership. Dr. Goldsmith and a fellow professor, Dr. Kim Pamplin in the chemistry department, are in their 14th year codirecting a program that enables high school chemistry and biology teachers to develop effective instructional strategies and integrate technology within their lessons. Dr. Goldsmith has served on several state committees for the Texas Education Agency. He served two terms as president of the Texas Council of Professors of Educational Administration.

The research interests of Dr. Goldsmith relate to effective principal practices and practicum design. He enjoys teaching in his church's inner city outreach ministry, where he helps equip those living in poverty to better handle life's challenges.

Dr. Goldsmith has been married to his wife, Mary, for 30 years and has three adult children—Abigail, Eleanor, and Nelson. Abigail and son-in-law Andrew Harmon are the parents of his two grandchildren, Luke Walling Harmon and Hilary Grace Harmon, for whom "Pa" enjoys being "Pa." Eleanor has taught fourth grade for two years in Taft, Texas, where her father began his teaching career. Nelson recently graduated with a degree in accounting and finance from Abilene Christian University. Llola, Dr. Goldsmith's chocolate lab, is spoiled and walks the good doctor every morning.

David E. DeMatthews is an assistant professor in the Educational Leadership and Foundations Department at The University of Texas at El Paso (UTEP). He received his PhD from the University of Maryland, College Park, in the area of educational policy and leadership. Dr. DeMatthews has also served as a high school social studies teacher in Baltimore City Public Schools and assistant principal and special education policy analyst for the District of Columbia Public Schools. Currently, Dr. DeMatthews works with graduate students teaching coursework related to school personnel, curriculum renewal, special education, and educational policy. He represents UTEP as the plenum session representative with the University Council of Educational Administration (UCEA) and has published frequently in a number of research journals, including *Teachers College Record, Educational Administration Quarterly, Journal of School Leadership, Leadership and Policy in Schools, Journal of Cases in Educational Leadership,* and *Education Policy Analysis Archives.* He is an active educational researcher and has studied school leadership, specifically examining how principals lead for social justice in high-poverty urban contexts and in regard to students with disabilities and linguistically diverse students.

1

Time Management and Your Leadership

So much time and so little to do. Wait a minute. Strike that. Reverse it!

—Willy Wonka, in *Willy Wonka and the Chocolate Factory* (Stuart, 1971)

SO MUCH TIME AND SO LITTLE TO DO

Principals, teachers, paraprofessionals, and auxiliary staff can all smile at Willy's time assessment. Harried, frustrated, and exhausted, principals lament the need for additional time to complete their assigned duties.

If you are reading this book, your reality is most likely "So little time and so much to do," whether you sit in central office, a campus office, a classroom, or a maintenance facility. You scramble to fit more and more into the allotted 24-hour day. Principals constantly seek ways to better manage time, increase efficiency, and have a positive impact on faculty and students. Historically, public education in the United States has been underfunded, and it is likely to remain so (Leachman & Mai, 2014). Regardless of the funding challenge, principals indirectly increase funding when they discover ways to increase their efficient use of time.

The universe is measured in time—past, present, and future. A person will work a finite period of time. Successful people use their allotted time efficiently and purposefully. As noted in Figure 1.1, Time Use on an Average Workday, most individuals spend approximately one third of their time in sleep and rest. Working obligations, family time and responsibilities, personal time, and leisure consume the other two thirds of a day's time.

Everyone is bound by time. There are no exceptions! Since the beginning, people have sought to expand their time. Around 323 BCE, Alexander the Great sought a river that "healed the ravages of age." A 16th century Spanish explorer, Juan Ponce de Leon, supposedly sought the fountain of youth rumored to exist somewhere in present-day Florida (Drye, n.d.). Today, we continue searching for ways to save time, buy time, or multiply time.

Figure 1.1   Time Use on an Average Workday

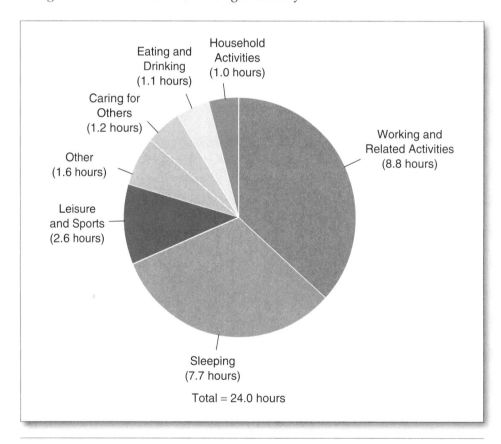

Source: Bureau of Labor Statistics, 2012.

Note: Data include employed persons on days they worked, ages 25 to 54, who lived in households with children under 18. Data include nonholiday weekends and are annual averages for 2012. Data include related travel for each activity.

If we work 40-hour weeks each year from age 20 to 65, we will have worked a total of 90,360 hours during our lifetime. Calculate your own lifetime work estimate. How well do you manage your time? A silent thief—a time stealer—resides amongst us. How can you recognize this thief and protect yourself from time robbery?

Allow me to introduce myself. I'm the *Silent Time Thief*. I knowingly, slyly, gradually, and silently steal time. To better learn time management tips, look for my *Silent Time Thief* icon and text boxes throughout this book. I look forward to stealing administrative time any way I can!

—*The Silent Time Thief*

Protection from time robbery begins with a visit to the Professional Standards for Educational Leaders (PSEL). These standards, developed by the nonprofit National Policy Board for Educational Administration (NPBEA; 2015), set the gold standard for school administration. While the PSEL standards' primary goal is to articulate what effective leadership looks like in a transformational public education system, the standards have much to say about the effective, efficient, and wise use of time.

REFLECTING ON YOUR TIME MANAGEMENT

The Principal's Guide to Time Management: Instructional Leadership in the Digital Age begins with an informal self-assessment examining time usage through six PSEL informed lenses: (1) vision, mission, and time; (2) leading, teaching, learning, and time; (3) the learning organization and time; (4) collaboration and time; (5) ethics, integrity, and time; and (6) the 21st century education system and time. The *Time Management Self-Assessment Instrument* (TMSI) located at the conclusion of this chapter provides a personal, informal benchmark of time management skills examined from a PSEL standards perspective. Subsequent chapters provide the reader opportunities to reflect on the appropriate TMSI time management lenses and their PSEL standards connections.

Vision and mission; leading, teaching, and learning; the learning organization; collaboration; ethics and integrity; and the education system operate in time-driven environments. Wise principals closely examine the impact of their time management decisions on themselves and those they serve.

Introducing Lens 1: Vision, Mission, and Time

Lens 1	Lens 2	Lens 3	Lens 4	Lens 5	Lens 6
Vision, Mission, and Time	Leading, Teaching, Learning, and Time	The Learning Organization and Time	Collaboration and Time	Ethics, Integrity, and Time	The 21st Century Education System and Time

Vision and mission are at the heart of academic success (Yukl, 2012). Weaving a school's vision into the school's culture requires principals to manage time carefully with the expectation that every student will meet with success, not just those students who come to school prepared and nurtured by their families. The expectation of success for every student is a weighty responsibility.

Time management is intertwined with the planning and implementation of the school's vision and mission. Time on task and student and faculty scheduling are instrumental in transforming the vision and mission into a reality. To hold all school stakeholders accountable, action plans driven by the school's vision and mission statements contain time lines for identified actions. Monitoring, implementing, and revising plans takes time. Efficient time managers use varied resources to support a school's vision and mission.

Introducing Lens 2: Leading, Teaching, Learning, and Time

Lens 1	Lens 2	Lens 3	Lens 4	Lens 5	Lens 6
Vision, Mission, and Time	Leading, Teaching, Learning, and Time	The Learning Organization and Time	Collaboration and Time	Ethics, Integrity, and Time	The 21st Century Education System and Time

The business of school is learning—not only for students, but also for faculty, staff, other stakeholders, and even the principal. Hoy and Miskel (2012) hold the principal responsible for nurturing the school's teaching and learning culture. The principal, after all, is the lead learner.

Nurturing the culture requires prudent use of school personnel and fiscal resources. It also requires principals to invest time leading, developing, and sustaining quality instruction. Time, along with other resources, must be aligned with leading, teaching, and learning. Chapter 3, "Leading, Teaching, Learning, and Time," further examines this PSEL lens. Additionally, Chapter 7, "The 21st Century Education System: Improvement, Time, and Technology," expands this topic and provides greater detail.

Time management involves more than scheduling and keeping students on task. Recruiting and hiring personnel who can effectively and efficiently carry out their duties is effective time management. Ill-prepared or underprepared employees are time thieves. Supervising and training poor hires consumes a disproportionate amount of a leader's time. An excellent resource for working with school personnel is *The Principal's Guide to Managing School Personnel* (Sorenson & Goldsmith, 2009).

Using effective teaching practices that close the learning gap for students who struggle academically is time-efficient teaching and learning. Time-efficient leaders devote time to monitor teaching and learning.

Introducing Lens 3: The Learning Organization and Time

Lens 1	Lens 2	Lens 3	Lens 4	Lens 5	Lens 6
Vision, Mission, and Time	Leading, Teaching, Learning, and Time	The Learning Organization and Time	Collaboration and Time	Ethics, Integrity, and Time	The 21st Century Education System and Time

Learning organizations are complex entities. Those that are successful have principals who develop caring, open cultures and positive climates that better address the growth and development of every member of the learning community. Developing and maintaining a caring, open culture and positive climate takes time. Within a trusting organization, individuals (students and staff) are known, valued, and respected, creating a robust, secure, and professional learning environment. Healthy learning organizations share ownership and accountability. Students are active members of the learning community, where they are academically and socially supported in a safe, secure, and technology-driven learning environment (see Chapter 4, "The Learning Organization: Culture, Climate, Technology, Safety, and Time").

Creating an effective learning organization requires a highly organized approach to operations and management founded upon the vision, mission, and values of the school. Senge and colleagues (2012) urge principals to connect policies and resource allocation to the school's vision and values. In today's school, modern technology and data systems improve school operations, providing the instructional leader additional time to focus on instruction and learning activities.

Effective learning environments save time by maximizing instructional time. Every minute of instructional time is precious. If only three minutes of class time are wasted for whatever reason in a six-period day, 54 hours—or more than 7.5 instructional days—are silently stolen during the academic year—time that can never be recaptured.

Likewise, time spent developing a positive classroom environment is time well invested; untold hours of instructional time are lost each year due to ineffective classroom management and instructional practices. It takes time to build trusting, productive relationships with students, fellow teachers, and other school stakeholders. It takes time to align policies, resources, and operations to the school's vision and mission.

Introducing Lens 4: Collaboration and Time

Lens 1	Lens 2	Lens 3	Lens 4	Lens 5	Lens 6
Vision, Mission, and Time	Leading, Teaching, Learning, and Time	The Learning Organization and Time	Collaboration and Time	Ethics, Integrity, and Time	The 21st Century Education System and Time

Developing trust and working collaboratively with faculty, families, community members, and other stakeholders requires investing time. There are no shortcuts in developing trust and collaboration; to think so is to deny reality. When community members are actively involved in campus life, they bring their talents and skills, and they expand time. Such collaboration encourages a school's community to use its diverse cultural, social, and intellectual resources, leading to valuable partnerships with a wide array of community organizations (see Chapter 5, "Collaboration and Time"). Collaboration creates an open culture and a positive climate where relationships are valued by families, care givers, school personnel, and other stakeholders.

Schools are often understaffed. Volunteer hours aligned with actions supporting the school's mission translate into a potential savings of tens of thousands of dollars in skilled labor costs. For example, if a school conservatively averages 10 volunteer hours per day, assuming a 180-day academic year, that campus would benefit from 1,800 volunteer work hours or 225 workdays. This is the equivalent of 1.25 full-time employees. Given that the Bureau of Labor Statistics (2012) reports the median paraprofessional salary is approximately $25,270 per year, the school in essence adds a value of $31,587 to its budget. If the same school averaged 15 volunteer hours a day, the campus would benefit from 2,700 volunteer hours or about 337 volunteer eight-hour workdays. This is the equivalent of nearly two paraprofessionals valued at approximately $47,311!

Introducing Lens 5: Ethics, Integrity, and Time

Lens 1	Lens 2	Lens 3	Lens 4	Lens 5	Lens 6
Vision, Mission, and Time	Leading, Teaching, Learning, and Time	The Learning Organization and Time	Collaboration and Time	Ethics, Integrity, and Time	The 21st Century Education System and Time

How can time possibly be connected to ethics and integrity? Surprisingly, ethics and integrity are deeply associated with time management—but in a unique way. Lunenburg and Irby (2006) declared the principal to be the "first citizen" of the campus and as such to influence the moral and ethical tenor of the school (p. 4).

What happens when principals fail to act ethically? What happens when principals fail to act with integrity? What happens when principals fail to act with fairness? What happens when principals fail to act morally? The answer to all four questions is the same—a violation of the professional code of conduct. Principals could be reprimanded or even lose hard-earned professional credentials. A formal reprimand, temporary suspension of credentials, or the revoking of professional credentials is a painful consequence for violating this standard. Not to be forgotten is the time spent in hearings, depositions, and investigations—time that could be better used serving students.

Thinking beyond one's self, what impact would a leader's unethical or immoral conduct have on other stakeholders in the organization? How will students react to an educator's unethical or immoral conduct? How will parents react? Community members? Is there any room for dishonesty or prejudice in a school setting?

Not only are the behaviors and reactions mentioned above traumatic for parents and community members, they also dramatically impact the students who have been entrusted to the school by their parents and guardians. Rarely—if ever—can any educator recover from such a breach of confidence. These inappropriate behaviors are always time thieves.

Introducing Lens 6: The 21st Century Education System and Time

Lens 1	Lens 2	Lens 3	Lens 4	Lens 5	Lens 6
Vision, Mission, and Time	Leading, Teaching, Learning, and Time	The Learning Organization and Time	Collaboration and Time	Ethics, Integrity, and Time	The 21st Century Education System and Time

School leaders must approach any discussion of the 21st century education system from a culturally responsive perspective guided by professional norms and ethical and moral principles. Schools do not operate in a vacuum. Principals must avoid getting so caught up in the day-to-day demands of leading a school that they lose sight of the larger perspective. The business of school is learning; leaders must use their time to influence, monitor, and promote learning.

Effective principals develop learning environments founded on time efficiency, data-based inquiry, technology enhancements, and continuous improvement (see Chapter 7, "The 21st Century Education System:

Improvement, Time, and Technology"). The mining, analyzing, communicating, and use of data are central to exceptional leading, teaching, and learning (DeMatthews, 2014a; Ubben, Hughes, & Norris, 2015). Others must be enabled to engage productively with change experiences; the principal facilitates this by promoting a collective direction, shared engagement, and mutual accountability.

If educators fail to advocate for their constituents, if they fail to influence decisions affecting student learning, if they fail to anticipate emerging trends, or if they fail to adapt their learning strategies; the leader will use more time cleaning up what was ignored than would have been spent in proactively addressing the situation. Once again the *Silent Time Thief* negatively impacts the school's various constituents.

FINAL THOUGHTS

In 1965, a popular rock group, The Byrds, recorded a major hit—"Turn! Turn! Turn! (To Everything There Is a Season)." The reader can hear this song and view some classic photos of the group performing at www.youtube.com/watch?v=Wga_M5Zdn4. The "Turn! Turn! Turn!" lyrics were adapted from the book of Ecclesiastes—a wisdom literature book found in the Old Testament of the Bible, written somewhere between 450 and 180 BCE. Twenty-four hundred years ago, time and time management issues challenged humanity. The writer of Ecclesiastes knew there was a time to plant and a time to reap, a time to dance and a time to mourn.

Today, humans are still challenged and fascinated by time. Many lament how fast the school days and academic years pass. As we journey together through this time study, "turn, turn, turn" through the pages of this book to discover ways to more efficiently and effectively manage time at work and at home. Time is unpredictable at best, short at worst.

DISCUSSION QUESTIONS

1. Select one PSEL standard. Review the standard and its supporting elements. Share three ways the selected PSEL standard addresses time management.

2. List three initial thoughts about the authors' contention that the PSEL standards address time management.

3. Discover a time management connection for each PSEL standard. Maintain a list. Add to and amend the list while progressing through the book.

4. List personal time management challenges. Keep the list readily available while progressing through the book. As you explore time and time

management, edit the list as needed. Chronicle your growing understanding of time management and its impact on your leadership skills.

5. How does your daily schedule compare to time use as illustrated in Figure 1.1, Time Use on an Average Workday? What conclusions can be drawn about your time management from this comparison?

6. Review your school's vision and mission statements. What connections can be made between your school's vision and mission statements and time management?

7. Create an ongoing list of your time management challenges in a location that will keep it in front of you. Review it and seek ways to improve your time efficiency.

8. Partner with a colleague to work collaboratively as a "time team." Share successes and failures in time management. Brainstorm new item management strategies and implement them. Discuss your progress with your partner. Hold each other accountable for improving each of your time management skills.

CASE STUDY APPLICATION

A SELF-REFLECTION ON YOUR TIME MANAGEMENT: TIME MANAGEMENT SELF-ASSESSMENT INSTRUMENT (TMSI)

This case study is an anomaly compared to the other case studies in this text. Why? Because you, the reader, are the subject of the case study.

As an active participant in this case study, you are asked to complete an informal instrument that provides you with an opportunity to examine and reflect on your time management skills as evidenced in the PSEL standards. The *Time Management Self-Assessment Instrument* (TMSI) contains 60 Likert-type items. Complete all items and score the instrument prior to reading any further in this text. (Scoring before reading further minimizes bias in your responses.) There are no right or wrong answers in this self-perception instrument. The survey provides informal feedback on your perceptions of vision, mission, and time; leading, teaching, learning, and time; the learning organization and time; collaboration and time; ethics, integrity, and time; and the 21st century education system and time. You are encouraged to complete the TMSI instrument again after reading this book or at a later date you deem appropriate. Compare the results. Reflect on your growth or lack of growth in time management skills.

TIME MANAGEMENT SELF-ASSESSMENT INSTRUMENT INSTRUCTIONS

The authors contend the PSEL standards and their accompanying items possess a time dimension. Therefore, a PSEL-informed informal instrument is in order to provoke deeper thought and reflection on how time is used in leadership.

Directions: Respond to the 60 performance standards on the TMSI by marking

  1—if you strongly disagree; that is, you fail to address this performance indicator;

  2—if you somewhat disagree that you fail to address this performance indicator;

  3—if you somewhat agree that you address this performance indicator; or

  4—if you strongly agree that you address this performance indicator.

Respond to "I spend the appropriate amount of time on this performance" indicator:

Item Number	Performance Statement *As an effective educational leader I*	Response			
1	Develop an educational mission for the school to promote the academic success and well-being of each student.	Strongly Disagree 1	Somewhat Disagree 2	Somewhat Agree 3	Strongly Agree 4
2	Promote the effective use of technology in the service of teaching and learning.	Strongly Disagree 1	Somewhat Disagree 2	Somewhat Agree 3	Strongly Agree 4
3	Develop and promote leadership among teachers and staff for inquiry, experimentation and innovation, and initiating and implementing improvement.	Strongly Disagree 1	Somewhat Disagree 2	Somewhat Agree 3	Strongly Agree 4
4	Develop the capacity, opportunities, and support for teacher leadership and leadership from other members of the school community.	Strongly Disagree 1	Somewhat Disagree 2	Somewhat Agree 3	Strongly Agree 4
5	Place children at the center of education and accept responsibility for each student's academic success and well-being.	Strongly Disagree 1	Somewhat Disagree 2	Somewhat Agree 3	Strongly Agree 4
6	Employ technology to improve the quality and efficiency of operations and management.	Strongly Disagree 1	Somewhat Disagree 2	Somewhat Agree 3	Strongly Agree 4
7	In collaboration with members of the school and the community and using relevant data, develop and promote a vision for the school on the successful learning and development of each child and on instructional and organizational practices that promote success.	Strongly Disagree 1	Somewhat Disagree 2	Somewhat Agree 3	Strongly Agree 4

(Continued)

(Continued)

Item Number	Performance Statement *As an effective educational leader I*	Response			
8	Build and maintain a safe, caring, and healthy school environment that meets the academic, social, emotional and physical needs of each student.	Strongly Disagree 1	Somewhat Disagree 2	Somewhat Agree 3	Strongly Agree 4
9	Align and focus systems of curriculum, instruction, and assessment within and across grade levels to promote student academic success, love of learning, the identities and habits of learners, and healthy sense of self.	Strongly Disagree 1	Somewhat Disagree 2	Somewhat Agree 3	Strongly Agree 4
10	Empower and entrust teachers and staff with collective responsibility for meeting the academic, social, emotional, and physical needs of each student, pursuant to the mission, vision, and core values of the school.	Strongly Disagree 1	Somewhat Disagree 2	Somewhat Agree 3	Strongly Agree 4
11	Safeguard and promote the values of democracy, individual freedom and responsibility equity, social justice, community, and diversity.	Strongly Disagree 1	Somewhat Disagree 2	Somewhat Agree 3	Strongly Agree 4
12	Promote adult-student, student-peer, and school-community relationships that value and support academic learning and positive social and emotional development.	Strongly Disagree 1	Somewhat Disagree 2	Somewhat Agree 3	Strongly Agree 4

Item Number	Performance Statement *As an effective educational leader I*	Response			
13	Model and pursue the school's mission, vision, and core values in all aspects of leadership.	Strongly Disagree 1	Somewhat Disagree 2	Somewhat Agree 3	Strongly Agree 4
14	Develop teachers' and staff members' professional knowledge, skills, and practice through differentiated opportunities for learning and growth, guiding by understanding of professional and adult learning and development.	Strongly Disagree 1	Somewhat Disagree 2	Somewhat Agree 3	Strongly Agree 4
15	Adopt a systems perspective and promote coherence among improvement efforts and all aspects of school organization, programs, and services.	Strongly Disagree 1	Somewhat Disagree 2	Somewhat Agree 3	Strongly Agree 4
16	Develop and support open, productive caring and trusting working relationships among leaders, faculty, and staff to promote professional capacity and the improvement of practice.	Strongly Disagree 1	Somewhat Disagree 2	Somewhat Agree 3	Strongly Agree 4
17	Lead with interpersonal and communication skill, social-emotional insight, and understanding of all students' and staff members' backgrounds and cultures.	Strongly Disagree 1	Somewhat Disagree 2	Somewhat Agree 3	Strongly Agree 4

(Continued)

(Continued)

Item Number	Performance Statement *As an effective educational leader I*	Response			
18	Infuse the school's learning environment with the cultures and languages of the school's community.	Strongly Disagree 1	Somewhat Disagree 2	Somewhat Agree 3	Strongly Agree 4
19	Use methods of continuous improvement to achieve the vision, fulfill the mission, and promote the core values of the school.	Strongly Disagree 1	Somewhat Disagree 2	Somewhat Agree 3	Strongly Agree 4
20	Build and sustain productive partnerships with public and private sectors to promote school improvement and student learning.	Strongly Disagree 1	Somewhat Disagree 2	Somewhat Agree 3	Strongly Agree 4
21	Implement coherent systems of curriculum, instruction, and assessment that promote the mission, vision, and core values of the school, embody high expectations for student learning, align with academic standard, and are culturally responsive.	Strongly Disagree 1	Somewhat Disagree 2	Somewhat Agree 3	Strongly Agree 4
22	Promote mutual accountability among teachers and other professional staff for each student's success and the effectiveness of the school as a whole.	Strongly Disagree 1	Somewhat Disagree 2	Somewhat Agree 3	Strongly Agree 4

Item Number	Performance Statement *As an effective educational leader I*	Response			
23	Create and sustain positive, collaborative, and productive relationships with families and the community for the benefit of students.	Strongly Disagree 1	Somewhat Disagree 2	Somewhat Agree 3	Strongly Agree 4
24	Assess and develop the capacity of staff to assess the value and applicability of emerging educational trends and the findings of research for the school and its improvement.	Strongly Disagree 1	Somewhat Disagree 2	Somewhat Agree 3	Strongly Agree 4
25	Develop shared understanding of and commitment to mission, vision, and core values within the school and the community.	Strongly Disagree 1	Somewhat Disagree 2	Somewhat Agree 3	Strongly Agree 4
26	Create and sustain a school environment in which each student is known, accepted and valued, trusted and respected, cared for, and encouraged to be an active and responsible member of the school community.	Strongly Disagree 1	Somewhat Disagree 2	Somewhat Agree 3	Strongly Agree 4
27	Use assessment data appropriately and within technical limitations to monitor student progress and improve instruction.	Strongly Disagree 1	Somewhat Disagree 2	Somewhat Agree 3	Strongly Agree 4
28	Recruit, hire, support, develop, and retain effective and caring teachers and other professional staff and form them into an educationally effective faculty.	Strongly Disagree 1	Somewhat Disagree 2	Somewhat Agree 3	Strongly Agree 4

(Continued)

(Continued)

Item Number	Performance Statement *As an effective educational leader I*	Response			
29	Confront and alter institutional biases of student marginalization, deficit-based schooling, and low expectations associated with race, class, culture and language, gender and sexual orientation, and disability or special status.	Strongly Disagree 1	Somewhat Disagree 2	Somewhat Agree 3	Strongly Agree 4
30	Manage governance processes and internal and external politics toward achieving the school's mission and vision.	Strongly Disagree 1	Somewhat Disagree 2	Somewhat Agree 3	Strongly Agree 4
31	Articulate, advocate, and cultivate core values that define the school's culture and stress the imperative of child-centered education; high expectations and student support; equity, inclusiveness, and social justice; openness, caring, and trust; and continuous improvement.	Strongly Disagree 1	Somewhat Disagree 2	Somewhat Agree 3	Strongly Agree 4
32	Develop and provide the school as a resource for families and the community.	Strongly Disagree 1	Somewhat Disagree 2	Somewhat Agree 3	Strongly Agree 4
33	Empower and motivate teachers and staff to the highest levels of professional practice and to continuous learning and improvement.	Strongly Disagree 1	Somewhat Disagree 2	Somewhat Agree 3	Strongly Agree 4

Item Number	Performance Statement *As an effective educational leader I*	Response			
34	Prepare the school and the community for improvement, promoting readiness, an imperative for improvement, instilling mutual commitment and accountability, and developing the knowledge, skills, and motivation to succeed in improvement.	Strongly Disagree 1	Somewhat Disagree 2	Somewhat Agree 3	Strongly Agree 4
35	Provide moral direction for the school and promote ethical and professional behavior among faculty and staff.	Strongly Disagree 1	Somewhat Disagree 2	Somewhat Agree 3	Strongly Agree 4
36	Institute, manage, and monitor operations and administrative systems that promote the mission and vision of the school.	Strongly Disagree 1	Somewhat Disagree 2	Somewhat Agree 3	Strongly Agree 4
37	Understand, value, and employ the community's cultural, social, intellectual, and political resources to promote student learning and school improvement.	Strongly Disagree 1	Somewhat Disagree 2	Somewhat Agree 3	Strongly Agree 4
38	Cultivate and reinforce student engagement in school and positive student conduct.	Strongly Disagree 1	Somewhat Disagree 2	Somewhat Agree 3	Strongly Agree 4
39	Ensure instructional practice that is intellectually challenging, is authentic to student experiences, recognizes student strengths, and is differentiated and personalized.	Strongly Disagree 1	Somewhat Disagree 2	Somewhat Agree 3	Strongly Agree 4

(Continued)

(Continued)

Item Number	Performance Statement *As an effective educational leader I*	Response			
40	Design and implement job-embedded and other opportunities for professional learning collaboratively with faculty and staff.	Strongly Disagree 1	Somewhat Disagree 2	Somewhat Agree 3	Strongly Agree 4
41	Act ethically and professionally in personal conduct, relationships with others, decision-making, stewardship of the school's resources, and all aspects of school leadership.	Strongly Disagree 1	Somewhat Disagree 2	Somewhat Agree 3	Strongly Agree 4
42	Manage uncertainty, risk, competing initiatives, and politics of change with courage and perseverance, providing support and encouragement, and openly communicating the need for, process for, and outcomes of improvement efforts.	Strongly Disagree 1	Somewhat Disagree 2	Somewhat Agree 3	Strongly Agree 4
43	Strategically develop, implement, and evaluate actions to achieve the vision of the school.	Strongly Disagree 1	Somewhat Disagree 2	Somewhat Agree 3	Strongly Agree 4
44	Foster continuous improvement of individual and collective instructional capacity to achieve outcomes envisioned for each student.	Strongly Disagree 1	Somewhat Disagree 2	Somewhat Agree 3	Strongly Agree 4
45	Develop and manage relationships with feeder and connecting schools for enrollment management and curricular and instructional articulation.	Strongly Disagree 1	Somewhat Disagree 2	Somewhat Agree 3	Strongly Agree 4

Item Number	Performance Statement *As an effective educational leader I*	Response			
46	Develop and maintain data and communication systems to deliver actionable information for classroom and school improvement.	Strongly Disagree 1	Somewhat Disagree 2	Somewhat Agree 3	Strongly Agree 4
47	Ensure that each student is treated fairly, respectfully, and with an understanding of each student's culture and context.	Strongly Disagree 1	Somewhat Disagree 2	Somewhat Agree 3	Strongly Agree 4
48	Promote the preparation of students to live productively in and contribute to the diverse cultural contexts of a global society.	Strongly Disagree 1	Somewhat Disagree 2	Somewhat Agree 3	Strongly Agree 4
49	Review the school's mission and vision and adjust them to changing expectations and opportunities for the school, and changing needs and situations of students.	Strongly Disagree 1	Somewhat Disagree 2	Somewhat Agree 3	Strongly Agree 4
50	Place children at the center of education and accept responsibility for each student's academic success and well-being.	Strongly Disagree 1	Somewhat Disagree 2	Somewhat Agree 3	Strongly Agree 4
51	Promote instructional practice that is consistent with knowledge of child learning and development, effective pedagogy, and the needs of each student.	Strongly Disagree 1	Somewhat Disagree 2	Somewhat Agree 3	Strongly Agree 4
52	Provide opportunities for collaborative examination of practice, collegial feedback, and collective learning.	Strongly Disagree 1	Somewhat Disagree 2	Somewhat Agree 3	Strongly Agree 4

(Continued)

(Continued)

Item Number	Performance Statement *As an effective educational leader I*	Response			
53	Conduct myself as a responsible, ethical, and accountable steward of the school's monetary and non-monetary resources, engaging in effective budgeting and accounting practices.	Strongly Disagree 1	Somewhat Disagree 2	Somewhat Agree 3	Strongly Agree 4
54	Advocate publicly for the needs and priorities to families and the community.	Strongly Disagree 1	Somewhat Disagree 2	Somewhat Agree 3	Strongly Agree 4
55	Maintain a presence in the community to understand its strengths and needs, develop productive relationships, and engage its resources for the school.	Strongly Disagree 1	Somewhat Disagree 2	Somewhat Agree 3	Strongly Agree 4
56	Employ valid assessments that are consistent with knowledge of child learning and development and technical standards of measurement.	Strongly Disagree 1	Somewhat Disagree 2	Somewhat Agree 3	Strongly Agree 4
57	Encourage faculty-initiated improvement of programs and practices.	Strongly Disagree 1	Somewhat Disagree 2	Somewhat Agree 3	Strongly Agree 4
58	Act according to and promote the professional norms of integrity, fairness, transparency, trust, collaboration, perseverance, learning, and continuous improvement.	Strongly Disagree 1	Somewhat Disagree 2	Somewhat Agree 3	Strongly Agree 4

Item Number	Performance Statement *As an effective educational leader I*	Response			
59	Develop and administer systems for fair and equitable management of conflict among students, faculty and staff, leaders, families, and community.	Strongly Disagree 1	Somewhat Disagree 2	Somewhat Agree 3	Strongly Agree 4
60	Tend to my own learning and effectiveness through reflection, study, and improvement, maintaining a healthy work-life balance.	Strongly Disagree 1	Somewhat Disagree 2	Somewhat Agree 3	Strongly Agree 4

Source: National Policy Board for Educational Administration (NPBEA), 2015.

SCORING INSTRUCTIONS FOR THE TIME MANAGEMENT SELF-ASSESSMENT INSTRUMENT

Record your score for each item using the TMSI Scoring Template. Calculate the sum of your scores for each of the TMSI six lenses:

1—vision, mission, and time;

2—leading, teaching, learning, and time;

3—the learning organization and time;

4—collaboration and time;

5—ethics, integrity, and time; and

6—the 21st century education system and time.

Divide the sum of the scores on each TMSI lens by ten for an average score reported to the closest tenth of a point (e.g., 3.6). Mark your average score on the TMSI Scoring Scale by placing an *X* on the scale.

Refer to your TMSI results as you proceed through the book. Consider completing and scoring the TMSI once again after reading the book. Compare the results. Consider completing the TMSI a year later or at a time you deem best for assessing your personal growth.

(Continued)

(Continued)

TMSI SCORING TEMPLATE

Lens 1 Vision, Mission, and Time		Lens 2 Leading, Teaching, Learning, and Time		Lens 3 The Learning Organization and Time		Lens 4 Collaboration and Time		Lens 5 Ethics, Integrity and Time		Lens 6 The 21st Century Education System and Time	
Item	Score	Item	Score	Item	Score	Item	Score	Item	Score	Item	Score
1		2		3		4		5		6	
7		8		9		10		11		12	
13		14		15		16		17		18	
19		20		21		22		23		24	
25		26		27		28		29		30	
31		32		33		34		35		36	
37		38		39		40		41		42	
43		44		45		46		47		48	
49		50		51		52		53		54	
55		60		56		57		58		59	
Total		Total		Total		Total		Total		Total	
÷ 10 =		÷ 10 =		÷ 10 =		÷ 10 =		÷ 10 =		÷ 10 =	

TMSI SCORING SCALE

Example score: 3.6   Strongly Disagree 1——2——3—X-4 Strongly Agree

Lens 1: Vision, Mission, and Time	Strongly Disagree 1——2——3——4 Strongly Agree
Lens 2: Leading, Teaching, Learning, and Time	Strongly Disagree 1——2——3——4 Strongly Agree
Lens 3: The Learning Organization and Time	Strongly Disagree 1——2——3——4 Strongly Agree
Lens 4: Collaboration and Time	Strongly Disagree 1——2——3——4 Strongly Agree
Lens 5: Ethics, Integrity, and Time	Strongly Disagree 1——2——3——4 Strongly Agree
Lens 6: The 21st Century Education System and Time	Strongly Disagree 1——2——3——4 Strongly Agree

With your plan in hand, begin a journey examining the relationship between your work, the PSEL standards, and time.

2

Vision, Mission, and Time

"I wish it need not have happened in my time," said Frodo.

"So do I," said Gandalf, "and so do all who live to see such times. But that is not for them to decide. All we have to decide is what to do with the time that is given us."

—J. R. R. Tolkien, *The Fellowship of the Ring* (1993)

TIME MANAGEMENT—AT THE HEART OF LEADERSHIP; VISION AND MISSION— AT THE HEART OF STUDENT SUCCESS

Frodo wished it—whatever "it" is—had not happened in his time. Gandalf felt the same way. Gandalf went on to include us with Frodo and himself wishing it had not happened in our times. Gandalf projects his thoughts on us. We decide what to do with the time given to us. In other words, we must discover our vision and mission and use our time while leveraging others' time to translate vision and mission into reality.

Were Frodo a principal today, he would realize that he, his school, and his school district are not autonomous bodies. An assortment of governmental bodies and nongovernmental agencies place rules and constraints on schools (Ingersoll, 2003). This results in schools consulting with outside forces in an effort to work within state, regional, and federal mandates, all of which impact a school's vision, mission, and time (Ingersoll, 2003).

Everything in education takes time, whether it is planning staff development, designing an accountability system, initiating a new instructional program, enhancing technology, or ensuring a facility is in good working order. But all is not lost. Time belongs to us. We do not belong to time. All of us possess the same 24 hours each day. Unfortunately, humans are inclined to focus on what they personally enjoy. If we are not careful, the important goes unattended. We choose to waste time, or we choose to partner with others, multiplying not only time but also our impact on society. Time management is at the heart of leading. It allows principals to effectively lead others. T. J. Kowalski (2013) portrayed time management as a necessity in managing schedules to ensure the essential aspects of work remain in the forefront. Absent a relentless focus on time management, vision and mission are likely to flounder.

Do stakeholders at your school know their school's vision statement? Mission statement? Getting personal, do you know your school's vision statement? Do you know your school's mission statement? Are your school's vision and mission statements appendages to documents and websites merely to keep the powers that be happy? What connections—if any—could possibly be made between vision, mission, and time? All are valid questions.

Vision and mission are at the heart of student academic success. A strong vision leads to supporting change, which creates innovation (Lick, Clauset, & Murphy, 2013). Making a school's vision and mission a reality requires principals to approach time management seriously with the expectation that every student will meet with success, including those who come with little to no nurturing and preparation. Success for every student does not allow principals to take this responsibility lightly. Vision becomes a problem when leaders and the team are not engaged or fully committed. This creates trouble for all stakeholders. Being disengaged and less than fully committed drags everyone down. Some are so blind they do not realize the problem lies within them. Sometimes, principals do not realize they are the problem. Why? They cannot see they *are* the problem (Arbinger Institute, 2002).

In the 2015 Professional Standards for Educational Leaders (PSEL), vision and mission are firmly linked to time, one of the scarcest resources in a school, and point the way to the school's desired future (Graham & Ferriter, 2010). The seven vision and mission elements of PSEL Standard 1 are shown in Figure 2.1, PSEL 2015 Standard 1: Mission, Vision, and Core Values.

Figure 2.1   PSEL Standard 1: Mission, Vision, and Core Values

Effective educational leaders develop, advocate, and enact a shared mission, vision, and core values of high-quality education and academic success and well-being of *each* student.

Effective leaders:

a. Develop an educational mission for the school to promote the academic success and well-being of each student.
b. In collaboration with members of the school and the community and using relevant data, develop and promote a vision for the school on the successful learning and development of each child and on instructional organizational practices that promote such success.
c. Articulate, advocate, and cultivate core values that define the school's culture and stress the imperative of child-centered education: high expectations and student support; equity, inclusiveness and social justice; openness, caring, and trust; and continuous improvement.
d. Strategically develop, implement, and evaluate actions to achieve the vision for the school.
e. Review the school's mission and vision and adjust them to changing expectations and opportunities for the school, and changing needs and situations of students.
f. Develop shared understanding of and commitment to mission, vision, and core values within the school and the community.
g. Model and pursue the school's mission, vision, and core values in all aspects of leadership

Source: NPBEA, 2015, p. 9.

A SCHOOL LEADER'S THOUGHTS ON VISION, MISSION, AND TIME

A conversation between Lloyd Goldsmith, author and former principal, and Steve Waddell, superintendent of Lewisville Independent School District (Lewisville ISD) located in the Dallas/Fort Worth metroplex, provides insightful information about ways to successfully develop and implement the vision and mission statements called for by the PSEL standards (S. Waddell, personal interview, March 6, 2015). Lewisville ISD comprises approximately 52,700 students, five high schools, and five ninth- and tenth-grade campuses. The student ethnic distribution is approximately 48% White, 28% Hispanic, 12% Asian American, and 9% African American. Thirty-one percent of the students are economically disadvantaged, and 14% are English language learners (Texas Education Agency, 2014).

It is easy to identify with Ralph and Alice. In the day-to-day struggle to meet personal needs and achieve goals—coupled with family responsibilities and work and social obligations—principals easily become hopeless rubber balls bouncing around aimlessly without thought to vision, mission, and time.

Source: Ralph and Alice cartoon by Alex Carruth.

A Voice From the Field—Part I

Lloyd: Steve, based on your experience as a successful superintendent, how important is vision and mission development?

Steve: I believe establishing vision and mission statements are extremely important. They are absolutely critical for academic success, regardless of the school or school district size.

Lloyd: What role do vision and mission play in academic success?

Steve: Vision and mission drive everything. High stakes accountability and standardized tests should not be the drivers of what schools districts are doing academically, but unfortunately, they have become just that. They have become the surrogate vision for districts and schools: to do well on these tests and let the tests essentially drive the curriculum of the school.

Lloyd: What happens when vision and mission do not drive a school district?

Steve: Without a clear vision and mission, a school district or campus has no sense of direction. It is absolutely imperative the vision and mission drive everything that goes on in the district or campus, not just academics, even though academics are our core business. You must know in what direction you are headed. The only way you can know that is to have a clear vision and mission.

Lloyd: Do you have a process for periodically reviewing your district's vision and mission statements to determine whether they are still appropriate?

Steve: You never fully accomplish your vision. It is something that is always out there. On the other hand, mission is something that can be accomplished. The vision is always in front of you. The best example for delineating between vision and mission that I have heard came from Philip Schlechty. People always confuse mission and vision. Schlechty said vision is when you think of NASA wanting to land a man on the moon by 1969, or today wanting to land a man or woman on Mars (Schlechty, 2005). When you buy into that example, your vision is always in front of you, but your mission is a shorter term objective that will help you accomplish your vision.

Lloyd: Yes, Steve, I see your point.

Steve: In our district, the vision and mission development process is so extensive. Our district is large. We have over 50,000 students. We involve thousands of people in establishing our vision and our goals. You always need to continually review what you are doing. We accomplish that each year by targeting parts of the goals we develop behind our vision and mission to see what we want to emphasize that year. Our plan was after about four years to refresh the mission statement. But you don't want to annually rewrite your vision, or even rewrite it every two or three years. Otherwise it is not a vision. The key is to involve enough people with enough breadth and diversity to say it is truly a legitimate vision. Shared vision is involving many stakeholders in developing the vision. It should not be the superintendent or the superintendent's cabinet or the board of trustees establishing the vision. Superintendents leave. Board composition changes. Where is the legitimacy of the vision? We involved about 3,000 people in the vision process from all over the district. We involved enough of the community that it is a legitimate shared vision. You don't want to go back and revisit that all the time. You have to give it long enough to make a difference. However, it is legitimate to revisit the mission every four or five years. You must go into a vision believing it houses something very large, much larger than any single entity.

Leaders like Steve Waddell understand devoting time to the development of a vision and mission is time well invested that produces handsome dividends. Engaging a school board and community in developing vision and mission statements takes time. Time is required to involve 3,000 of the district's various stakeholders in the vision and mission development process. One can be easily tempted to take shortcuts in this process. Shortcuts must not be taken. When time is invested, vision and mission intersect in a robust developmental process. The participation of various stakeholders lends authenticity to the district's vision and mission, and this filters down to the specific vision and mission of each campus. These are linked to the district's vision and mission statements, which are tailored to support the district's vision and mission as a whole. The vision and mission are connecters between a district and its campuses.

A Story About Vision, Mission, and Time

Silver, Berckemeyer, and Baenen (2015) share a story of a teacher whose husband died from colon cancer. The grieving teacher took her husband's body back to his hometown. A week passed and she depleted her paid sick leave days. Unbeknownst to her, her colleagues developed a schedule where they rotated covering her classes during their preparation periods. This mission-related behavior allowed the teacher to forego paying for a substitute. Her colleagues initiated an action plan that benefited not only the teacher, it benefited her students as well. These teachers made sure the students learned the curriculum during the teacher's absence. Win–Win!

This story oozes vision, mission, and time. The teachers ensured the students mastered the material during their colleague's time of grief (vision and mission). They voluntarily gifted their time to prepare for and cover her classes (time). The teacher in crisis received donated time when she needed it. Vision, mission, and time share a symbiotic relationship. Vision + Mission + Time = making it happen, regardless.

GOAL WRITING

Roland Barth, who was a successful principal for a number of years before joining the faculty of the Harvard Graduate School of Education, coined the term *craft knowledge*—knowledge gained from a collection of life experiences and hard physical labor (Barth, 2001). Craft knowledge is essential for those who want to collaboratively develop rich goals promoting a sense of community. Establishing goals is a fundamental step all self-disciplined leaders utilize and the one step that many are—unfortunately—inclined to skip and blame it on time (Sorenson & Goldsmith, 2013). Setting goals requires self-discipline and self-accountability. If you, your school, or your school district fails to establish goals, ignores goals, or creates loosely written goals replete with loopholes, your school will definitely fail to make its vision and mission a reality. Solid, clear goal writing demands strategy and time.

Goals motivate principals and teams strive to accomplish their district and campus vision and mission statements. Locke and Latham (1990) identified four reasons goals improve performance: (1) goals point toward the task, (2) goals mobilize effort, (3) goals increase persistence, and (4) goals encourage finding new strategies when the current strategies no longer work. Goal writing is a crucial component in making vision and mission a reality. Donohue's (2011) seven-step goal-writing strategy is an effective way to develop goals.

Step 1: Make sure the goal you are working for is something you really want, not just something that sounds good. When passion does not exist among the stakeholders for a goal, it is doomed for failure. Your goal must be consistent with your values.

Step 2: Ensure campus goals do not contradict district goals or go beyond the physical and fiscal resources in the school's campus improvement or action plan. For example, if a campus planning committee establishes a goal to improve student mathematics performance by hiring three additional mathematics teachers, and the committee knows there is little to no possibility of funding additional faculty positions, the committee sabotages its own work and needlessly frustrates colleagues at both the campus and district levels.

Step 3: Develop goals in six areas of your life: family and home, financial and career, spiritual and ethical, physical and health, social and cultural, and mental and educational. Donohue reminds us of the importance of living a balanced life. Personal life goals in these six areas eliminates the non-integrated thinking referenced in Step 2.

Step 4: State goals positively. Write what is desired rather than what is not. For example, write "95% of our students will pass the state mathematics exam" as opposed to the negative "less than 5% of our students will fail the state mathematics exam." Think positively in goal setting; think positively in all aspects of life, both public and private.

Step 5: Incorporate specific wording in the goal. It makes a difference. "At least 80% of students will improve their reading skills" is a vague goal. Specificity is added when the goal is revised to "80% of all students as well as 80% of each of the following subpopulations—male, female, White, Hispanic, African American, students qualifying for free and reduced-price lunch, and students receiving special education services—will increase their reading comprehension by at least one grade level by the end of the academic year as measured by the state's reading exam." Specificity clarifies expectations and dampens the efforts of those who seek to hide behind ambiguous wording to avoid academic accountability.

Step 6: Incorporate high expectations. For example, an attendance goal of 91% is not nearly as rigorous as an attendance goal of 97%. Likewise, setting a goal of 100% attendance is unrealistic. Establishing goals that push us beyond the established data patterns raises expectations for all.

Step 7: Put goals in writing. There is something positive about placing goals in writing and keeping goals in front at all times. Going about day-to-day business and challenges, principals and teams can easily lose sight of campus goals. Goals can become vague in stakeholders' memories. Keeping goals physically in front also keeps them in front of all parties.

What About SMART Goals?

SMART goals were introduced in the November 1981 issue of *Management Review* (Doran, 1981). Since then hundreds of interpretations by a plethora of authors have permeated the SMART goal literature (www.smart-goals-guide.com/smart-goal.html). The acronym SMART is used around the world for establishing all sorts of goals, including career goals, health goals, financial goals, and—in schools—academic and achievement goals. Today, many definitions and interpretations exist for SMART goals. One popular interpretation for SMART goals is the following:

S   Specific

M   Measurable

A   Achievable

R   Realistic

T   Time-based

Some interesting variants of the SMART acronym include these:

S   Specific, significant, stretching, stimulating, simple, strategic

M   Measurable, meaningful, motivating, manageable, maintainable

A   Achievable, attainable, appropriate, agreed, accepted, ambitious

R   Realistic, relevant, rewarding, resourced, robust, reviewable

T   Time-based, time-bound, time-lined, tractable

A Tool Kit for Quality Professional Development by Patricia Roy (2007) describes SMART goals as follows:

Specific. Exactly what will be measured? Specific goals focus on student needs. Strategic goals are determined in part by analyzing achievement and student behavior data. Commonalities and differences among student groups become apparent as data are disaggregated.

Measurable. Are measurable terms employed? Measureable goals contain information on how change is calculated. An instrument must be identified to measure whether a desired outcome has been achieved. Using multiple measures increases the confidence that such actions made a difference.

Attainable and Aligned. Are the goals aligned to campus needs, district goals, and state standards? Are they attainable? Attainable goals contain actions that the school can take with existing resources. A baseline is established to determine whether the goal is obtainable. The amount of time and resources that are available to accomplish the goal must be identified. A balance must be established when setting a goal that will excite the team but not be so unrealistic that the team players become discouraged.

Relevant/Results-Based/Real World. Is the goal results-based, indicating an outcome? Results-based goals require specific measurable and observable outcomes. Results manifest in different ways, such as an increase in student achievement in an identified area, or improved performance defined and measure by a rubric. Results-based goals require a clear and specific description of the results of the school's activities.

Time-Bound. When will the school evaluate whether it has met the goal? A sense of urgency makes goals more compelling. A clearly defined time frame prioritizes the goal for all stakeholders. (Roy, 2007, pp. 3–5)

Figure 2.2, SMART Goal Example, provides an illustration of a SMART goal. The goal is **S—specific** because it identifies who is involved, in this case all students on the campus. The goal is **M—measurable** because a mastery level of "meets or exceeds" is established. The goal is **A—attainable** because a reasonable time as well as a reasonable mastery measurement metric is established. The goal is **R—results-based** because it is connected to the state writing assessment. The goal is **T—time-bound** because it is defined by the academic year. All five components must be clearly identifiable for a goal to be considered a SMART goal.

Figure 2.2   SMART Goal Example

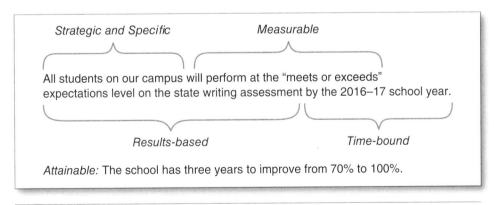

Source: Maxwell & Bardwell, 2014.

Anne Conzemius and Jan O'Neill, in *The Handbook for SMART School Teams* (2014), take SMART goals a step further and advocate for SMART schools. Conzemius and O'Neill posit that SMART goals alone will not expand a school's capacity for improvement, but when applied systematically throughout a school, SMART goals will have enormous impact. Conzemius and O'Neill call for four actions in creating SMART schools:

- All stakeholders must know the priorities and expectations and align efforts to achieving them (because consensus was obtained on strategic, specific, and attainable goals).
- All stakeholders know the school's definition of success and how, when, and who will measure it (because all stakeholders agreed on what is measurable).
- As a component of the overall results-oriented strategy, all stakeholders are involved in discovering an avenue to achieve the priorities (within the framework of their own work) and collectively identify what is or is not working as planned.
- Initiatives have a greater opportunity to succeed and become part of the school's culture when they are continuously improved, based on well-informed decisions, and provided targeted resources. (Conzemius & O'Neill, 2014, p. 7)

FOSTERING A SCHOOL TECHNOLOGY VISION

The digital age and associated technologies are presenting new challenges and unique opportunities for school principals. Principals must navigate these technologies and change their schools in the new digital era. Principals must embrace, prepare for, and lead in this new learning environment. Central to these responsibilities, as noted previously in this chapter, is developing a vision, specifically a vision of technology integration. Principals must lead schools with a clear vision of how technology will be utilized to enhance learning experiences for all students, and moreover, aid teachers in becoming more effective and efficient instructors. However, consider this assessment by Michael Karlin from his April 25, 2013, *Ed Tech Round Up* blog:

> Today it is almost impossible to spend any time during a day without being exposed to technology. In the privacy of one's home, smart digital devices are everywhere—the television, connected thermostat, washing machine, coffee maker, baby monitor, door locks, lighting, activity tracker, crock pot, alarm clock, smart phones, land-lines, security camera, appliances, and too many other smart devices to list. On the other hand, if you spent the day in a typical classroom you would likely find almost the opposite— little technology, few digital devices to improve instruction.

A sad commentary that is too often true. Digital technology places significant pressure on principals and faculty—pressure to change, to adjust, to improve, to become more instructionally effective and more efficient in management of time. At the core of these change processes is the school leader. If the principal lacks a vision and fails to define the school's mission (to be developed collaboratively with all stakeholders), then the principal will fail to harness the power of digital technologies, and students will be left behind.

Madrid School Develops a Tech-Savvy Vision

Sam Cade was beginning his fourth year as principal at Madrid School. He had assembled a fine team of educators, and together they had made significant instructional progress working with a student body that included a large percentage of English language learners. What concerned Sam late one afternoon was a very good teacher, Rudy Davillo. Rudy had come into Sam's office and asked why the principal was not paying more attention to the technological needs of students and faculty. Principal Cade was not only intrigued by the question, he felt that Rudy had posed a question that demanded an answer. Sam decided to conduct a serious investigation by examining empirical research to determine how principals can develop digital expertise and utilize technology to improve leadership and instructional practices. Principal Cade felt he was somewhat competent in this new digital era. He used a desktop computer, a laptop, a tablet, a smartphone and apps, tech systems in his car, and even a trusty old digital camera. However, he felt a failing in developing a digital vision for Madrid School. Sam was embarrassed Rudy Davillo had to inspire him into recognizing a digital vision must be developed.

Principal Cade immediately turned to his computer and sent an e-mail to several members of his team. He invited his assistant principal, Betty Jo Bradley, and several teachers from the differing grade levels and departments to join him the first of the next week to examine their campus vision and determine how technology could be better integrated not only into the vision but also extensively into the instructional program. Sam wanted the team to brainstorm how technology could become an effective partner in teaching, leading, and learning, and how technology could save time and produce greater academic achievement.

Betty Jo Bradley, Madrid's assistant principal, received and read the e-mail and immediately walked into Sam's office. She was delighted to learn that Sam was taking a digital era lead. She recommended that Sam give serious consideration to the needs and opinions of both some tech-savvy teachers and some other teachers who were anything but. Sam had done so, but he and Betty Jo devised an additional faculty list to include counselor Joe Carson, parent liaison Charley Pratt, and teachers Kate Benaderet, Homer Bedloe, Lisa Douglas, and of course, Rudy Davillo. Both Sam and Betty Jo knew this would be an exceptional team to work on the digital vision issue.

Come Monday the following week, after the dismissal of students, Sam, Betty, and Rudy convened the Madrid School Visionary Task Force. Several individuals made it to the meeting. Some did not.

(Continued)

(Continued)

Sam Cade:	Hello, folks. Good afternoon. We've got some serious work to do, and I appreciate your willingness to serve on this task force. Betty Jo and I, at the urging of Rudy, have done some serious thinking and research, and we strongly believe that a digital vision must be established at Madrid School.
Betty Jo Bradley:	Sam is right, and thank you, Rudy, for initiating this meeting. We have work to do, so let's get to it!
Rudy Davillo:	Thank you, Sam and Betty Jo. I'd been reflecting over summer break and realized that we were behind the curve technologically. That's why I spoke to Sam last week. The bad news? Yes, we're behind the curve. The good news? Sam, Betty Jo, and I have been working to bring research and data to you so we can develop a strong digital-age vision and vision statement for our school.
Homer Bedloe:	Folks, I'm honored to be selected for this committee work, but you all have to know that I'm about as technically illiterate as they come. Yep, I can turn on my computer, check e-mails, and enter attendance and grades, but after that, if there are any technical glitches, I'm calling my good friend, Rudy, or one of my colleagues, like Lisa, Kate, or Joe.
Charley Pratt:	I strongly resemble those remarks! I'd rather be asked to serve as the C. & F. W. Railroad engineer than be called "tech-savvy"!
Kate Benaderet:	Well, here's my recommendation—let's all work together and become tech-savvy. I think we should look at the following: First, what makes for a highly effective tech-savvy principal? Second, how can the leadership team best ensure that faculty and staff are tech-savvy, instructionally focused, and efficient time managers? Third, what can we do as a team to implement a technological vision and statement to ensure our students achieve and succeed?
Lisa Douglas:	I believe those are excellent starting points, but I think we better determine what the research stipulates relative to technological implementation, time management, and instructional excellence before we jump into the proverbial deep end.

Joe Carson:	Lisa's right! She probably knows technology better than any of us. She even has a digital kitchen toaster that's amazing! I'm even thinking of getting one. Back to business: If we're to develop a digital vision and vision statement, we better have our facts, research, data, and acts together!

Thus began a series of task force meetings that culminated with the following recommendations for a Madrid School digital vision and vision statement.

The Madrid School Visionary Task Force collaboratively decided upon six potential digital vision statements. Examine each of the statements below, and then respond to the questions on page 38.

Technology Vision Statement 1. Technology is changing the way we live and work, and it will continue to evolve. Technology has the power to enhance the teaching and learning processes, to stimulate creativity and self-discovery, and to enable us to communicate more effectively, work more efficiently, solve problems, and access and analyze information. Students and faculty will understand, incorporate, and be comfortable using technology.

Technology Vision Statement 2. Technology is the digital-era tool for learning that expands our instructional program and maximizes the effective use of our time and the capacity of all teachers and student learners. It is our digital vision that students be engaged in a stimulating academic environment and a challenging curriculum that is technology driven, student centered, and focused on inquiry-based learning.

Technology Vision Statement 3. Madrid School has the responsibility for developing curriculum and applying instructional methods enriched with technology. Our digital vision ensures that students and teachers are proficient users of new technologies.

Technology Vision Statement 4. We envision students, faculty, and administration at Madrid School being engaged in learning, leading, and teaching, focusing on technology to create inquiry-based and hands-on learning. Technology will support learning across the curriculum and subject areas. All will be fully active using current technology, software, tools, and applications.

Technology Vision Statement 5. Technology will enable all Madrid School learners (student, faculty, and administration) to become effective, efficient, and productive in educational and life pursuits. Students, faculty, and administration will develop digital competencies necessary to incorporate and utilize technology as a tool to create, access, analyze, synthesize, evaluate, and communicate information.

Technology Vision Statement 6. Madrid School students will acquire lifelong learning skills though involvement in meaningful, real-world digital experiences. Teachers will be supported by administration as they utilize technology to create instructional materials, develop and deliver instructional methods and strategies, and evaluate student learning.

> **Question 1.** Reflecting on what you have read in this chapter, which one of the six digital vision statements do you consider most appropriate for Madrid School?

> **Question 2.** Could a better digital vision statement be developed, based on what you have read in this chapter? How? By what means?

> Share your responses to these questions with peers and/or colleagues.

SEVEN HABITS FOR TECH-SAVVY PRINCIPALS

1. **Develop a vision.** Transform your school into a student-centered, technology-focused learning environment. Use instruction with hands-on technology as a means of empowering students to become more digitally relevant, technically competent, and timely learners.

2. **Collaborate as a team.** The term *collaboration* can be changed into a principal-oriented question: "How can we work together?" Collaboration allows for open conversations among faculty, students, and administration. Faculty can technically collaborate with students, and students with faculty, via digital tools such as education-focused Twitter communities, blogs, discussion boards, and a Padlet Wall (www.padlet.com).

3. **Seek new ideas.** Create focus groups, brainstorming sessions, or task forces (à la those at Madrid School) to regularly meet after school hours to examine how to integrate technology into the curriculum and instructional program, to discover new digital tools, and to share ideas about utilizing technology in classrooms to enhance student learning. Recall, "All of us are smarter than any one of us!"

4. **Innovate and facilitate.** Revolutionize and modernize a school by helping others transform responsible instruction to include the use of technology. This means allowing students to use web-enabled mobile devices, tablets, social media, audio and video technology, and other web-based resource tools. Principals must make a conscious decision to help and trust (but always verify) teachers and students with technology. Administration must provide digital resources that will aid teachers with instruction to further increase student achievement.

5. **Take risks.** How does a principal take a digital risk? Here's one idea: Permit students to access their mobile devices during the school day—obviously for instructional purposes. Students have their devices, so permit them to use them to become better learners and technologically advanced citizens. If faculty do not permit students to use their devices for educational purposes during the day, let's not kid ourselves—the students will use their personal devices for their own vices!

6. **Allocate resources—fiscal, material, and human.** Funding digital devices is always difficult. Sorenson and Goldsmith (2013) in their bestselling text, *The Principal's Guide to School Budgeting*, make no bones about it—principals have to become experts at doing more with less. *Think differently.* To use a well-worn phrase: "Think outside the box!" Collaborate with faculty, students, parents, and community members as to what new technical materials can replace materials of the past. Here's an example: Stop purchasing sets of textbooks; use online curricular supplements instead. Use the money saved to purchase needed digital tools that are real-world oriented, technologically relevant, and practical for the 21st century. *Think dollars!* Another example: US history textbooks—you need 200 for your 11th graders. The texts cost $125 each. You can save $25,000 by not buying new history textbooks. The authors strongly suspect that everything found in the text can be found online, and what is found online may be actually more historically accurate and relevant. *Think people!* Find human resources on campus or within the district or the community who can provide expertise or funds for digital initiatives. *Think innovatively!* Consider this example: Why purchase labs—computer, language arts, foreign language, et cetera? Instead, ask community corporations to fund digital purchases for your students and faculty. Tablets for a whole class cost a fraction of what a lab would cost. Tablets do the same work, are more personal and easily accessible, and enable effective and efficient teaching, leading, and learning. Just think, no more headaches, conflicts, and time consumed when scheduling classes into labs. Remember, labs cost a fortune and are on their way to obscurity, if not antiquity, the day after their purchase. Negotiate with companies to acquire other digital devices for educational purposes. Again, it is time, especially during this era of fiscal constraint, to think differently, to think dollars, to think people, and to think innovatively. It's time for the visionary leader to *think digitally!*

7. **Lead learners are lifelong learners**. Change and transformation in schools will not occur until principals become connected learners and digital modelers. Commit to learning about technology, and then share what you've learned. Principals are always willing to express their expectations of faculty and students. Now is the time to model what you expect by using practical and innovative methods that integrate digital tools into the curriculum and into the classroom. Student learning will be enhanced, academic achievement will increase, and time will be saved.

TIME MANAGEMENT AND TECH-SAVVY, INSTRUCTIONALLY FOCUSED LEADERSHIP

Principals must

1. Make time for technology (learn how in Chapters 3, 4, 5, 7, and 8 of this text);

2. Model how to use technology;

3. Provide and lead professional development in the use of technology;

4. Support technology adopters and risk takers, and communicate and champion technology;

5. Provide technology resources and tools;

6. Integrate technology; and

7. Expect technology-driven teaching and student learning and work.

Principals must recognize that the visionary benefits of integrating technology in schools are numerous:

- Teachers can create individualized instruction and assessments better tailored to individual student needs;
- Students can work at their own pace and receive one-on-one instruction through virtual lessons;
- Lessons can be more engaging, interactive, collaborative, and relevant, and they can be designed for multiple intelligences;
- Assessment results can be delivered immediately;
- Students with special needs can access modified forms of instruction and assessment;
- Advanced students can extend their learning opportunities outside the traditional curriculum; and
- Technology is a timesaver for educators (Gudenius, 2010).

TECHNOLOGY TIMESAVERS FOR VISIONARY EDUCATORS

Educators are the same everywhere—*busy!* Envisioning, incorporating, and integrating technology into their work frequently seem to be overwhelming expectations and tasks. These tasks demand more of educators and their valuable time. What's a principal to do? In reality, focus faculty on the campus digital vision and on technology as a timesaver. When integrated, technology makes teaching, leading, and learning more efficient and, actually, more effective. In reality, technology allows teachers more time to focus on the needs of their students. Consider a few of the technology timesavers listed here, and incorporate them into your daily campus routines.

1. Declutter your inbox with *Unroll.Me*.

2. Use *IFTTT*. This web-based service empowers individuals with creative control over apps such as Gmail, Facebook, Instagram, and Craigslist.

3. Use *Remind* to send important reminders to colleagues and students.

4. Use *Google Calendar*. Employ *Boomerang Calendar* to schedule, in one click, group meetings with other busy professionals.

5. Bookmark your favorite websites using *Diigo*.

6. Can't keep up with all those personal passwords? Use *PassCaddy*.

7. Use *Google Apps* for yourself and your students. Everything can be saved here and accessed anytime and anywhere. With *Google Apps*, students can turn in their work and you can provide feedback digitally.

8. Use a tablet to manage your classroom. Here's how: Connect the tablet to your LCD projector or SmartBoard, and use apps to connect with students, conduct student polls, and informally check for understanding.

9. Use *Smore* to create classroom newsletters or as a resource for student projects. *Smore* allows for helpful links, saving hours of time making copies, as all is stored in one place.

10. Save time by sharing and creating documents using *Doctopus* (Google Docs).

11. *Flubaroo* aids teachers when making multiple-choice or fill-in-the-blank tests or assignments. Plus, this digital tool will grade the tests and assignments.

12. Administrators will appreciate *FormMule*. This digital tool takes notes/scripts during classroom observations or in follow-up conferences. Additionally, it shares appraisal feedback immediately by automatically forwarding e-mails with results.

13. Need to organize your classroom learning management system? Try one of these digital systems—*Schoology*, *Edmodo*, *Moodle*, or *Google Classroom*.

14. Teachers can save time by selecting an online lesson plan book. *Planbook* is an excellent digital tool for this purpose.

TIME MANAGEMENT AND CAMPUS PLANNING

It goes without saying that more academic learning time—time teachers and students spend with each other on academic tasks—results in greater student achievement (Denhan & Lieberman, 1980; Ybarra & Hollingsworth, 2001). Thus principals must be intentional in leading stakeholders to align district and campus planning with time management priorities.

Kowalski (2013) defines time management as consciously planning and governing schedules in order to address the most pressing and significant aspects of work. Schmoker (2006) reminds us if we seek to create better schools, we must discover efficient means to do so. Time usage must be aligned with priorities. Likewise, Schmoker (2006) calls on principals to monitor and authenticate evidence that administrators and faculty are targeted on that narrow fundamental action set with the greatest impact on instructional quality. Yukl (2012) offers nine time management guidelines designed to help leaders become intentional with their time management. Yukl's time management guidelines are as follows:

- Recognize the reasons for demands and limitations;
- Expand the variety of choices;
- Determine what you want to accomplish;
- Analyze time usage;
- Plan daily and weekly activities;
- Avoid unnecessary meetings and activities;
- Defeat procrastination;
- Take advantage of reactive activities; and
- Set time aside for reflective planning.

Time management is intertwined with planning and implementing the school's vision and mission, as is evidenced in Figure 2.3, Campus Planning Template. The campus planning template demands timely action

Figure 2.3   Campus Planning Template

Goal II: Provide a curriculum that addresses the basic skills to increase student academic performance. **Objective 1:** Explore and implement programs that will increase overall student achievement. **Strategy 1:** Continue current instructional programs.					
Action(s) Implementation(s)	Responsibility Staff Assigned	Time Line Start/End	Resources	Audit (Formative)	Reported/ Documented
		May 2016 – March 2017			
Evaluation (Summative): All disaggregated student groups will obtain 80% or greater mastery on State Assessment of Academic Progress.					

as well as accountability. Actions must be described with specificity. Individuals responsible for implementing the actions are identified. Time is assigned to the activity, providing beginning and ending points, and resources are clearly identified. Means of formative assessment are established, as is a system for reporting on and documenting progress toward the goal, objective, and strategy. Finally, summative evaluation is specific and measurable.

Time on task, student scheduling issues, and faculty and staff schedules are crucial in making vision and mission a reality. Action plans driven by the school's vision and mission statements must contain time lines for identified actions in order to enforce ongoing accountability. Monitoring, implementing, and revising plans designed to fulfill the school's mission and vision require efficient use of time. The principal who manages time efficiently also uses varied resources efficiently while supporting the school's mission effectively.

The Sorenson-Goldsmith Integrated Budget Model, Figure 2.4, aligns campus resources with the school's vision and mission. Leadership is

Figure 2.4   Sorenson-Goldsmith Integrated Budget Model

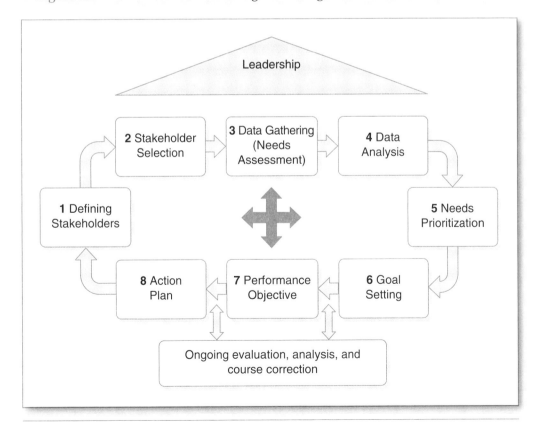

Source: Sorenson & Goldsmith, 2013, p. 81.

placed at the top of the model not to symbolize top-down leadership but to represent the shepherding and alignment of the school's resources with its vision, mission, and time. Component 8, the Action Plan, aligns these three factors while assigning accountability to the appropriate stakeholders. Action plans must be active documents, open to change and modification and frequently revised and updated. The bottom box in the model, "Ongoing evaluation, analysis, and course correction," constantly interacts with the eight numbered components of the budget model. The double pointed arrows illustrate the constant adjustment and course corrections needed to maintain the alignment among vision, mission, and time.

For a school's vision and mission to become a reality, time becomes an important commodity—a finite commodity—that always appears to be in short supply. Lambert (2003) declared that leaders become imprisoned by time. According to Lambert, leaders feel most victimized by time when:

- The number of tasks and agendas make them feel pulled in multiple directions and powerless to affect their conditions;
- Meetings are ineffective, leaving them feeling more tired than when they arrived (see the Chapter 3 case study, Death by Meeting!);
- No decision-making processes exist, leading to inertia;
- Directives disrupt work and require changes in direction; and
- Leaders work hard but don't feel successful.

Time can be a tyrant that controls lives; it hides, steals, and eats up space. That's what I do best!

—*The Silent Time Thief*

Demands escalate, but available time remains constant, even as the decision-making process requires more time (Graham & Ferriter, 2010). It is up to principals to effectively and efficiently manage time. Principals must determine how to use time. Principals must purposely set aside time for reflection. Not doing so interferes with the ability to distill the important from the unimportant. Likewise principals must invest time in others with whom symbiotic relationships have been established. The authors invest time with each other through collaborative writing. Doing so creates synergy and reveals insights that clarify both writers' thoughts and writing. Likewise the authors schedule time for breaks and fellowship. It is important to reserve time for reflection and fellowship. Principals who fail to do so are likely to lose their ability to delineate effectively between what is important and what is unimportant.

Personal Time Management

Christa Metzger solicited input from school leaders on a variety of their personal growth leadership practices. Six themes were identified. Balance, one of Metzger's identified themes, was defined as balancing life and work, balancing professional and private life, and prioritizing and allocating time prudently (Metzger, 2008). These school leaders identified seven time management practices to balance one's life:

- Create time each day with nothing scheduled;
- Remain after everyone leaves for an opportunity for quiet time;
- Find time for what's important;
- Take time out to breathe—deeply and slowly;
- Use after hours/Saturdays to target pet or priority projects;
- Develop to-do lists synced to electronic devices (then let them go); and
- Establish priorities for yourself (Metzger, 2008, p. 125).

Many if not most principals look at this list and readily consider incorporating some of the time management techniques into their work. Others ignore this dimension of their professional lives. However, all benefit from reflection on time management strategies. Begin by identifying one of Metzger's time management strategies and practice it. Reflect to see if a positive change occurs in your leadership skills. Once the first time management strategy is mastered, select another one. Continue until you have mastered all of these strategies. Personal reflection combined with professional growth in time management makes for stronger, better principals.

One Way to Defeat the *Silent Time Thief*

Personal Reflection + Personal Growth =
Improved Time Management Skills.

I dare you! Try to defeat me!

—The Silent Time Thief

The creation story in Genesis, the first book of the Bible, has the Creator resting on the seventh day. The authors use the seventh day as a time for rest, a time for renewal, a time to meditate, a time to adjust their perspectives. Some might consider a day of rest to be wasting time. But it isn't. It is investing time. Rest, reflection, and renewal allow the authors to address Stephen Covey's "first things first" decree (Covey, 2004). While it is initially awkward to take time for rest and it provides a potential source for angst, it improves personal effectiveness.

Flaherty (1999) reminds principals they exist in three time openings—past, present, and future. When considering Flaherty's position, principals realize what they are completing was initiated in the *past* by doing it in the *present* with an outcome in the *future*. Flaherty is implying existence in all three time openings simultaneously—past, present, and future. Savor traditions from the past, but also be excited about the future. However, principals must begin their workday in the present, for it is there they encounter the day.

Time Use and Effectiveness

Educators in general and principals in particular must understand the relationship between time use and effectiveness. Horng, Klasik, and Loeb (2010) conducted one of the first large-scale observational studies of principals' time use, examining it with respect to school effectiveness. They organized principals' use of time into six categories: administration, organizational management, day-to-day instruction, instructional program, internal relations, and external relations. Some of their findings are shown in Figure 2.5, Principal Time Usage.

Figure 2.5   Principal Time Usage

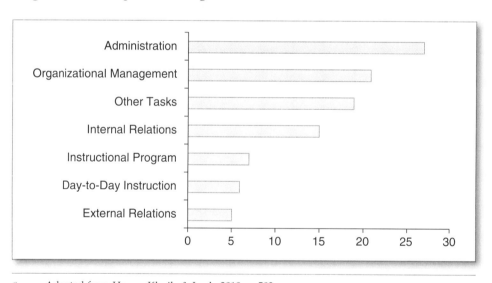

Source: Adapted from Horng, Klasik, & Loeb, 2010, p. 502.

Principals allocate more of their time, approximately 26%, to administrative obligations, including discipline and compliance requirements, than to any of the other six time use categories. Organizational management—including items such as the school budget and staff and personnel matters—consumed about one fifth of principals' time. Fifteen percent of their time was spent dealing with internal school relationships, including developing rapport with students and connecting socially with staff. Five percent of the principals' time was devoted to external relationship tasks such as fund raising. Surprisingly, the campus instructional leaders in this study spent about six percent of their time on instructional programs and five percent on day-to-day instruction. Day-to-day instruction includes informally coaching teachers and conducting classroom visits. Finally, during 20% of their working hours, the principals' behavior did not fit into any of the six broad categories.

 How does one thwart the *Silent Time Thief*? The following list revisits nine thwarting strategies. Using an acrostic, "time thief" is spelled out and defined.

1. *DaTa* are used to assess organizational effectiveness and promote organizational learning.

2. *VIsion* is at the heart of academic success.

3. ***M****ission* is a reality that requires principals to approach time management.

4. *Tim**E** management* is essential for principals leading stakeholders in district and campus planning.

5. *SMAR**T** goals* increase accountability by being specific, measureable, achievable, realistic, and time based.

6. *Leaders**H**ip* must be intentional on time management.

7. Consciously *plann**I**ng* and controlling your schedule ensures you attend to the most important and demanding aspects of your work.

8. It is important for educators in general and leaders in particular to understand the relationship between time use and ***E****ffectiveness*.

9. Vision and mission point the way to a school's ***F****uture*.

DA**T**A
VIS**I**ON
MISSION
TIM**E** MANAGEMENT

SMAR**T** GOALS
LEADERS**H**IP
PLANN**I**NG
EFFECTIVENESS
FUTURE

—The Silent Time Thief

FINAL THOUGHTS

Many make periodic eye appointments to have their vision checked. This exam usually includes monitoring the eyes for any disease or abnormality. Often the pupils are dilated to allow the doctor to view the eye's inner recesses. This exam also involves an acuity check to determine the sharpness of vision that begins with reading large-font letters and progressing to smaller and smaller fonts until the patient can no longer distinguish the letters. If acuity meets the 20/20 standards, the patient departs. If not, a prescription for corrective lenses or contact lenses is dispensed.

Read Figure 2.6, Vision Chart, and determine whether you can find the authors' hidden message.

Figure 2.6   Vision Chart

Did you observe vision, mission, and time in Figure 2.6? Is your vision 20/20? Taking a "vision exam" is a good way to close this chapter. The vision chart's embedded message reads, "Everyone needs a vision and mission driven by time."

Maybe principals are like Frodo, frequently wishing that "it"—whatever "it" is—had not happened in their time. But it did happen, and exceptional principals must act with the time provided. In other words, exceptional principals are responsible for discovering the vision, mission, and time relationship. Exceptional principals are responsible for using time to translate vision and mission into reality. Gandalf reminds principals: Decide what to do with the time provided.

One More Point

Will Rogers, a social commentator born in 1875 on the Dog Iron Ranch in Indian Territory (Oklahoma), provides principals with old but timely advice—"Even if you are on the right track, you'll get run over if you just sit there" (n.d.). Timeless advice. Vision. Mission. Time.

DISCUSSION QUESTIONS

1. Using the six lenses of the PSEL standards, provide three examples for each of Horng, Klasik, and Loeb's (2010) principal time use categories (as shown in Figure 2.5, Principal Time Usage), as manifested on your campus. If a category or categories is/are not evidenced on campus, what do you suggest to address the omission(s)?

2. Identify five challenges principals face in managing time. What strategies can be used to meet the identified challenges?

3. Christa Metzger identified seven time management practices for balancing personal and professional lives. The practices are as follows: (1) Have some "white calendar" time each day. (2) Stay after everyone has gone to find quiet time. (3) Make time for what's important to me. (4) Take time to breathe deeply and slowly. (5) Come in after hours or on Saturday to concentrate on a special project. (6) Make a to-do list, write things, and then let them go. (7) Set priorities for myself. Rank Metzger's time management practices in order of usefulness. How do these practices impact time, vision, and mission?

4. Interview a principal. Ask how he or she manages vision, mission, and time. What connections can you make from this interview to the content of this chapter?

5. Review your campus plan's goals using the information on SMART goals located in this chapter. Are your school goals SMART? If so, congratulations. If not, what changes need to be made to make them SMART goals?

6. Identify a campus need. Construct a SMART goal and develop a plan to address the need. Be certain to consider vision, mission, and time.

7. Yukl (2012) offered nine time management guidelines. Reflect on personal time management using Yukl's guidelines. Identify three behaviors you exhibit that support these guidelines. Identify three behaviors that you could improve and how you would make the improvements.

8. Lambert (2003) identified five ways she felt victimized by time. Share two times when you experienced being victimized by time.

9. What technology time savers do you use? How do they save time?

10. Select a technology from the *Technology Timesavers for Visionary Educators* list to consider adopting. What made this app appealing to you?

SELF-REFLECTION ON LENS 1: VISION, MISSION, AND TIME

In Chapter 1, "Time Management and Your Leadership," you completed the *Time Management Self-Assessment Instrument* (TMSI). In this chapter we examined TMSI Lens 1—Vision, Mission, and Time. It is time for self-reflection. Review your responses on the TMSI Scoring Template for Lens 1, Vision, Mission, and Time. Consider the material from this chapter and its association with the items from Lens 1. What beliefs were reinforced? What items are you reconsidering? Why? Would you change your score on any of the items? If so, why? Remember, as you progress through this book, examine your use and understanding of time in association with the PSEL standards.

CASE STUDY APPLICATION

THE MADGE SIMON SCHOOL

Madge Simon School (MSS) is named after a revered high school mathematics teacher in Windy Palms Public School District (WPPSD), a suburban school district located near the coast. Thirty years ago, WPPSD had fewer than 400 students. Today there are 4,600 students, and enrollment is expected to climb rapidly to 6,600 students, as two major foreign corporations are investing $1.2 billion in two industrial plants. The district is anticipating an influx of students speaking Asian languages as well as basic English. Within the past two years, the district has enrolled approximately 300 Spanish-speaking students.

MSS has had three principals in the last six years. The previous principal resigned for "personal reasons." One third of the faculty and staff have been on the campus for fewer than three years. WPPSD's superintendent, Dr. Neaux, realized this campus was likely to experience a "perfect storm"—an influx of new students with language challenges, a faculty of which 40% have been at MSS for three or fewer years, and a new principal.

Dr. Neaux convened a meeting with the campus planning committee. She shared the "perfect storm" scenario with the faculty and staff. Everyone appreciated the superintendent's frankness and honesty. She requested the committee nominate a pool of ten faculty and four staff members to be considered as a search committee for a new principal; this approach had never been taken in this school district. Dr. Neaux selected five faculty and two staff members from this pool to serve on the search committee. For the first time, trust was developing between the campus and the superintendent's office—something everyone appreciated.

The search committee involved all campus stakeholders in hiring the principal—once again, this was something that had never happened before at MSS. The superintendent and the search committee agreed upon a pool of three applicants. All three were vetted and interviewed by the superintendent and the campus planning committee. Following district hiring procedures, Dr. David Roberts was chosen by unanimous decision of the committee and hired as the next principal of MSS.

After a few days of meetings, being welcomed by such groups as the MSS PTA executive committee and the MSS custodial team, and attending a faculty/staff meet and greet, Dr. Roberts attended a Kiwanis Club meeting, where he introduced himself to the community. Dr. Roberts also visited First Family Church, whose members were predominantly minorities, located two blocks away from MSS. The pastor invited Dr. Roberts to speak for 15 minutes about his vision for MSS at the Sunday morning assembly. After several more days of meetings and being introduced to other school and community groups, it was time for Dr. Roberts and his team to get down to business.

(Continued)

(Continued)

Dr. Roberts sensed a new excitement in the air at MSS. The campus planning committee convened for the first time since he assumed the principalship. He assured the faculty he was "in for the long haul." This statement was followed by strong unsolicited applause. Dr. Roberts asked the committee if they believed it was appropriate to review the campus vision and mission statements. He shared his desire to breathe life into these statements and allow them to "be the beacon" for the school. There was applause. Excitement was building.

The new principal introduced the faculty and staff to PSEL Standard 1 and the seven elements. Each person received a copy of this PSEL standard along with a table containing assorted data on MSS.

Dr. Roberts divided the faculty and staff into teams of three or four members. He then asked each team to brainstorm at least three ways each of the PSEL Standard 1 elements could manifest itself at MSS. He told them that he and the faculty would get together and share their brainstorming results.

APPLICATION QUESTIONS

Brainstorm two or three ideas using the seven elements of PSEL Standard 1 to improve Madge Simon School. Once these ideas have been created, develop a plan for using them in creating the MSS vision and mission statements.

Selected Data From the Madge Simon School

Indicator	Madge Simon School	Windy Palms ISD	State
Total Enrollment	370	4,600	–
Attendance Rate	96.0%	95.7%	–
Student Ethnicity and Other Student Data			
African American	2.7%	1.4%	12.8%
Hispanic	58.7%	53.6%	50.8%
White	34.5%	41.2%	30.5%
Asian	2.7%	1.0%	3.6%
Two or More Races	0.8%	2.0%	1.7%
Economically Disadvantaged	55.4%	43.4%	60.4%
Limited English Proficient	6.5%	2.1%	16.8%
Mobility Rate	19.4%	18.8%	17.8%

Teachers by Experience			
Beginning	0.0%	1.1%	4.6%
1–5 Years	33.1%	22.1%	28.7%
6–10 Years	31.7%	22.6%	22.3%
11–20 Years	24.9%	29.4%	26.6%
Over 20 Years	10.3%	24.3%	17.9%
Expenditures			
Instructional Expenses per Student	$3,890	$4,117	$5,061

3

Leading, Teaching, Learning, and Time

My candle burns at both ends;

It will not last the night;

But, ah, my foes, and, oh, my friends—

It gives a lovely light!

—Edna St. Vincent Millay, "First Fig,"
in *A Few Figs From Thistles* (1921)

STRUCTURE IS THE KEY TO LOCKING OUT THE *SILENT TIME THIEF*

A memorable light, yet a short-lived glow! Edna St. Vincent Millay, American poet and playwright, had it exactly right. The beauty of her poem is much more than the rhythmic lyrics. The poem reveals exactly what happens when the instructional leader spends too much time on a light to lead by, but soon finds the *Silent Time Thief* (poor time management) has transformed the light into nothing more than a heat that burns. What is missing from this particular leadership equation is structure, the key to locking out the ever-intruding silent thief—representing the loss of time. Lazear (1992) reveals that structure, for some school principals, is perceived as nothing more than a bandage—helping a little when the principal senses it's either too late or too early to start a particular task. Actually, structure is a gift—a gift that apportions time to fit the task or tasks at hand. Such aptly relates to the words of the famous German writer and thinker, Wolfgang von Goethe (1749–1832): "The day is of infinite length for those who know how to appreciate and use it" (as quoted by Andrews, Biggs, & Seidel, 1996). Goethe, centuries ago, revealed what every instructional leader must recognize and understand today: Structure your time, and your tasks will be completed in appropriate time, if not record time. You think to yourself, "How?"

I Need a 27-Hour Day

James Van Horn served as principal at Sands School, and he always seemed to have too many tasks to complete, even with the help of Sandra Rios, the school's assistant principal. James often told anyone who would listen: "I need a twenty-seven-hour day!" Unfortunately, James had a problem—he frequently overcommitted, choosing to take on more than he could handle, and he refused to delegate. James would say, "Well, I feel bad if I ask someone else to do the work. Sandra is busy enough as it is, and I don't want her or any of the faculty to think I'm dumping on them." Understand, it wasn't as if James didn't have the drive, the initiative, or the competence to do the work. He just needed more time, and often James would chuckle to himself, "Sometimes more body parts—an extra set of hands, a couple more brains, and maybe, four more legs—all would be helpful." However, his dilemma was no laughing matter! The question constantly on his mind was one all principals consider: "How can I get done what needs to be done in the time I have?"

Structuring one's time, one's day, is a difficult proposition. There are always, it seems, too many fires to extinguish—teachers need to talk to the principal and only the principal! The same is true of parents. The instructional leader serves on numerous districtwide committees, regularly responds to central office directives, interacts with the superintendent, and, as always, handles numerous unpredictable demands. These demands, interactions, responses, committee responsibilities, parents, students, and teachers simply take over—they work as the *Silent Time Thief*—stealing valuable time from an already busy schedule and further disabling the leader from working effectively and efficiently to improve instruction and learning. What's a leader or a prospective leader to do? Consider the following principles of time management:

1. **Know thyself.** Develop an awareness of yourself and your leadership position. Recall from Chapter 1, "Time Management and Your Leadership," after completing the *Time Management Self-Assessment*

Instrument, how you were able to recognize your strengths, and just as important, recognize those areas to target for personal and professional growth. Principals must develop a personal awareness of individual and unique needs, styles of leading, characteristics and skills, and leadership-oriented practices. Know your responsibilities, list the main tasks associated with your leadership role, and then determine the amount of time you actually use to accomplish each task. Keep a daily log for added structure, if needed. An electronic calendar is an excellent tool for detailing times, tasks, and length of time needed to accomplish said responsibilities.

2. **Structure time.** Understand the essential goals and objectives or functions of the leadership positon before you structure your time. Consider the following: As part of your professional development, you attend a time management workshop. You come into the office the next morning fired up—ready to go! Prior to faculty, staff, and students arriving, you develop a daily to-do list. You think to yourself, "I'll accomplish more today than I've ever accomplished on any previous day!" However, within the first 30 minutes of the day, even before the first bell rings, your to-do list has been flittered away. You say to yourself, "What a waste of time to go to that workshop. The best of my intentions to manage my time more efficiently have gone up in smoke! I just don't understand what's wrong with me—why can't I manage my time like some of my colleagues?"

Here's why: You simply overlooked the main functions of the leadership role and position. You failed to plan for the usual inundation of requests from faculty, staff, custodians, parents, and students that occur every morning prior to the first bell. Prior planning is an essential element in structuring time. With prior planning comes contingency planning—handling the daily interruptions. These cannot be willed away. They will always be present. Don't forget to expect the unexpected. Always insert time for disruptions. They will be there—they will never disappear. So, don't stress, place the unexpected into your daily to-do list—on your daily agenda or in your digital device—and move forward. Your day will go better, guaranteed!

3. **Establish priorities.** The most important aspects of leading must receive your attention first, and thus the majority of your time. When you devote the majority of time to the smallest number of high-priority tasks, a direct increase in time efficiency occurs. Think back to Chapter 2, "Vision, Mission, and Time," and recall that research reveals that principals, inefficiently, spend the greatest percentage of time on the least important facets of the leadership role (Horng, Klasik, & Loeb, 2010).

4. **Simplify the work.** Increase personal efficiency and effectiveness by implementing "work simplification." Rid the daily to-do list of all management functions. Delegate those duties to someone else—someone trustworthy and dependable. However, recall the old adage, "Inspect

what you expect!" Forget politics; simply adopt the message of the following quote attributed to the late president Ronald Reagan: "Trust but verify!" Good advice, no matter your political persuasion. Delegate duties such as these:

- Completing maintenance request forms;
- Walking the building looking for potential safety hazards;
- Conducting bus duty;
- Monitoring the cafeteria; and
- Checking textbooks in and out.

The authors by no means wish to imply that the duties noted above are frivolous. However, these duties are administrative, managerial by nature. Most managerial duties can be "managed" by someone other than the instructional leader—by an assistant principal, office clerk, head custodian, receptionist, or, in some cases, student worker. Here's the magic question: Why are you—the instructional leader—hanging onto these routine duties? Surely you have more demanding instructionally oriented responsibilities that need immediate attention!

5. **Increase personal efficiency and effectiveness**. Work smarter, not harder! You've heard that philosophy since you were a kid. Good advice then, even better advice today. What falls into the realm of working smarter?

a. Reduce all managerial duties as much as possible;

b. Establish priorities—complete the most demanding (typically instructionally focused) duties first;

c. Structure time—use the latest in digital, time management technology (smartphone, tablet, even the old reliable laptop or desktop computer—see Chapter 8, "Technology: Staying a Step Ahead of the *Silent Time Thief*") to efficiently organize your time and tasks; and

d. Know your strengths and weaknesses. Know who you are, and target for improvement any deficiencies that inhibit you from effectively serving as an instructional leader and further impede your ability to efficiently manage your time.

Underestimating the time it takes to complete an administrative or instructional task actually makes the task seem longer and less enjoyable. Prioritize your tasks and time, or I'll readily take from both!

—The Silent Time Thief

Listed below are six additional recommendations for school principals relative to saving time:

1. Mikoluk (2013) suggests principals *get help from experts*—talk with administrative colleagues who have their acts together with respect to time management. Let these individuals assist you in creating a more structured schedule, allowing additional time to complete day-to-day tasks while working efficiently toward long-term goals.

2. Cookson (2013) advises principals to utilize a technology tool, *RescueTime*, an application that monitors how instructional leaders utilize their computers, focusing specifically on web-surfing habits and time spent working with certain reports and documents.

3. Gretchen Schilie, a principal in Seoul, South Korea, advocates the best time saver is a *space saver*. "I learned from a mentor administrator to deal with each issue or sheet of paper or e-mail at hand as soon as I can—instead of setting it aside and saying I will get back to it" (Hopkins, 2012, p. 6).

4. Beth Burt, a Texas elementary school principal, alludes to the fact that her *secretary* has taken on responsibilities that end up saving this principal valuable time. Her secretary organizes the mail; then the secretary and principal review it together. Burt relates the following: "First, we do all things that need to be signed, then we go over any communication from the district office, then other important mail, then things to read, and lastly junk. As we go through it together, we accomplish the mail and signing of papers very quickly" (Hopkins, 2012, p. 4). Principal Burt highly recommends a workshop entitled "How to Work Less, Play More, and Still Get the Job Done in a Normal School Week" (www.the-breakthrough-coach .com/curriculum/two-day.php).

5. Peggie Robertson (2006), a former elementary school principal in Virginia, proposes the use of *electronic devices* to help manage time as a principal. Apps endorsed by the University of New South Wales (UNSW Sydney, 2014) include, but are not limited to, the following:

> **Wunderlist 2,** a platform for creating to-do lists and for setting those all-important reminders. *Wunderlist 2* offers native apps for iOS, OS X, Windows, and Android, as well as a web-based service accessible from anywhere.
>
> **Tom's Planner,** a web-based scheduling tool that allows for creation of different task categories (seen side by side), allowing for better planning.
>
> **Evernote,** a free web-based filing cabinet for all notes a principal may take, whether the notes are actually notes or thoughts or sketches or something else. *Evernote* comes with native apps for iOS, OS X, Windows, and Android, as well as a web portal.

Google Calendar and Documents, an online calendar, filing system, and word processor that principals can use to update schedules and exchange documents online, anywhere, at any time. Principals can create shared calendars to help organize group work, or share resources such as an important study book, manual, curriculum guide, budget planner, et cetera. Documents can be created and shared online and others can edit them—this is a real time saver in group work. Refer to Chapter 8, "Technology: Staying a Step Ahead of the *Silent Time Thief*," for a greater analysis and screenshot examples of digital tools for the busy principal.

6. Sam Nachin, Jr., MBA, an educational consultant, recommends the following:

> I personally use *Wiggio* (www.wiggio.com). Best part, it's free. Principals can use this website to either create different "groups" in school, or have the entire staff as one "group." With this website a principal can create to-do lists with assignments to people, host virtual meetings and conference calls, manage events and appointments on a shared calendar, develop surveys/polls, manage files uploaded to the website, and send group emails/text/and other digitally-oriented messages, both automated and manually, to different group sets or to the entire staff. (Nachin, 2015)

Source: Ralph and Alice cartoon by Alex Carruth.

THE INSTRUCTIONAL LEADER

The term *instructional leader* has been humorously defined as a "ten-thousand aspirin job"! In fact, Copland (2001) described the instructional leader as a super principal whose qualifications include the following:

> Wisdom of a sage, vision of a CEO, intellect of a scholar, leadership of a field general, compassion of a counselor, moral strength of a nun, courage of a firefighter, craft knowledge of a surgeon, political savvy of a senator, toughness of a soldier, listening skills of a blind man, humility of a saint, collaborative skills of an entrepreneur, certitude of a civil rights activist, charisma of a stage performer, and the patience of Job (p. 528).

The authors do not wish to suggest that the instructional leader must be a super principal, nor do we wish to imply that the instructional leadership role demands medication in order to survive the job. However, the role is demanding, requiring a principal to have a high level of competence and expertise when it comes to the instructional program, appropriate teaching and learning, and technology—especially in this digital age.

The Instructional Program

Guthrie and Schuermann (2010) relate that a school year is composed of approximately 5,000 hours. We sleep approximately 3,000 hours a year. Bottom line, we spend the vast majority of our time as leaders at work, pursuing an almost divine mission—a calling, much like that of a minister, priest, or rabbi. In other words, this calling is a critical aspect of a principal's life. This calling is of significant importance to the clientele served—students. Time is of the essence when it comes to leading, teaching, and learning. Two decades ago, Milton Goldberg (1994), director of the National Education Commission on Time and Learning, wrote what remains most viable today: "Time is a resource that must be used more creatively and effectively" (p. 114). What defines a "best-practice" or "student-centered" instructional program, and what are principles of effective instruction? What barriers to student learning exist, and how are they overcome? Finally, high expectations in any instructional program equate to high student achievement.

A Best-Practice/Student-Centered Instructional Program

Effective instructional programs are student centered based on the incorporation of research-based, best-practice, and student-centered approaches. For example, effective programs are aligned with curriculum. Exceptional principals examine instructional programs to determine what is actually taught and learned in comparison with what the curriculum mandates. Do variances occur? Absolutely! Recall that high school teacher who preferred to focus the second semester of American History on World War II? Remember that middle school English teacher who so loved certain aspects of American poetry that she had overlooked in the curriculum the critical inclusion of other literature and grammar instruction? Recall that elementary school teacher who continuously shared with her second graders information about dinosaurs, resulting in other aspects of the science curriculum being completely ignored? Once again, "inspect what you expect" and "trust but verify." The instructional leadership role demands efficient use of time to best ensure students are on task and learning. Appropriate and effective learning guarantees academic success! Focus time and efforts on the instructional program, and student achievement will increase.

What else makes for effective instructional programs and excellence in student learning? Frequently examine what is tested and how the testing is administered. Be certain that curricular variances do not occur—in other words, know what curriculum should be taught and when. Be familiar with the curriculum guides. Recognize what must be included in the writing and revisioning of curriculum to include state and national standards and assessments. Effective instructional programs must include benchmarks; specified local standards; relevant professional development; teacher and student monitoring, evaluation, appraisal, and modeling; and continuous data analysis and programmatic assessment.

The instructional leader must ensure the development of a campus improvement or action plan and a needs assessment process. The campus improvement plan cannot be a document that ends up abandoned somewhere within a teacher's file cabinet. It must be a living, breathing instrument that serves as a measure for monitoring change, improvement, and student success. The same is true of a needs assessment. Far too many principals provide lip service when it comes to conducting a needs assessment and programmatic evaluation. Finally, all data collected must be analyzed in a prudent and appropriate manner. In other words, if instructional leaders are not competent in the data analysis process, they are caught in a never-ending undertow pulling them further and further out to sea, away from the safety of the shore—to the end of what was once a most promising career in school administration! Effective principals recognize that each of the above noted considerations leads to excellence in instruction, better utilization of time, and increased student learning and achievement.

Principles of Effective Instruction

Instructional leaders, working in collaboration with faculty and staff, must take time to clarify and plan what is to be taught, to include thinking about the content as what students need to learn. Collaboration with faculty includes cofacilitating discussions to create inclusive classrooms to meet the needs of all students, exploring types of knowledge and skills students must acquire to be successful in the future, and using culturally relevant pedagogical approaches that differentiate content and process (DeMatthews & Mawhinney, 2014). As noted previously, principals must find time to provide guidance to faculty about what to teach (state and local standards) and help the faculty prepare to teach. Effective teachers assess student understanding of the standards and lesson content. They organize the lesson content for better student understanding, and they choose methods for analysis (benchmarking) to determine whether students have learned the content.

Principals must grasp the concepts of effective instruction by helping teachers gain a clear understanding of what Price and Nelson (2007) refer to as the "big ideas"—those fundamental concepts that connect to smaller ideas. Big ideas assist teachers in determining what to teach and how to focus time on specific yet essential learning outcomes.

A Teachable Moment—Learning Curriculum and Instruction

Chuy Uranga, principal at Allamoore School, recognized a need to help his science teachers with taking big ideas and streamlining them into teachable moments. These teachers were in the first three years of their careers. Advantages and disadvantages existed with their lack of teaching experience. Chuy knew the teachers were trainable and not set in their ways, as sometimes was the case with his more senior faculty. However, being new to the profession, these teachers were frequently weak in classroom management and curricular expertise. Chuy jumped at the opportunity to coach the new faculty. Most of the new faculty were lost—there seemed to be no better way to describe their inexperience. So, as the instructional leader, Chuy began at the beginning. He planned to meet with the science department team in the school's conference room and begin the session with a simple lesson—"connect a big idea with a smaller, more detailed or specific teaching concept." So, Chuy—previous to the meeting—e-mailed the faculty with the following assignment:

Hello Science Department Members.

Tomorrow afternoon, in planning time, we will make essential connections between a major instructional idea and a specific teaching concept, based on our scope and sequence chart within the science curriculum guides.

(Continued)

(Continued)

Contemplate the following "big ideas" and be prepared to share how one can take such a global concept and narrow the focus into a detailed teachable moment. Consider these three items:

1. The interactions of desert mammals within their environment shape both the characteristics of the mammals and the environment.

2. Biology students, prior to conducting experiments related to desert mammals, read to become more informed about the Chihuahuan desert.

3. Conducting experiments and writing evaluative and analytical reports about the associated research requires technical expertise.

Chuy concluded the e-mail with the following assignment:

Be prepared to showcase, with your colleagues, how to make items 1–3 teachable moments.

Prior to the end of the school day, the science teachers met in the science department hallway, between bells, as students passed from class to class. The teachers looked at one another, grinning. Ellie said to Lisa, "The guy's a history major—taught American history and coached football prior to becoming a principal. Here's what's scary: He knows our curriculum." Lisa responded, "Yeah, we better be just as prepared and respond appropriately and correctly to the assignment. You know, Ellie, it's nice to work with a leader who understands curriculum and instruction. My husband, Sam, teaches English at one of our feeder schools, and his principal is lost in space. He's considering ability grouping students—can you believe it?" Ellie responded, "I guess we're lucky, but we better be prepared! Let's get with Abbie, Nelson, and Ryan and get started on this assignment."

Pause and Consider

- Place yourself in the role of Chuy Uranga, principal, and Ellie, Lisa, Nelson, Ryan, and Abbie—the five science teachers at Allamoore School. All parties must be prepared to examine and then discuss the proposed principle of effective instruction as noted in the vignette. What would be your response to the assignment? How would you turn a global or big idea concept into a specific or detailed teachable moment? Choose one of the three big ideas, and discuss and explain.

- Again, place yourself in the role of Chuy Uranga, principal, and think about the time aspect of this scenario. Is this a role for Mr. Uranga to fulfill, or should this role be delegated? Explain.

Effective Instructional Leadership and Time Management

In the previous scenario, Chuy Uranga, principal at Allamoore School, understood curriculum and instruction. He had excellent experience with technological devices. However, he constantly reminded himself, "I can't keep up this pace—I'm spending day and night at school. My family looks at me like I'm a stranger. I've got to find more time or lower my expectations. I can't even find time to think. I need some peace!" Consider again, "What's a principal to do?"

Think about the old adage "There's a time for everything and everything in its time." Humans are often predisposed to avoid unpleasantness, conflict, and difficult aspects of life. Mr. Uranga certainly fell into at least one of these categories—he would have preferred to avoid the work he was responsible for, the high expectations he had set for not only himself but for members of his faculty and staff. All were overwhelming him. Time was fleeting, and peace was often an afterthought.

Service as a principal often creates conflict—sometimes personal conflict and inner turmoil. It's obvious that Mr. Uranga wanted to be the best leader he could be, and he desired the best for and from his faculty and staff in order for his students to receive opportunities to learn and achieve. To work through such internal turmoil, to find the time, and to avoid the *Silent Time Thief*, that is, the loss of valuable time, Mr. Uranga—like any other administrator—needed to realize there is a time for everything and everything in its time. The question asked by Mr. Uranga, and one frequently asked by the best of school principals, is "How?"

Listed below are seven recommendations:

First, define the problem in terms of the needs of all parties. Mr. Uranga, as principal, had the competence and knowledge to lead his faculty toward excellence in instruction, but he needed more time. His faculty had the time (of course, the science team might argue they too needed more time), but they lacked the instructional competence and related skills.

Second, communicate! Discuss possible solutions, but avoid being evaluative, critical, or judgmental of any recommendations or solutions posed. Principals must be active listeners. Leaders must hear what is being said and then rephrase the message back to the speaker to be certain that they understand it. Then, begin a problem-solving and decision-making process. Success, as it relates to time management and the instructional program and student learning, is all about hearing and doing. Hear the suggestions, and *do* solve the problem.

Third, test, pilot, evaluate, and implement what is to be taught and learned.

Fourth, decide whether the solution is viable—is it working in its pilot form? If so, does it continue to be acceptable to all parties?

Fifth, place into action the agreed-upon solution. Put into practice what works.

Sixth, re-evaluate the solution, the process, the initiative, or the program. Make certain it is working for the best benefit of students and their learning, and, again, determine whether the solution is acceptable to all parties, especially when they are asked, "Is the solution better ensuring increased student achievement?"

Seventh, schedule time for inactivity. You probably read the previous sentence at least twice and thought to yourself, "I must have misread that sentence, or there must be a serious misprint. Did I really read that correctly? Inactivity, stop working? Who are these authors kidding? Are they really suggesting that I stop working? Are they nuts?"

There is precedence for this final recommendation. Research concludes that leaders frequently become victims to the "perpetual motion" syndrome, a chronic condition that dates back in the literature to the 19th century (Dircks, 1861/2012). Principals frequently believe that they must be active—busy with being visible, busy with student issues (discipline, for example), busy with hall duty, busy with completing forms and reports, busy with bus duty, busy observing teachers, busy meeting with parents, and busy conducting and attending meetings. Busy, busy, busy! Principals believe they must always be moving, always working, and they must always be on the go! Stop and consider the following: "I should build into my schedule a time to think and reflect!"

The exceptional principal finds time to think, reflect, plan, and keep abreast of current research and instructional trends. Scheduling periods of inactivity is okay. Schedule this time and close the office door. Don't feel guilty! Inform office staff there are to be no interruptions unless there is an emergency or a crisis. Better yet, find a place in another part of the building that is seldom frequented by other members of the faculty and staff. Go to that quiet place and think and reflect.

One of the authors had such a place—near the rear corner of the materials center at his school. There was a desk in that obscure part of the center, hidden behind a couple of very large bookshelves, bookshelves very high and wide, and the area was seldom stumbled upon by anyone on campus. When someone did walk back to that particular area (which was uncommon) and the author was there, both parties were often startled. Nevertheless, the author (then principal) typically found the place to be a quiet haven—a place to think, to clear the muddled administrative mind. Here was a place to reflect upon certain instructional and/or administrative issues, concerns, and/or problems. This was a place for meditation and in some instances, prayer.

Yes, this place provided an escape from the entrapment of the perpetual motion syndrome! It worked, and the author found an opportunity for the much-needed thinking time to prioritize tasks, if not life. And the really good news is the place worked, as the vast majority of tasks and decisions on the author's mind did not need immediate action or resolution. In actuality, the time required for the author to think through the issues or concerns or problems or instructional and/or learning considerations did save valuable time, even reduced stress, and more times than not, relieved the author—at least for a short period of time—of the burden of leadership. Fewer errors were typically the result, and the solving of the problem at hand was more often than not a one-time deal. This is what Mr. Uranga, principal at Allamoore School needed—a little calm, a little time, a little reflective period, and a lot of peace! Also, time is saved!

PRINCIPLES OF INSTRUCTIONAL CAPACITY AND MAXIMIZED STUDENT LEARNING

Sorenson, Goldsmith, Méndez, and Maxwell, in their text, *The Principal's Guide to Curriculum Leadership* (2011), assert, "Principals must establish curricular expectations on the basis of personal content knowledge, an understanding of instruction and instructional strategies and activities, and an awareness of how to properly evaluate curriculum design" (p. 55). Additionally, these same authors write, "Curricular leadership demands high principal expectations" (p. 55). Principals must be experts in their role as instructional leaders, always finding the time to coach or train or teach their faculty. Nothing less will do!

The Learner-Centered Expertise of Principals and Faculty

Twenty-five years ago, in a text no longer in print, *The New Manager's Survival Manual* (1989), Clay Carr alluded to the following relative to successful leaders: These leaders get results by developing successful followers, by building influence in an organization, and by increasing opportunities for enhanced student learning. This dated text reveals what remain truisms of school leadership to this day:

1. Know what to do;

2. Know how to do it well;

3. Have the tools to do it well;

4. Have the time to do it well; and

5. Take responsibility for doing it. (p. 17)

Elwood Cubberley wrote in an even earlier book, *Public School Administration* (1916), a century ago, the following about leading public schools:

Our schools are, in a sense, factories in which the raw products [students] are to be shaped and fashioned into products to meet the various demands [curricular, instructional, and business-oriented mandates] of life. The specifications for manufacturing [teaching] come from the demands of the Twentieth Century civilization [politicians, courts, and federal/state dictates], and it is the business of the school [principals and teachers] to build its pupils according to the specifications [state and local standards] laid down. This demands good tools (goals), specialized machinery [technology], continuous measurement [benchmarking and data analysis] of production [learning] to see if it is according to specifications, the elimination of waste [time management] in manufacture, and a large variety [diversified populations] in the output. (p. 33)

In a sense, nothing has changed over the past 25 or even 100 years with the exception of the date on the calendar and certain advancements in technology. The desire for students to learn and succeed, for teachers to effectively teach, for principals to be excellent instructional leaders, for new curricular and instructional enhancements to be achieved, and for time to be managed efficiently—these considerations continue as clarion calls for exceptional leadership and instructional expertise in learning.

If expertise is a measure of improved instruction and learning, what defines the exceptional instructional leader and faculty? Guthrie and Schuermann (2010) espouse the following: The best, the successful school principals and teachers, are those who

- apply strategic thinking (the constant appraisal of the learning environment and the recognition and application of change).
- plan operational details (the combination of sociopolitical processes and analytic techniques designed to improve the school's performance and efficiency).
- possess policy knowledge and formation. (Policy is a uniform plan or course of action, and therefore the associated change cannot be viewed as a one-time-only undertaking. Principals must be cognizant of education policy and its related implications insofar as the instructional program is concerned.)
- know the law (legal conventions, constitutions, cases, and court decisions as correlated with the curricular and instructional program).
- understand instructional programs (determining forces dictating instruction and perspectives on the assessment of quality learning as aligned with state standards).
- assess student learning and performance effectively and regularly (examining time for instruction, determining subject areas to be tested, and identifying appropriate aggregation of student subgroups to best compose a schoolwide measure of performance).

- make data-based decisions (understanding why and how to appropriately analyze data) and understand people. (Schooling translates to people, and exceptional people equate to exceptional schools.)
- partner with parents and communities.
- incorporate technology.

Cover (2014) believes that expert instructional leaders and teachers possess "the skill and the will" to bring about increased student learning and achievement and overall instructional and curricular improvement. Cover defines *skill* as effectively delivering the latest and greatest professional development to a less-than-enthusiastic group of individuals, and *will* as meeting a deadline that everyone else expected to be met yesterday! The best principals utilize skill and will to the greatest benefit of students and faculty. If *will* means getting the job done, what expert leadership and faculty *skills* are essential to doing so?

Important principal and teacher skills include the following:

- Creativeness
- Technical competence
- Intelligence
- Self-confidence
- Dependability
- Energy
- Tolerance
- Adjustability
- Sociability
- Achievement orientation
- Assertiveness
- Communicative ability
- Active listening ability
- Moral and ethical behaviors
- Quality orientation
- Participative and inclusive orientation
- Research orientation
- Change orientation
- Cultural sensitivity
- Ability to motivate others
- Spiritual orientation
- Purpose orientation
- Servant orientation
- Team accommodating

Now deceased, Thomas J. Sergiovanni, in his book, *Rethinking Leadership* (2007), wrote about leading, teaching, and learning qualities frequently exhibited by expert principals and faculty:

- They will be people of substance.
- They will be people who stand for important ideas and values.
- They will be people who are able to share their ideas with others in a way that invites them to reflect, inquire, and better understand their own thoughts about the issues at hand.
- They will be people who use their ideas to help others come together in a shared consensus.
- They will be people who are able to make the lives of others more sensible and meaningful. (pp. 82–83)

These points, as well as those in the previous lists, are the essence of leadership, whether characterizing or describing a school principal or a campus faculty member. These points are reflective of those leaders and teachers who strongly desire to best ensure effective and appropriate student learning, in a timely manner!

Instructional Design, Enhancements, and Interventions

Newly designed instructional programs must be developed, with written curriculum, to reveal cognitive and affective skills, concepts, and learning outcomes as general approaches to instructional enhancements and interventions to best address the diversity in schools today. This requires time! Lemov (2015); Hattie (2012); Sorenson, Goldsmith, Méndez, and Maxwell (2011); Lohr (2003); and Seels and Glasgow (1998) identified critical elements of instructional design, to include effective methods by which principals and teachers can analyze, design, develop, implement, and evaluate instruction, instructional enhancements, and interventions, and save time.

School principals can effectually and efficiently implement instructional design, enhancements, and interventions by applying the following time-saving phases, functions, and outcomes relative to the development of curricular and instructional programs and the improvement of student learning.

The *Analysis Phase* provides the school principal—in collaboration with the faculty team—an opportunity to conduct a needs assessment as well as a curricular/quality analysis (see Chapter 3 in *The Principal's Guide to Curriculum Leadership*) as a means of identifying and initiating appropriate learning goals and behavioral objectives. Additionally, an analysis of all relevant data in relation to student achievement and accountability standards is essential to the instructionally oriented problem-solving and decision-making process.

The *Design Phase* affords the school principal, again in collaboration with faculty, a process by which assessment instruments, instructional methods, techniques, and strategies can be designed and developed to better enhance leading, teaching, and student learning and achievement. This process also allows for content area to be formulated.

The *Design Phase* helps the principal and team to identify the characteristics and needs of each learner, specifies outcomes, establishes benchmarks of academic achievement via assessment instruments, and provides opportunities to plan for strategies for determining a program's overall effectiveness. Within this important phase, planning confirms and defines the instructional needs of student learners, clarifies academic outcomes, and further identifies subskills that must be taught and learned. This process also aids the principal and team in determining the scope and sequence of curricular and instructional content.

The *Development Phase* is an important step in the design of instructional and curricular programs, in which a principal and team formulate curricular actions and instructional (teaching/learning) activities and then purchase necessary supplies and materials essential for student success. In the *Development Phase,* quality control is essential. Within this phase, leaders and teachers ensure that curriculum guides are developed that are appropriate for the learners and that the instructional activities are appropriate relative to the desired outcomes. At this phase, assessments must be included, materials and activities must be aligned with instructional strategies, and assessment feedback must support intended instructional enhancements and interventions.

At the *Development Phase*, principals must serve as advocates for the students by

- Working with faculty to ensure that all instructional activities are aligned with learning outcomes;
- Ensuring that all materials, activities, and assessments are aligned with instructional strategies; and
- Evaluating all aspects of the programmatic design process and making revisions as necessary.

The *Implementation Phase* is critical to programmatic functioning, as the principal and faculty are able not only to plan for instruction implementation, but also to manage the process while delivering important aspects of leading, teaching, and learning. During this phase, curriculum guides, materials, and supplies are provided to teachers and students, and continued analysis and assessment occurs.

Furthermore, the *Implementation Phase* is the critical stage in ensuring appropriate, time-efficient, and effective instructional design, enhancements, and interventions. Here, the principal—always working collaboratively with team and in the best interest of students—must provide required professional development, examine and analyze teamwork effectiveness, and determine whether additional feedback is required.

The *Evaluation Phase* is the final step in initiating instructional design, enhancements, and interventions. At this phase, the principal and faculty are able to conduct formative and summative evaluations and, further, revise instruction based on the evaluation the program.

The critical instructional design process prompts a principal to consider several important questions as defined by Gustafson and Branch (1997). These questions serve to guide a principal and faculty through the design, development, and implementation phases:

1. What are the instructional/academic needs of the learners? Have the learners actually been asked this question?

2. What prior experiences, beliefs, and values have guided the learners in relation to the content and context of the instructional program?

3. What learner characteristics, skills, and information needs serve to guide instructional problem solving and decision making? Have the students been involved relative to this question?

4. What curricular and/or instructional changes are desired?

5. By what process will said changes positively impact leading, teaching, and learning? What do the students think?

6. What learning activities will be provided to learners to stimulate change or improvement in thinking, learning, and performance—of all participants, that is, students, teachers, and leaders?

7. What programmatic designs and changes requiring alignment among outcomes, goals, assessments, and learning activities result in effective instruction and student learning? Should the students have a voice in this process?

8. How do the students respond to the instructional strategies, methods, and techniques? Are these effective? Have the students been asked?

9. Should any instructional design, enhancements, and/or interventions—prior to the formative evaluation process—be modified based on the results of pilot testing and student interactions and feedback?

The authors realize that the information provided in this section of the text may be new or even intimidating to readers, especially the part about involving students. You may ask yourself, "How do I get this process started; where do I begin?" "Should I actually involve the students?" "How much time will this take?" Read the following vignette, and then pause and reflect upon the questions posed.

Dancing to the Tune, but Singing the Wrong Song!

Dr. Donna Arnold had been working with the teachers and a small group of students at Wildwood at NorthPointe School. Dr. Arnold had served as principal for the previous four years and recognized that substantial instructional changes had to occur, or students would continue to suffer academically and even behaviorally. Dr. Arnold had decided to bring in a team of administrators (principals and assistant principals from surrounding schools and districts, much like in Instructional Rounds) to assess—with an outside eye—the teaching and learning situation. This assessment was not Dr. Arnold's brainchild. In fact, one of the teaching teams had come to Dr. Arnold the previous fall and said, quite frankly, something had to give—something had to be done! With that initial statement and several follow-up conversations, the outside instructional designers were brought in to Wildwood at NorthPointe School. After several design, enhancement, and intervention sessions, some actually involving greater incorporation of technology, the following conversation occurred—an exchange between

Dr. Arnold and the teaching team requesting assistance. Team members were Savannah, Nehemiah, Grace, and Timothy.

Savannah: You know, Dr. Arnold, I've been a teacher for the past 10 years, and I've been involved in a couple instructional design trainings, but today, I had a unique experience. I came to understand that the instructional design team, along with books and models I've learned from, emphasizes the work of the designing team, but little regard is provided for team interaction with our student learners.

Grace: Yeah, Savannah, now that you mention that, I have noticed the same thing. I think I understand your point, but what exactly are you asserting?

Dr. Arnold: What are you two referring to?

Savannah: Well, here's the scoop: We all understand the premise behind initiating instructional design, enhancements, and intervention—to improve student learning and achievement. That's the easy part. The differing phases—you know analysis, design, development, implementation, and evaluation—are all readily understood. Our professional development sessions were very helpful. However, the problem, as I see it, is quite straightforward. We're dancing to the tune but singing the wrong song!

Dr. Arnold: What in the world are you talking about, Savannah?

Nehemiah: I'll tell you what she's talking about! She's referring to how little attention our students receive in the process of designing instruction. Isn't this process supposed to be for the students and all about the students?

Dr. Arnold: Of course, Nehemiah. Go ahead, folks, tell me more.

Savannah: This is how it all unfolded. Timothy noticed the problem first. He realized that instructional design, especially the model, emphasized the tasks of the designers—how they are to perform during the process of instructional change, enhancements, and interventions. More important, he noticed how little regard is provided for interacting with our students.

Timothy: Yeah, you know how it is with all aspects of learning—some students just naturally get it; they intuitively understand what their involvement is to be in the process. The problem is related to those students who really don't understand!

(Continued)

(Continued)

Grace: Let's make it better for our students. Let's ensure our outside designers are receiving more effective training and preparation when it comes to interacting with students. These folks seem to be able to effectively initiate and follow through with the instructional design process. They just have poor interactive skills with students. They are probably so focused on the process that they don't think about interacting with the students—to get the students' feedback. These students are smart. They know the difference between good and bad instruction. If we or anyone else thinks differently, they are selling students short—way short!

Savannah: Yes, our students are clearly frustrated when it comes to applying skills when interacting with the design team, skills that are not typical to our coursework—like using technology. The designers don't know how to really relate to the students, and what's scary, these people are educators! That worries me! Maybe some of these administrators have been away from the classroom way too long, or they don't know the essential aspect of collaborating with students when building a new instructional program.

Dr. Arnold: So, what you four are telling me is quite simple: We need to provide the team with more professional development, especially as it relates to interacting with our students. Well, folks, here is the magic question—When? I have limited time. I've got so much paperwork back in the office that I could be covered with it!

Nehemiah: We understand, Dr. Arnold, and you are exactly right! They need training, "student" training! Plus, we can assist you, Dr. Arnold, with the training if it saves time!

Timothy: What I'm wondering is whether these designers actually understand the process themselves—especially the student interaction part. You know what, Dr. Arnold? The training and process model needs to be updated to include the student interaction part.

Savannah: Let me add one more item, especially as it relates to the inclusion of technology-oriented skills. Here's what I heard from a couple of our students—you all know Sam and Lisa. Listen to what Sam had to say. This student is really into technology, big time. Sam tells me, "Miss, I don't think that man knows anything about technology." Lisa says, "You need to get my dad up here. He's an expert! He fixed our big-screen TV, and you know how difficult that can be!" [Everyone laughed!] So see, our students know what the problem is—they figured it out before we did as teachers.

Our design team doesn't know or possess the technological skills to be developed and initiated to better enhance our teaching and learning!

Dr. Arnold: You know what I think, from our perspective as faculty who have actually had extensive experience in initiating instructional design, enhancements, and interventions? Our design team actions are probably not atypical. You're right Savannah; they've been dancing to the tune, but singing the wrong song!

Pause and Consider

- Should students be included in instructional changes, enhancements, or interventions, even elementary school students? Explain.
- What is missing, beyond student interactions and involvement, in relation to the design team at Wildwood at NorthPointe School?
- Dr. Arnold states, "I have limited time." What time management skills can be employed by Dr. Arnold to better assist with ensuring that the instructional design process works more efficiently? Not certain? Need more "time" ideas? Read on.

SAVING TIME WHEN TIME COUNTS

There is never enough time, right? In the previous scenario, Dr. Arnold, like all principals, was in search of more time. All principals, including Dr. Arnold, would be wise to consider the following:

The way we spend our time defines who we are.

All great achievements require time.

We can only speculate that all principals have calendars filled to capacity, and yet, more time is needed. Recall the commercial airline napkin with the following embossing: "Your calendar doesn't have blackout dates. Neither does ours!" Here are a few time-saving tips that might help Dr. Arnold and every other principal or prospective principal, especially when it comes to handling the paperwork, hard copy or electronic:

1. **Throw it away, delete it, or simply get rid of it.** Wow, that's easy, but how? Here's how:

2. **Delegate it.** Give it to someone else to read, do, file, or respond to.

3. **Act on it.** Throw it away or respond to it or file it. Straightforward and simple!

4. **File it temporarily.** At least set it aside until action is required or until additional information has been gained to better follow through. If follow-through is required, incorporate the "tickler" file system. Here's how it works:

   o **What is it?** The tickler file is a simple, back-to-basics filing system made up of 43 folders—one for each day of the month (numbered 1–31), plus one for each month of the year, each labeled with the name of the month.

   o **What does it do?** The tickler file permits a principal to gain control over paperwork relative to action that needs to be taken on a particular date in the future, but not today. (So, now you've created some additional time!) For example, a principal will be attending an out-of-town leadership conference on the 20th of the month. She or he will simply file the travel itinerary, directions, confirmation numbers, tax exemption form, conference agenda, meal tickets, et cetera, in the folder labeled number 20.

   o **Where to obtain one?** Why purchase a tickler file when you can make your own using file folders and a labeler (even the old reliable pencil will do!). Of course, to save time (but not money), you can buy the infamous tickler file at Amazon.com for a reasonable price. Go to www.amazon.com/gp/product/B000J09O1W/ref=as_li_ss_tl?ie=UTF8&camp=1789&creative=390957&creativeASIN=B000J09O1W&linkCode=as2&tag=simplify101-20. Even better, digital tickler apps are also available.

   So, tickle yourself organized!

5. **File it permanently.** If you are working with hard copies, use an organized file system beyond the tickler file, or better yet, have someone else (clerk, student worker, secretary, administrative intern) file hard copies for you in a place where either you or your filing helper can promptly find it for later use. Even better, incorporate an e-organized file system. It saves time and paper!

School principals frequently fail to maximize instructional time. Here's how to address this age-old problem:

- Engage students in time-on-task learning activities. (See in Chapter 5, "Collaboration and Time," how North Star Academy in Newark, New Jersey, is able to incorporate this recommendation.)

- Minimize noninstructional time, that is, time used for classroom transitions, locker breaks, recess, and homeroom period.
- Provide faculty with classroom management techniques for minimizing student interruptions and other disruptive behaviors.
- Emphasize student attendance—the greatest loss of student learning time results from students arriving late or missing school entirely.

Remember, by establishing these organized and maximized methods, time-on-task learning will occur! Otherwise, I'll gladly steal valuable instructional time!

—The Silent Time Thief

FINAL THOUGHTS

Exceptional principals understand structure is essential to being organized and incorporating efficient time management. Leaders must have an awareness of their strengths and weaknesses, establish priorities, simplify their work, and increase personal efficiency and effectiveness by incorporating time-saving and instructionally focused activities.

Exceptional principals guide a strong, best-practice, student-centered instructional program by incorporating a series of principles of effective instruction and efficient time management techniques by (1) defining the instructional problem at hand; (2) communicating effectively to all stakeholders; (3) piloting and evaluating what is to be taught and learned; (4) deciding if the solution is viable; (5) practicing what works and works well; (6) re-evaluating, constantly; and (7) scheduling time for inactivity—to think, reflect, meditate, and even pray about instructional issues and possible solutions.

Exceptional principals possess a high level of learner-centered and technological expertise. They know what to do, do it well, have the right tools, have the time, and take responsibility for what has been done!

Exceptional principals utilize leadership skills to complete the tasks before them. These leaders are people of substance who stand for important ideas and values. They share their ideas to help faculty become better teachers and students become better learners. These principals bring about consensus through collaborative decision making and problem solving, and they make the lives of others better—more sensible and meaningful.

Exceptional principals understand and are able to communicate and coach methods of instructional design, enhancement, and intervention utilizing a series of phases (analysis, design, development, implementation, and evaluation) to bring about a significantly better curricular and instructional program—all for the benefit of students and their achievement.

Exceptional principals save time when time counts. They understand and incorporate procedures for handling hard copy and electronic or digital paperwork, and most important of all, exceptional principals regularly avoid the *Silent Time Thief*!

Finally, exceptional principals know the answer to this riddle:

What is free, yet priceless? You can't own it, but you can use it. You can't keep it, but you can spend it. Once you've lost it, you'll never get it back. What is it? TIME!

Note to the Reader: This chapter readily and effectively correlates with Chapter 7, "The 21st Century Education System: Improvement, Time, and Technology."

DISCUSSION QUESTIONS

1. Why is structure such an important aspect of a principal's repertoire (skill set)? How does structure relate to efficient time management and instructional leadership? Explain.

2. Examine how you structure time in your own role as principal. What percentage of your daily principal activities is instructionally focused? Managerial-administrative focused? What do your calculations reveal about how you use your time as an instructional leader?

3. Of the seven principles of effective instruction and efficient time management techniques (see pages 65–66), which one do you believe is the most important or provides the best guidance to a principal or prospective principal? Be specific in your answer.

4. The learner-centered expertise of a principal or faculty member is frequently measured by "skill and will," as noted on page 69 of the chapter. Examine the listing of important leader and faculty skills, and select three you perceive as essential to the instructional success of a program and to the academic success of the learner. Provide examples to support your answers.

5. Which aspect of the instructional design, enhancement, and intervention process is critical to ensuring that you have the most effective instructional program? How can a school principal incorporate technology into this process to best safeguard time management? Be specific in your answers.

6. Sergiovanni (2007) wrote of expert principals and teachers, "They will be people of substance" (p. 82). As a principal or a prospective principal, how would you define *substance* as it relates to Sergiovanni's statement? Explain with examples. Does time management factor into your definition? Why or why not?

7. The principals (Mr. Van Horn, Mr. Uranga, and Dr. Arnold) in the vignettes within the chapter had time management issues or concerns. Differing time management techniques were used by each of these characters. Specifically identify one time management technique that would best assist each character in becoming a much more effective instructional leader.

SELF-REFLECTION ON LENS 2: LEADING, TEACHING, LEARNING, AND TIME

Return to Chapter 1, "Time Management and Your Leadership," and reflect again on the *Time Management Self-Assessment Instrument* (TMSI). In this chapter, you examined Lens 2: Leading, Teaching, Learning, and Time. Review your responses on the TMSI Scoring Template for Lens 2, Leading, Teaching, Learning, and Time. Consider the material in this chapter and how it relates to Lens 2. What beliefs were reinforced? Which items are you reconsidering? Why? Would you now change your score on any of the items? If you would, why? How does this chapter relate to your use and understanding of time in relation to the PSEL 2015 standards? Explain.

CASE STUDY APPLICATION

DEATH BY MEETING!

John Singer "Buz" Sawyer was a troubleshooter for the Crane School District. Because he was called a troubleshooter, one could very well expect Buz to be the excellent and efficient school leader who was brought into different schools in the district to ensure positive and essential change. His job was simple—make things right. He took his work seriously; faculty, staff, administrators, parents, and community members readily recognized Buz had a job to do and that he would do it exceptionally well. *Timely action* was a term that was often associated with Buz.

Buz was directed by the superintendent of schools to meet with Roscoe Sweeney, principal at Frontier School. Roscoe had been experiencing time management issues as related to meetings and instructional improvement. Roscoe "ran" his meetings autocratically. Empowerment, participative leadership, team influence, and digital-technological competence were terms of no endearment to Roscoe. His father, Randolph—or "Big R," as he had so often been called—had been a top-down administrator, and Roscoe admired and respected his father and saw no reason to be anything different.

Buz walked in to Roscoe's office one Monday morning, and, without any pretext, stated, "Roscoe, we've got work to do, so let's get with the program!" Roscoe grimaced and said, "Buz, I like and admire you. I know things aren't right here at Frontier School. But, you know what? I don't know if I can change." Buz simply responded, "Roscoe, you've got to change; your instructional program must change, or you'll be jingling the change in your pocket on some street corner blocks away from this building!" Roscoe got the message! He knew the facts—he'd been called into the superintendent's office and told change was coming, so he had to either get on board or face the consequences. Roscoe was determined to get on board!

Buz worked collaboratively with Roscoe Sweeney and other members of the faculty, including Christy Jameson, Peggy Marsh, Pepper Barrera, and Teddy Rowe—all members of the site-based decision-making (SBDM) team. Collaborative team work was the favorite and most recommended style that Buz utilized. He believed in it and he stood by it. So, that Monday morning at Frontier School began with Buz recognizing that Roscoe needed some team meeting and time management skill development. Buz had the skill. Did Roscoe have the will?

Buz determined that if the school was to be successful, it had to move away from the old model of top-down management, autocratic meetings, and wasted time. After interacting with the school's SBDM team and Roscoe, Buz thought the best beginning solution was to initiate a "real" site-based decision-making process, not some lip-service model like the one that had been in use at Frontier School. Buz suggested, and the team readily agreed, that the new or real SBDM meetings might be called "work-out" meetings, because that would be the intended outcome—to work out any instructional issues, concerns, or problems. The SBDM team loved the idea and asked whether they and other faculty members would be able to openly ask questions and speak up at work-out meetings. Buz quizzically looked at Christy, Peggy, Pepper, and Teddy and smiled, saying, "Of course. That's the whole idea. Work together, interact with all members of the faculty, make decisions, solve problems, save time and energy, and increase student achievement!" Christy said, "Great—let's go to work. I've got an issue that needs to be addressed!"

"Tell us the issue," said Buz. So Christy began to unload about an instructional issue affecting everyone at Frontier School. Roscoe just sat and listened to Christy as she shared with Buz and the rest of the team. Roscoe didn't know whether he should step out of the meeting to provide a more open and sharing environment or simply stay in place and keep his mouth closed. Buz picked up on Roscoe's mental dilemma and said, "Roscoe, this is your school, and your input and feedback is essential. Move up here with me and let's get to the heart of this matter and find a solution!" Roscoe smiled, jumped up, and moved around the conference table to sit next to Buz and Christy.

Christy began detailing the problem. In a nutshell, this was the concern: "When we meet, it is always 'this way and this way only'! We have too many meetings, and those in attendance don't have a clue as to what the meetings will be about. Mr. Sweeney, excuse me, sir, dominates the proceedings, and our meetings last too long. There never seems to be a focus, let alone any instructional solutions, and let me tell you—it is death by meeting!"

Buz looked at Roscoe and asked, "Roscoe, is she hitting the nail on the head?" Roscoe nodded affirmatively. Buz then stated there were ten keys to effective and timely meetings, saying to the SBDM team and Principal Sweeney, "Fortunately, you have hope. Many meetings are a complete waste of time, and they don't have to be. There is a cure to your dysfunctional and long-lasting meeting ills! The really good news: The cure is right before us, it's inexpensive, and it's an easy pill to swallow. Actually, the cure saves lots of valuable time!" Everyone clapped, and even Roscoe smiled, saying, "Well, let's get on with it, Buz!"

Buz asked the team if they had any ideas as to what the ten keys were. They actually named at least four of the ten. Prior to impressively concluding this initial meeting on time, Buz had a chance to describe all the effective meeting keys:

1. **Be prepared.** In actuality, little time is required to prepare for a meeting. However, the preparation payoff is significant—time is not wasted, and immediately, all parties understand why the meeting was called. Business can be conducted both effectively and efficiently.

2. **Have an agenda.** Agendas drive meetings. In many respects, an agenda is the GPS, determining how to get to the meeting's destination. Immediately, participants recognize the meeting's goals, and they recognize what will

(Continued)

(Continued)

be discussed, examined, and/or solved. Agendas save an abundance of the time often wastefully expended at the beginning of a meeting; they are especially effective if they are provided at least a day prior to the meeting. Better yet, if the meeting is scheduled for midweek to late in the week, the agenda should be distributed on Monday afternoon. This multiplies the effectiveness and efficiency of the meeting, as participants know in advance what will be addressed and can plan accordingly.

3. **Start on time and end on time (even sooner).** Leaders who arrive late to a meeting or shoot the breeze during the first few minutes of a meeting are doing a terrible disservice to the participants. Leaders who start on time emphasize that the meeting and the agenda items are important. Ending on time is also essential. Respect the meeting participants by not droning on and on after the meeting's ending time. The participants have work to do, and continuing to hold them hostage both irritates and demoralizes team members.

4. **Have fewer but better meetings.** Call a meeting only if a meeting is absolutely necessary! When a meeting is called, there should be a good reason for it to be called. Why discuss the travel reimbursement policy when an e-mail to all team members will do the trick? Include in the e-mail the following concluding line: "If you have any questions, feel free to contact me." Don't be tempted to call a meeting if an e-mail or text message or a telephone conversation will do the trick. People hate meetings. These same people will love you if you aren't continuously calling meetings, especially those that waste time!

5. **Think inclusion, not exclusion.** Not every member of a team needs to be at every meeting. Why would all of the department chairpersons wish to sit in on a meeting with the principal and the social studies department, especially when the session is about implementing the new social studies instructional standards? Include only those people who are relevant to the meeting, including individuals who are experts in a particular area and can offer insight relative to an issue, concern, or problem.

6. **Keep a focus.** Ruthlessly keep meetings on the agenda items at all times. Stay on topic, and seek input from all parties.

7. **Solve problems and make decisions.** This is what meetings must be about—address the problem, solve it, and make a decision how to proceed. Meetings with no purpose, no direction, and no relevant actions are, again, a complete waste of time. Talk about death by meeting! People are dying to get out of meetings and have other work and responsibilities.

8. **Use time efficiently.** PayScale (2015a, 2015b) provides interesting, important data regarding national averages of salaries for teachers and principals. These salaries can be correlated with money wasted when time in meetings is utilized ineffectively and inefficiently. Average salaries are listed in the chart below and are broken down into daily rates, based on 185 teaching days per year and then divided by the average working hours per day.

Teacher	Annual Salary	Work Days	Daily Work Hours	Daily Rate	Hourly Rate
High School	$46,445.00	185	8	$251.05	$31.38
Middle School	$43.190.00	185	8	$233.46	$29.18
Elementary School	$42,216.00	185	8	$228.20	$28.52
Principal	$84,528.00	225	10	$375.68	$37.56

Sources: Data from PayScale, 2015a, 2015b.

Meetings must be timely and purposeful, because meetings are costly. The chart above permits a principal and district leaders to recognize an aspect of meeting time that is frequently overlooked—time is money. Wasted time is wasted money. Point: If you are a high school principal meeting with a team of teachers (math department, for example), chances are there will be at least four to six teachers present. Using the chart above, you can figure the administrative hourly rate along with the hourly rate of six teachers present at a meeting. Then consider the meeting is 2 hours in length. Multiply 2 hours times the hourly rate of six teachers and a principal, and you recognize this meeting cost the district more than $450. More important, the district lost valuable instructional time, as teachers were away from their students. Now, calculate the cost of a meeting in your school.

Question: Was this meeting a worthwhile expenditure in time, money, and purpose?

Question: Would the attendees be more productive not attending this meeting?

Question: Is there a true need to call this meeting and to attend this meeting?

Question: Do principals waste instructional time and district money in drawn-out meetings when an e-mail would save time and money?

(Continued)

(Continued)

These four questions naturally lead to other questions: Are all meetings necessary? As a principal, am I prepared to lead meetings effectively and efficiently? Am I inviting only those who really need to attend a meeting? Did I begin the meeting promptly? Will I proceed through the agenda punctually? Will I conclude the meeting within the designated time frame?

Each question posed, and possibly others you may have thought of while reading this, probably reflect the concerns exemplified in these two quotes—"Have you ever heard anyone complain a meeting was too short?" "Regret for time wasted is more time wasted." Don't waste time—especially other people's time, and don't waste district money with unnecessary and/or ill-prepared meetings!

1. **Get feedback.** Prior to closing a meeting, ask for feedback. This is an exceptional method of measuring the effectiveness of the meeting. A principal will find out what was right about the meeting as well as what went wrong. The latter serves as an opportunity for the principal to obtain ideas as to how to make subsequent meetings more insightful and effective. Think about this quote, "You will never see yourself as others do unless they tell you!"

2. **Incorporate digital meetings.** Digital or electronic meetings ("e-meetings") can be used in place of traditional face-to-face sessions. The most common form of an e-meeting is conducted through web-based software (for example, SMART Meeting Pro, Christie Brio, ThinkTank, MeetingSphere, Monsoon Anonymous, yaM [yet another Meeting], and even digital instructional needs tools such as Snapwiz), which permits school leaders and team members and other groups from around the district, state, nation, or world to facilitate meetings without physically relocating to an agreed-upon location. The most important aspect of web-based e-meetings is the standard functionality of the process—agendas are organized inviting participants to contribute; discussions are conducted; participants vote via numeric scales, rank ordering, or on ballots; and multiple methods are available to assess the utility and impact of the meeting. Additionally, minutes can be taken automatically, and synchronous (participants meet at the same time) and asynchronous (participants contribute at different times) meetings are available. Advantages over face-to-face meetings include the following:

   • Conversations dominated by one or more members are curtailed.
   • Anonymity provides for increased openness and less personal interaction. Individuals feel free to comment without fear of criticism, negative evaluation, or other forms of retribution.
   • Any-place (online) capability is available.
   • Increased participant availability is ensured.
   • Interactivity and participation are increased by parallelization (by placing interactivity and participation into a certain location).

- More sophisticated analysis by voting and analysis in real time works to a school's advantage.
- Less effort is necessary for preparation because of the availability of meeting templates.
- Automatic, comprehensive, and neutral documentation is the final result.

APPLICATION QUESTIONS

1. As a principal or a prospective principal, do you think Buz Sawyer appropriately and effectively handled Principal Roscoe Sweeney? Why or why not? Would you have done anything differently? Explain.

2. Many books and websites regarding efficient and effective meetings state that a principal should not begin a meeting 1 second late. What are the positives and negatives relative to this assertion? How does it affect or relate to time management? Explain.

3. How could Principal Roscoe Sweeney be assisted as an instructional leader beyond what Buz Sawyer was doing or attempting to do in the scenario?

4. Which of the ten keys to effective meetings is most appropriate to effective instructional leadership? How? By what means?

5. What is appealing about digital meetings? What is not? How can a principal effectively and appropriately utilize digital meetings as an instructional tool? Provide an example.

The Learning Organization

Culture, Climate, Technology, Safety, and Time

I want to work in a trusting way. I must begin to make myself known as a trusting, caring, and up-front member of this organization, and be the example of what I strive for.

—Jonathon Lazear, entry for August 26
in *Meditations for Men Who Do Too Much* (1992)

CREATING A POSITIVE CLIMATE AND OPEN, TIME-EFFICIENT CULTURE

School culture and climate are frequently described as overlapping concepts. There are, however, some distinctions. Culture is viewed as the values and norms of a school. Culture is what teachers, students, and parents "think" (their attitudes and beliefs) about a school. On the other hand, climate is viewed as the behavior or personality of a school. Climate is the behaviors or personality that leads teachers, students, and parents to love a school and to be a part of the school.

The two terms, *culture* and *climate,* are frequently connected, often interchangeable, yet different. Bottom line: No matter the application of the terms, a causal relationship exists between the principal's role and organizational culture, climate, and change. Point: Principals are critical to establishing open cultures and/or positive climates and thus bringing student-centered change to a school.

Effective principals create a learning community that has an open culture and a positive climate. This is a community of strong interpersonal relationships, effective technology implementation, efficient time management, safety, and transparency (DeMatthews, 2014b). Within this community, students are known, valued, and respected. This community exemplifies a culture in which the security and emotional protection of all students is a norm. This community exemplifies a climate of care, appreciation, trust, and respect. All stakeholders feel welcomed and loved. As a result of the community culture and climate, students desire to excel and achieve. Lazear (1992) was right: The best cultures and most effective organizational climates are based on trust, care, and being an "up-front member" and leader of the team.

The Common Good: Shaping Schools
Into Cultures of Openness and Positive Climates

Sorenson and Goldsmith (2009) in their text, *The Principal's Guide to Managing School Personnel*, underscore the need for effective leadership in shaping school climate and culture for the common good. What is the common good? From a leadership perspective, common good is defined as a learning community where students are treated with dignity, no matter their race, color, creed, background, experiences or lack thereof, or their intellectual capacity. Common good recognizes that all students can learn and is a form of assurance, if not insurance, that all students will work and learn in a protective (physically, emotionally, sexually) environment. How? By what means?

First, as noted above, effective principals shape schools into cultures of openness and positive climates protective of all students. Principals can develop schools of this kind by initiating essential strategies such as modeling trust, actively listening to all parties, improving methods of collecting and analyzing data, being moral and ethical in all aspects of leadership, encouraging others, and simply caring. These essential strategies, which establish learning environments designed to improve the culture and climate of a school as well as the common good for all students, include the following:

- **Model trust and respect.** You can fool adults, but you can't fool kids! Students can read an adult like a book, especially if the adult is less than genuine in telling the students what to do or not to do. Principals must realize that their modeling behaviors have to be built on a high level of trust and respect. Students must know that their principal cares for them and appreciates all of their efforts. First, however, their principal must be moral, ethical, trustworthy, and respectful.

- **Listen.** Active listening is the key to an open culture and positive climate. One of the authors of this text frequently asserts "People have two ears and one mouth. Listen at least twice as much as you speak." Wise advice. Active listening provides a principal with insights. Insights allow for corrective action and strengthen both leadership and followership. Active listening is a process by which a principal gains essential understandings when interacting with others. Active listening helps create a culture and climate of protection, trust, respect, and care. How does a principal "actively" listen? Consider using this helpful guide: (1) Provide eye contact. (2) Pick up pencil and paper and write down what is being said. (3) Repeat aloud what you have heard and written down. (4) Ask for clarification in case you have misunderstood something stated.

- **Improve data collection and analysis**. An essential element to an open culture and positive climate is having complete confidence in determining which academic areas must be targeted for growth, improvement, and achievement. Effective data collection and analysis is powerful. The best principals utilize ongoing data collection, analyses, and decision making. The best organizational decisions are correlated with facts. Facts don't lie. Truth, transparency, and open communication—based on effective data collection and analysis—build a strong community of leaders, teachers, and learners.

- **Be moral and ethical.** Moral and ethical leadership is not happenstance. Moral and ethical behaviors are studied and learned and lead to honest interactions. Moral and ethical leadership is based on a high level of personal integrity (see Chapter 6, "Ethics, Integrity, and Time"). A lack of integrity is a leadership flaw with serious if not damning consequences. The best of schools are built on a foundation of leadership integrity. The followership trusts and respects the leadership team and vice versa. Reflect upon who you are. Are you an individual of great integrity? Consider who influences you. Does this person model the highest level of moral and ethical conduct? Are you being influenced by the right person—a person of integrity?

- **Encourage others.** An open culture and positive climate are based on how a principal provides support, comfort, and hope to members of the learning community—especially the students. Write a positive note, greet individuals with a smile, share a cheerful "hello," and extend a friendly handshake. Let people know you care and are concerned about them. Use humor, frequently. Humor is the medicine that heals a hurt and uplifts others. It fills the air with sweetness, cleanses a disheartened soul, and lightens a heavy load. Humor is the one encourager that brings a smile, a hearty laugh, and more often than not, a moment of joy. Remember, never use humor at the expense of another individual. That's not humor. That's an insult disguised by a laugh or smile.

- **Care.** The principal who doesn't care isn't leading through best example, inspiring with passion, living through loving, touching the human soul, or leaving an indelible mark on the future. The principal who doesn't care will never make a difference. The principal who cares is the leader who doesn't listen when the head says, "Who cares?" Instead, the principal who cares is the one who listens to the heart whisper, "Who cares? You do!" This principal states, "Yes, I care. I will always care."

Second, effective principals recognize that an open culture, overlapped by a positive climate, has a phenomenal impact on student learning. A review of eight research studies (Abelein, 2013; Boyd, 1992; Heck & Marcoulides, 1996; Hoy, 1990; Kramer, Watson, & Hodges, 2013; MacNeil, Prater, & Busch, 2009; Maslowski, 2001; Sundell, Castellano, Overman, & Aliaga, 2012) reveals an open school culture and positive climate can have definite and conclusive effects on the following:

- Academic achievement, including
  - ○ Significant increase on mathematics performance,
  - ○ Positive gains in all academic subjects, and
  - ○ Increase in scores on standardized tests.
- Student engagement and social skills development.
- Attendance rates for students, teachers, staff, and administrations (increase).
- Continuous critical inquiry (increase).
- Collaborative decision-making and problem-solving (increase).
- Disciplinary incidents (decrease).
- Student suspension days (decrease).
- Teacher burnout and turnover rates (decrease).
- Student attitudes toward schooling (positive).
- Teacher, student, and community attitudes toward change (positive).
- Overall school improvement in these areas:
  - ○ Goal focus;
  - ○ Communication;

Source: Ralph and Alice cartoon by Alex Carruth.

- Power equalization;
- Resource allocation;
- Cohesiveness;
- Morale;
- Innovativeness;
- Organizational structures;
- Instructional practices;
- Teacher, principal, and student academic expectations;
- Student rigor and engagement in instruction;
- Knowledge and skill development; and
- Time management, principal leadership, and increased academic achievement.

Third, principals who lead schools with open cultures and positive climates better manage their time, and, as a result, improve instruction in their schools along with student management and discipline (Educational Research, 2015; Horng, Klasik, & Loeb, 2009; Spiro, 2012; Turnbull, Haslam, Arcaira, Riley, Sinclair, & Coleman, 2009).

Using Technology, Saving Time, and Maintaining Discipline to Create an Open and Positive Learning Environment

Leticia Moreno is an administrator in a major metropolitan West Coast city. She works in a high-poverty school located in an immigrant-filled barrio dotted with gang-related activities and crime. Developing an open culture and positive climate is essential to successfully meeting the needs of adolescent students.

Leticia interacts daily with middle school students, many whom are prone to possess concealed weapons, not necessarily to initiate criminal activity, but for personal protection. Leticia is a strong instructional leader, yet regrettably, she spends a large percentage of her administrative day interacting with students who have made ill-fated decisions resulting in disciplinary action and, in some tragic situations, death. Leticia's no pushover. At the same time, she has a big heart and deep love for the students, their families, and the faculty she is privileged to serve. Here's one of Leticia's stories:

One summer afternoon I was at home when I received a call from local police asking for an administrator to go to school, because the body of a middle school–age student had been found (not on school premises), and law enforcement needed someone to identify the deceased student. Quickly, I threw on my blouse and jeans and arrived at school as soon as possible. After entering the school building, a police officer and I searched yearbooks for a photograph that would identify the body, yet no picture was found.

I suggested to the officer that I visit the girlfriend of the student we thought was the victim; she lived in nearby federal housing, to determine if she had a photograph of the student we thought was the victim. The officer agreed and offered to drive me in his cruiser. I immediately replied, "Absolutely not!" The last thing a school administrator needs is to arrive in a police cruiser in a community of gang activity and crime where she is trusted and respected. He agreed, and I traveled in my own vehicle to the girlfriend's home. I was greeted by the girlfriend's mother, and as is the custom, I was offered something to eat, which I respectfully declined. I asked the mother's permission to speak to her daughter, and she gave it.

I spoke to the teenage girl and asked her if she had heard from her boyfriend. She asked me if he was in trouble and I said no. She said she had not heard from him. I asked her to log on to her Facebook account and message him. We searched through the potential victim's Facebook page and noticed he had recent selfies posted only a couple of hours previously that day. I was relieved and almost cried when I saw his reply message pop up saying "hello" to his girlfriend. I took photos of the Facebook account and messages and e-mailed them to the police officer on duty.

The account above reveals how Facebook can be an asset in administrative investigations, aiding principals and assistant principals in locating victims or perpetrators of fights, bullying, arson, vandalism, murder, or just about any other disciplinary or criminal action related to schooling. Many students, for example, post information about fights or other inappropriate or illegal information on Facebook, and this information can help with disciplinary investigations.

While many principals greatly exaggerate the amount of time they spend on instruction, more times than not—as noted in the previous vignette—administrative time is spent on student management and disciplinary issues. Such is part of the leadership role. However, the previously noted studies reveal that effective school leaders who have developed open cultures and positive climates will intentionally focus and spend time on instruction by (1) conducting formal and informal walkthroughs; (2) planning with teachers curricular changes and instructional initiatives; (3) leading instructional meetings with faculty; (4) collaborating with decision-making committees; (5) reviewing lesson plans; (6) initiating and leading professional development sessions; (7) orienting and supervising new faculty; (8) analyzing data; (9) assessing teacher, parent, and student perceptions via survey instruments; and (10) working directly with students—specifically, students at risk of failure. These same studies illustrate the complexity of the principal's role, the management side of the role, and—more important—essential principal time-use methods and exceptional measures of school leadership effectiveness.

Fourth, schools exemplified by open cultures and positive climates have principals who ensure that the learning environment is built on the precept that time is more valuable than money. Anyone can get more money, but no one can get more time. It is important the school leader understand that time is a valuable commodity. Often, principals understand the following about time: Use it or lose it, or use time wisely, or waste time and reap the consequences. What do principals often fail to comprehend about time? How should principals use time to best benefit students, faculty, staff, and parents? Read on.

MANAGING TIME AND BUILDING A STRONG LEADING, TEACHING, AND LEARNING ENVIRONMENT

Principals frequently manage time poorly. What must be accomplished in any given hour, day, or week is not necessarily impossible if time is managed properly. What makes for the best-organized school principals? Following are five basic time management tips to help principals cope with job demands and better develop an open and caring culture and a less stressed climate.

- **Make lists.** The evening before or the morning of the workday, use timesaving technology and make a list of items to do. This to-do list prioritizes tasks needing to be completed, and such lists are essential in beating work overload. With to-do lists, a principal appears focused, reliable, productive (saving time), and valuable to stakeholders. Additionally, a principal will be less stressed. Finally, software-based to-do approaches are more efficient than paper lists, in spite of the learning curve. Specialty software for this purpose includes Microsoft Outlook, Gmail, Remember the Milk, Todoist, and Toodledo (see Chapter 8, "Technology: Staying a Step Ahead of the *Silent Time Thief*"). These task and time management tools remind the user of events or tasks that will soon be overdue, they can be synchronized with smartphones and e-mail, and they can be shared with others, including, but not limited to, the school secretary and assistant principal. Digital to-do lists can also be shared with faculty, which is especially helpful when collaborating on a project.

- **Set goals.** Your to-do list should correlate with established personal and professional goals. Goals keep a principal and team focused. Goals broaden opportunities for success. Goals help leaders and faculty maintain perspective (see Chapter 2, "Vision, Mission, and Time"). Effective principals set goals for themselves and for the learning community. These goals should always be just slightly out of reach, but never out of sight. Remember, one day at a time, one step at a time, one realistic goal at a time.

- **Prioritize activities.** Ensure that items on goal-oriented to-do lists are in priority order. This afternoon, you need to have a personal school photo, attend a special education eligibility or annual review meeting, set a parent–principal conference regarding a student who has recently exhibited some disturbing behavioral issues, walk two miles, attend a campus fundraising function, meet with a team of teachers regarding an instructional concern, and help the Parent–Teacher Association (PTA) executive committee decide when the next semester meetings should be scheduled. It doesn't take a rocket scientist to determine what is priority one, two, three, four, et cetera. You know the drill. Just in case a reminder is needed, think students first, faculty second, parents third, and everything else fourth. (An appropriate prioritization is found at the conclusion of the chapter on page 106.) Make the priority listing, save time, complete all tasks, look successful, and be less stressed!

- **Know your daily cycle.** If possible, handle the most trying and demanding aspects of your leadership role during the part of your day cycle when you are most alert and productive. You know that time of day. One of the authors of this text is at his best in the early to midmorning hours. Another is at his best in the late afternoon to evening. If possible, schedule those trying tasks, events, and problems to be solved during your daily cycle.

- **Use technology.** Technology is improving education. Why? How? (1) It allows for better collaboration; (2) valuable research is easily and quickly accessed; (3) the greatest ever, most accessible expanse of material and resources is at your fingertips via the Internet; (4) online learning is a most credible and timely option; (5) student learning outcomes are significantly improved; (6) meaningful work is created; and (7) productivity and efficiency are increased (Blumengarten, 2014; EdTechReview Editorial Team, 2014; Saxena, 2015). Understand the adage, "Principals will not be replaced by technology, but principals who do not use technology will be replaced by those who do" (Reven, 2014)!

You Waste More Time!

She finally had enough and blurted out, "You waste more time looking for stuff you've misplaced, mislaid, or lost than anyone I've ever known. Thank goodness your head is attached to your neck or we'd be looking for it too!"

Two principals, husband and wife, Pete and Gladys, are technological gurus. They didn't achieve their status as digital experts overnight. They sought out answers, they learned, and they realized that as administrators, they had to learn fast or sink when seeking to find and save time. What they found is technology, the greatest timesaver ever. The couple uses technology in all aspects of leading and learning and even in their personal lives. Their repertoire of techie tricks includes a small, coin-sized digital device that easily attaches to any item. Stick it on, clip it on. With this device comes a cell phone app that tracks and locates in seconds any item the device has been attached to.

In their offices, Pete and Gladys attached the tracking device to sets of keys, tablets, smartphones, purses, wallets, books, and other items worth keeping up with. One of the two is apt to lose something in a heartbeat, in the administrative offices, in the classrooms, in the gym or cafeteria or library, and even in the restroom. Not anymore. Now the time wasted tracking down the lost item is minimal. What a timesaver! Want one? Simply go online and search for "tracking device."

Think of the words of legendary college basketball coach and amazing leader John Wooden (n.d.), "If you don't have time to do it right, when will you have time to do it over?" Use technology appropriately. Lead effectively. Work efficiently. Save time!

Ever sat in a restaurant and watched a young couple, high school age or early- to mid-20s? The couple eagerly awaits their meal. Notice, however, the minimal conversation and personal interactions.

(Continued)

(Continued)

The young couple seems entranced by their individual electronic devices. Wonder why? The couple is of a culture, a generation, that finds itself intrigued, perhaps obsessed, by mobile and other digital tools and software. As they sit and await their meal, the couple busily navigates their personal devices, texting, searching, posting, e-mailing, and messaging. This is what the younger generation does.

Ever watched children, as young as age three or four, sitting with their parents, riding the urban metro system, or, like the couple above in the restaurant, waiting at a fast-food eatery for an appetizing kid's meal? These kiddos are hands-on busy with their tablets or mobile devices, extending their little fingers, rapidly moving their bright eyes, and stretching their insatiable intellects as they play the latest kids' music, game, or educational activity, or read interactive or other e-books, or manipulate material on interactive websites. This is what the youngest generation does.

Now, consider the value of incorporating technology into the administration or management of schools, and most certainly into instructional programs. Technology is to 21st century America what the advent of electricity was to 20th century America. Both indispensable! Neither could ever be perceived, in its era, as anything but a prized and treasured development.

Tidbit of Advice: Ignore technology as a means of enhancing the modern learning organization, and you become your own time thief, robbing yourself, your students, and your faculty of a most requisite teaching, leading, learning, and time-saving tool!

—The Silent Time Thief

CREATING SAFE, EFFECTIVE, AND EFFICIENT OPERATIONS AND MANAGEMENT

Effective principals create efficient operations and facilities by properly managing time, focusing on work-related areas such as faculty, public relations, personnel and relationships, school law, food services, student discipline, school safety, school budgeting, pupil transportation, student services, master scheduling, curricular and instructional programs, and school wellness—to name just a few areas in which the principal is the school manager. It was William Sharp and James Walter in their classic text, *The Principal as School Manager* (2012), who wrote, "These areas cover important roles for the principal, which occupy much of a principal's time, are visible to the community, and sometimes are the criteria on which a principal may be judged" (p. xi). In the next few pages, we will examine one of these time-consuming yet extremely critical managerial areas: school safety. All said, we must be grateful for those who have made the principalship their profession, if not their mission in life!

School Safety

Principals must ensure a safe learning environment for all. This takes time, competence, significant research, and a serious acquisition of funds. Sharp and Walter (2012) write, "It seemed a shame that the second edition of this book had to include a chapter on school safety, but violence has become so commonplace in our society that administrators must deal with it, in varying degrees, on a routine basis" (p. 121). At the turn of the 21st century, Kemerer and Walsh (2000) had to write in *The Educator's Guide to Texas School Law*, "This is the first time the word 'murder' has appeared in the Texas Education Code. We've come a long way. Or have we?" (p. 286).

Today, principals must contend with numerous aspects of school safety, including identifying students predisposed to violence, and, more often than ever before, personnel predisposed to violence. How serious is the problem? Recognize that every workday in the United States

- Over 16,000 threats are made to school personnel;
- More than 700 school employees/leaders are attacked at school; and
- Almost 44,000 school employees/leaders are harassed.

Now, consider these statistics:

- One out of four employees is attacked at school;
- Fifty percent of US schools experience incidents or threats of workplace violence; and
- Sadly, sometimes tragically, 25% of schools ignore the warning signs. (National Center for Victims of Crime, 2014; Seckan, 2013; Workplace Violence Research Institute, 2012).

What's a principal to do? What a principal cannot do is state, "I don't have time!" Read the following scenario. Think as you read: Is my school safe? Have I made time for a safe school?

School Safety and Technology, or How We Came to Save Student Lives and Time!

Providing for the physical safety and security of students is by no means a new school challenge. However, how a school meets this challenge reveals much about the culture of the school and the effectiveness of its leader and team interactions. In the aftermath of the December 14, 2012, shooting of 20 students and six staff members at Sandy Hook Elementary School in Newtown, Connecticut, many school principals and teams took immediate action to increase campus

(Continued)

(Continued)

safety and security to better protect students. But none were quicker than those individuals serving at the Flax Road School. Here's the story of how a school principal and team used technology to protect students, and how technology and time became cultural factors in preserving lives on campus.

The Flax Road School Story

Dr. Kim Bremner was in her sixth year as principal at the Flax Road School. Kim had created an amazing culture at the school by exhibiting respect for others, being trustworthy, and being open and transparent in all aspects of leading. During the second semester of her sixth year leading the school, Dr. Bremner met with the school's site-based decision making team, and they reached a very important decision—student safety must be Priority 1 at the Flax Road School. The principal and team held several meetings following the tragedy in Newtown, Connecticut, including numerous town hall meetings with parents and community members, and implemented the Flax Road Safe School Technology Primer and Plan. Indeed, the plan was a primer, a simple teaching and learning tool. Straightforward in many ways, it dictated results—all for the safety and security of students, faculty, staff, and other individuals on campus.

Dr. Bremner and team found the essential technological resources (Dr. Bremner believed in the adage, "I'll find the money," not "show me the money") that would save time in the event of a crisis and, more important, save lives. Read what Dr. Bremner and faculty did at the Flax Road School. The principal and team:

- Sought district, local, state, and federal grant dollars. One funding source was the Readiness and Emergency Management for Schools Grant Program. This discretionary grant supported the school by providing funding to strengthen the crisis preparation/management plan, train school personnel and students in emergency response procedures, communicate emergency plans and procedures with parents, and coordinate with local law enforcement and other public health agencies; and aided in the purchase of prudent technological devices designed for school safety.

- Provided for school safety digital devices, including

  o Wearable panic buttons for every employee. These buttons immediately alert police when an emergency occurs.
  o A digitally connected camera security system that was light-years better than the old analog system with its fuzzy images.
  o Medical alert devices (yes, just like the one "Grandma" advertises—"I've fallen and I can't get up"). Stationary buttons were mounted under desks and counters in the school's reception areas and administration offices.

○ Iris scan technology to replace outdated and less-than-reliable identification card systems. This form of technology is noninvasive and presents no health risks. With iris scan or biometric technology there is no need for cards, which may be lost, forgotten, or stolen. It reduces staff monitoring requirements and serves as exceptional door access security.

○ Sensory devices to detect the presence of guns, knives, razor blades, bombs, and fire; as well as to identify potential problems in the school's utility systems and threats from inclement weather. These were installed to protect students and others, to deter crime, and to avoid other potential crises.

○ A school-based virtual private network. This was initiated as a means of linking Flax Road School to other schools and community agencies to ensure timely and secure sharing of school safety information.

○ A virtual school resource officer (SRO) software program. This used a geographic information system to map and analyze incidents in or near the school.

○ Way-finding apps for students to use on their mobile devices, on or off campus. These created maps and digital images to help them when they felt they were potential victims of crime.

○ An anonymous reporting channel for students to report incidents. This digital application included toll-free hotline numbers for both voice and text messages, and dedicated computer terminals in public locales and on-campus computers from which individuals could send anonymous e-mails.

• Provided for student emotional and academic security via technical devices. Acknowledge that many students, especially those who are learning disabled, can feel insecure, stressed, or disoriented if they are academically unprepared, or if they are not certain as to what assignments need to be completed or what homework is due the next day, or if they simply feel less than knowledgeable about certain aspects of instruction. Haven't we all been there and experienced such feelings of insecurity? Listed here are several technology tools used by the Flax Road School to help students with advance preparation, followed by tools to help students ask questions:

○ Lesson plans are posted online, and students can access information, tutoring help, and other resources and materials;

○ Text-to-speech software support on classroom websites permits students to hear the material, thus reinforcing and scaffolding learning and comprehension; and

○ Classroom blogs and wiki sites enable students to share their understanding of lesson topics, materials, and assignments.

(Continued)

(Continued)

Now, let's examine technologies for asking questions. Acknowledge, again, that many students who struggle in class are frequently inhibited from asking questions aloud or in private because of insecurities associated with shyness or not wanting to reveal their personal academic deficiencies or struggles. The principal and faculty at the Flax Road School developed the following digital tools to aid academically insecure students by advancing more respectful, timely, and accommodating opportunities for questioning. Students can

- E-mail questions to an online learning platform to be answered anonymously;
- Use web-based social sites such as Twitter to create anonymous questions, which can be shared during class sessions; and
- Use real-time polling software, via mobile devices, to check for understanding of the lesson content.

These layered technical/safety/security approaches were put to a timely test at the Flax Road School when a gunman entered the school reception area early one spring morning. The gunman, who had become estranged from his wife and family, was intent on finding his twin children, doing fatal harm, and then committing suicide. He was stopped immediately as a result of school security devices and interventions, and lives were saved—including his own.

Pause and Consider

- Place yourself in the role of Dr. Kim Bremner, principal, at Flax Road School. How did this principal utilize technology to enhance school safety? To better manage or save time? Explain and discuss.
- Which of the noted school safety digital devices are available at your school? Which devices are not, and why not? Discuss.

FINAL THOUGHTS

Exceptional principals are charged with developing collaborative cultures of productive relationships and trust, promoting climates of collective efficacy (worth, effectiveness, and efficiency), and nurturing cultures of shared accountability. These responsibilities may seem overwhelming, especially when considering the words of actress/comedian Lily Tomlin, "We are all in this together—by ourselves." The good news? We're not in this by ourselves. We have help, and the help we have is each other! Exceptional principals are doers. They bear the burden and responsibility of "doing" not alone, but by incorporating the assistance of many. Exceptional principals transform learning environments by changing the culture from closed to open, advancing the climate from negative to positive, and by moving a learning community from "many ones" to "one of many"!

Exceptional principals incorporate the knowledge and expertise of others, most notably as related to improving the instructional program. Remember, "All of us are smarter than any one of us!" Exceptional principals seek out individuals of substance, strength, intelligence, and ability. Exceptional principals put these competent people to work—always using, never abusing. Yes, we are all in this together—each lending a helping hand, offering a kind word, sensing a time to step up—not out, and taking the reins of leadership at every beck and call. Every person can, in some form or capacity, lead. Leading is helping, offering, sensing, and bringing about a high level of competence and excellence—all to best benefit students!

Exceptional principals model trust, actively listen to others, effectively collect and analyze data, encourage others, and are moral and ethical in all aspects of leadership—on or off campus. Exceptional principals manage time effectively and efficiently. They make to-do lists, set goals, prioritize activities, and use technology.

Exceptional principals understand in this digital age that technology cannot be ignored. Technology is that lending hand, that step-up required, and that leader behind the scenes who aids the lead leader. Technology is essential because it helps a principal manage and save time in creating effective and efficient operations and management systems.

Exceptional principals develop and ensure safe learning environments, recognizing the serious challenge posed by those predisposed to violence, and using every possible means to protect students. These principals make time to seek funding sources to increase campus security. They provide school safety digital devices and layer technology, safety, and security approaches to save time and lives.

Finally, exceptional principals use time wisely. They block out time for the important business. They share, in a timely manner, their plans with others. They make time and create daily interactions with faculty, staff, students, and parents. They find time to develop a vision and establish goals. These principals take time to share their vision and goals with all stakeholders. Exceptional principals take time to make time!

DISCUSSION QUESTIONS

1. Consider the six methods of shaping schools into a culture of openness and a positive climate protective of students. Of the six methods identified, which ones do you believe to be essential to (a) effective leadership, (b) instructional and curricular improvement, (c) technology enhancement, and (d) time management? Provide examples to support your answers.

2. Based on your reading of this chapter, in what ways can principals better manage their time, and as a result, improve instruction? Be specific in your answers.

3. Time, technology, and school safety are strongly correlated in the research literature. Why are technology and time so critical to a safe school and positive learning environment? Provide detailed explanations in your answers.

4. "Time has a wonderful way of showing us what really matters."— Margaret Peters (www.quotationspage.com/quote/38969.html). Consider this quote in relation to school safety, in relation to school leadership. How does the quote connect? Explain in detail.

SELF-REFLECTION ON LENS 3: THE LEARNING ORGANIZATION AND TIME

Return to Chapter 1, "Time Management and Your Leadership," and reflect once more on the *Time Management Self-Assessment Instrument* (TMSI). In this chapter, you examined Lens 3: The Learning Organization and Time. Review your responses on the TMSI Scoring Template for Lens 3, The Learning Organization and Time. Reflect upon the material within this chapter and how it relates to Lens 3. Which of your beliefs were reinforced? Which items are you now rethinking? Why? Would you change your score on any of the items? If you would, why? How does this chapter relate to your use and understanding of time in relation to the PSEL 2015 standards? Explain.

CASE STUDY APPLICATION

AS THE SUN SETS SLOWLY IN THE WEST, OR HOW TO DEVELOP A LEARNING COMMUNITY

Sunset School, located in the Hill Country, near Union State University, is far from being a picturesque school. The Hill Country, on the other hand, is a beautiful year-round vacation spot. People flock to the locale in any season. It is a charming region of the state, with meandering creeks and rivers, spacious parks, bed-and-breakfast cottages, and animal and plant life to amaze both the casual and regular observer.

Sunset School, unlike the area in which it is located, is far from striking. Somewhat like the community it serves, it is old and run down, less than scenic. The people in the school, however, are quite charming and absolutely pleasing. Sunset School is found in a community that has as its largest employers the school system and the state fishery. The community is older, with many of the residents at or near retirement age. Nevertheless, younger families are moving to the district. Most of the faculty are in their 50s and have been with the school system for years. They, too, are reaching retirement age. The principal, Olive Estes, is in her mid-60s and will be retiring at the end of the next school year. Olive is a vivacious leader and she sparkles with excitement in showing Sunset School to all visitors. Old and run-down the school may be, but neither Principal Estes nor any faculty and staff show any signs of being derelict in their duties, and they certainly are not neglectful when it comes to the student body.

Bill Rand, assistant principal, is a long-time community member and has worked for the local school system for 42 years. He states, "This is a great school and learning community. I have no plans to retire unless, of course, the new principal that replaces Olive is a cantankerous sort." Bill works at the fishery during the summer months, after his school contract ends. He is beloved in the community. He further amplifies, "Olive has developed a rich learning and working environment. Our school may look like it's on its last legs, but once you step inside, you notice immediately that all is alive, well, and in good spirits. Have you ever noticed that some of the most attractive and stunning school exteriors are anything but inside? We're just the opposite! We just wish Olive had more time to devote to further school improvement."

Assistant Principal Rand further describes how the Sunset School climate and culture were established. "You see, Principal Estes is a special leader—I'd call her an exceptional leader. She fosters an open, tolerant, and trusting culture. She values the viewpoints of all stakeholders. She is one who encourages open dialogue and always has a 'student-first' attitude. She's contagious. We've all bought in to her thinking, and as a result, we work collaboratively to develop, promote, and implement a shared vision that places student learning and achievement first and foremost. As a result, quality teachers stay. Less than industrious teachers

(Continued)

(Continued)

left long ago, after Olive became principal. Why, you might ask? Olive is a strong believer in measurable goals and outcomes that are student-focused, and instructionally centered. Additionally, she monitors and evaluates progress toward our collaboratively determined goals. If we're not working, students are not working, and thus, our goals are not working! That's what Olive always says and believes. So, those who won't work, don't work here long!"

Lorena Ellebracht, a longtime resident, has been involved at Sunset School since the early 1960s. Her children went to school at Sunset, so have her grandchildren, and currently, she has three great-grandchildren attending the school. Lorena relates why Sunset School has been such a success, especially in recent years. "Let me tell you, we may have a small community. We may have a school system that doesn't have a strong tax base. We may have a school in need of upgrading and a few coats of paint. What we do have at Sunset School, and there's no maybe about it, is a leader in Olive Estes. She involves all members of the learning community—students, faculty, staff, business leaders, parents, grandparents, and even great-grandparents, like me. She champions an instructional program that maximizes student learning and achievement. She just needs more time! Now, look here: Our school may seem ragtag at first glance, but we will stand up against any school system when it comes to our students and their outstanding achievement!"

Tommie Syfan is one of the younger parents; she came to the Sunset School community from a neighboring school system that, in her words, was "inadequate, irrelevant, and unable to sustain academic and social supports that are essential to driving learning and teaching expectations and student success." Mrs. Syfan asks, "Have you observed our technology infrastructure? It's state of the art. While the school system has limited dollars to maintain the outward appearance of the building, Principal Estes has sought and found digital funding in the form of grants, foundation dollars, community fundraisers, and state funding initiatives. We have a better and safer school because of technology! Even community members are permitted to use the school's technology. Using a laptop I check out from the school, I e-mail my out-of-state parents all the time. Let me tell you about Mrs. Estes: That woman is a real leader, and she has a 'seek and you shall receive' attitude when it comes to finding technology dollars. She just needs more time!"

Carrie Tuttle has taught kindergarten at Sunset School for the last 17 years. She is described by Principal Estes and Assistant Principal Rand as being a "lead teacher," a "master teacher." She spoke with a patient and loving voice, "We are so fortunate to have our leadership team. Both Mrs. Estes and Mr. Rand are exceptional leaders. They trust the teachers and we trust them. There is an atmosphere of mutual respect, and they listen to us. If you have a problem or an issue as a teacher, their office doors are open. Both provide their cell phone numbers to us, and we can call if we have a need. Both are moral and ethical people. They are actively involved in their church and synagogue. Both teach young people—Mrs. Estes teaches an arts and crafts class at her church on Saturdays, and Mr. Rand is a scout leader. Mrs. Estes has established a community of lifelong learners and leaders who base all 'student-first' decisions on extensive research, data collection, and analysis. Both of our administrators are so encouraging. They give lots of pats on the back and frequently send us notes describing positive aspects of teaching and learning they have observed. Now, don't get me wrong—neither is a pushover. They expect the best, and we give the best. So do our students! You know what? They care. You do understand the meaning of the word *care?* It's seen on posters throughout our school. *Care is recognizing that every individual is the most precious thing in the world!"*

To conclude this case study, and to use the vernacular of the 1940s technicolor travel documentaries known as *Fitzpatrick Travel Talk*, we close with "As the sun sets slowly in the west, we wave goodbye and bid a fond farewell" to Sunset School and all those who make it a special place for leading, teaching, learning, and achieving. We also recognize the obvious: Sunset School is administered and managed efficiently, effectively, and expertly.

APPLICATION QUESTIONS

1. The case study reveals a great deal about Sunset School—the students, faculty, stakeholders, and administrative team. What is revealed specifically that relates to the material detailed in the chapter?

2. Consider the concluding statement: "Sunset School is administered and managed efficiently, effectively, and expertly." How, and by what means? Is time a perceived element? Explain.

3. Now that you have read the first four chapters of the text, suggest what could assist Principal Olive Estes in gaining more time, as was noted by each of the case study stakeholders. Provide examples to support your answers.

4. How would you describe the culture and climate at Sunset School? Who is responsible? How does this person (or how do these persons) affect the climate and culture, and by what means? Is it actually possible to have a school like the one in the case study narrative, or is it simply an unrealistic narrative in today's era of federal, state, and district assessment and accountability? Relate your answer to personal examples and relevant research. Provide a detailed response.

5. Regarding research, which of the following statements, all of which are correlated with the development of an exemplary learning community, best exemplifies Sunset School? Provide examples to support your answers.

(Continued)

(Continued)

- ○ Establishing a learning community is a collaborative process.
- ○ Optimal learning and achievement requires participation of all stakeholders.
- ○ Learning communities must have leadership that develops an ethos that supports a vision and mission of students first.
- ○ Creating a powerful learning community must have as its foundation: (a) strong leadership, (b) a culture of continual learning, (c) a positive climate based on collaboration and teamwork, (d) instructional expertise, (e) technology in this digital era, and (f) time.
- ○ Experimentation must be cherished, reflection must be consistent, renewal must be continuous, and school-community partnerships must be collective.

6. Which of the following, as noted within the chapter, can be inferred either directly or indirectly about Principal Olive Estes and/or Assistant Principal Bill Rand? Explain how you reached your conclusions.

- ○ Models trust and respect.
- ○ Listens.
- ○ Utilizes improved data collection and analysis.
- ○ Models moral and ethical behaviors.
- ○ Encourages others.
- ○ Cares for personnel.

7. One can readily perceive that Sunset School will soon change, notably with the retirement of Principal Olive Estes. How might her retirement affect school culture and climate? What must a new principal expect and anticipate? Can the current culture and climate be maintained by the new principal? If it can, how—by what means? If not, why not?

Answers for Page 94

Consider the following priority order:

1. Parent-principal conference regarding a student who has recently exhibited some disturbing behavioral issues.

2. Attend an admission, review, and dismissal (ARD) meeting.

3. Meet with a team of teachers regarding an instructional concern.

4. Attend a campus fundraising function.

5. Help the Parent-Teacher Association (PTA) executive committee decide when the next semester meetings should be scheduled.

6. Walk two miles (yes, your health is more important than a school photo!).

7. Now, have a personal school photo taken.

What order would you choose for your priority listing?

5

Collaboration
and Time

Two Keys to Instructional Success

Observe life, look around and pay attention, engage and interact with others, and make a difference!

—Mark Sanborn, *You Don't Need a Title to Be a Leader: How Anyone, Anywhere, Can Make a Positive Difference* (2006)

COLLABORATION—FIRST AND FOREMOST!

Collaboration might very well be defined as a mindset that ignites a passion within a community of learners to build a common vision and mission. Mark Sanborn is correct, as noted in the opening quote: Every encounter and every interaction is an opportunity to gain knowledge and expertise, and to move the collective school community forward. For school principals, each encounter is an opportunity to make a difference—a positive, collaborative difference! From each encounter, a principal has the opportunity to grow, to learn, to change, to add another level of awareness, to gain greater insight, and again, to make a collaborative difference! Simply put, collaboration is a problem-solving approach that requires the integration of all parties.

Principals who effectively collaborate utilize the following approaches. They

- Seek integrative and inclusionary solutions;
- Understand the real objective of leading is to learn;
- Obtain insights from people, including parents, with different perspectives;
- Gain commitment by incorporating the ideas of others into a consensus; and
- Work to develop a culture of collective and equal power.

Collaboration is the one leadership tool that takes time to learn and incorporate, but the effort is time well spent! The emergence of effective school leadership is based on how well a principal can understand existing school conditions and build capacity by fostering a collaborative environment through a culture of trust and mutual respect. When the principal does this, individuals feel empowered to take risks and be creative, and in turn, they feel secure in offering suggestions and solutions for the enhancement of the organization (Green, 2013). So, let's make this easy—what is collaboration? Collaboration is clearly defined with one question a principal must sincerely and regularly ask followers: "How can I work with you?"

How Can I Work With You?

Far too many principals prefer to think things through, seek solutions, solve problems, and make decisions without looking for assistance from others. It just seems easier to do it on your own! Consider a recent important decision you have made. Did you actually seek input from others, or did you think to yourself—"I don't have time to seek out others and gain their perspectives. I can do this myself!" Did that approach to leading actually work? Maybe so—more often no! You are now thinking, "Come on, who has time for this, and why should I make time when I can decide things on my own? And by the way, who would I seek out if I did, in fact, decide to obtain input from others?"

Faculty Have a Vested Interest

Seek input from faculty first. They are in the trenches doing the critical work of teaching and guiding learning. Who knows and understands instruction and students better? Gaining faculty insight is frequently the surefire method of acquiring new and different perspectives, multiplying suggestions, expanding solutions, and ensuring that good decisions are made on crucial instructionally focused questions. And, just as important, getting advice from faculty and interacting with them actually saves time. How? Consider the following seven secrets of exceptionally productive principals who collaborate with others:

1. Seek means and methods from those who are a lot smarter, who've had more experience and practice.

2. Obtain from others their best ideas, always giving appropriate credit.

3. Keep a handwritten journal, or, to save time and productivity, an e-journal on a computer or handheld device (tablet or smartphone). Insert ideas you gain from others—their thoughts, suggestions, recommendations—as well as important notes and reminders.

4. Never be afraid to ask the opinions of subordinates. They actually know best! Recall the words of Andrew Carnegie about "being introduced to the broom" at an early age. In other words, intimately know and understand the most lowly tasks and those who perform them. You may not do the grunt work, but you better know how it is done. Equally important is personally knowing those who do the grunt work, and most important is listening to and crediting them!

5. Avoid the office during work hours—more can be gained and learned by being out and about, being visible, and interacting with faculty, staff, and students.

6. Avoid arriving at meetings 10 or 15 minutes before they begin. Much can be gained in "just" 10 or 15 minutes, so don't give that time away. Never feel bad about protecting time!

7. Steer clear of unsolvable problems. Don't waste personal time or the valuable time of others by continuing to address a problem that is impossible to solve. If at first the insights gained from those trusted most have failed to help solve a problem, move on. Principals recognize there are two or three more problems to solve for every one unsolvable, time-consuming conundrum!

Vestiges of institutionalism, or "tradition" if you prefer that term, actually restrict a principal's use of time and that of a faculty. Each year, it is not unusual to hear both teachers and principals decry their lack of meeting time. Then, life is further complicated with all members of a learning community realizing how crowded their calendars become and how nearly impossible it is to get all parties together at one time in one location. So, principals and teachers actually restrict themselves with the notion that committee work must be done at a specific time and locale. Principals all too often paint themselves into a "no-time" corner with no visible way out. Foolish! There are simple time-saving tips and management solutions.

TIME-SAVING TIPS AND MANAGEMENT SOLUTIONS

The lives of principals are always busy. Every school day seems to bring even more craziness to a principal's schedule. Sometimes, even the best of principals think to themselves: "It's enough to make you want to give up!" Of course, rarely is this a viable solution to the overwhelming aspects of leading. Time-saving tips help bring solutions to management issues. Time-saving tips help relieve stress—especially when schedules are packed. Conduct a Google search of "time-saving tips," and at least 85 million links appear presenting a multitude of options for the busy person, ranging from "do less" to "delegate" to "get priorities done first" to "focus on one project at a time" to "learn to say no" to "avoid meetings." When it comes to collaboration and meetings, few—if any—principals can afford to say no or simply avoid essential meetings. Consider the following collaboration and time-saving tips.

Asynchronous Collaboration

Listservs can free faculty and principals to collaborate via flexible schedules (asynchronous communication/collaboration). The authors suspect most principals know how these work, but, as a bonus, a few tools—some free— are provided! Asynchronous communication or collaboration is the transmission of data or information, generally without the use of an external clock signal, where said data or information can be transmitted intermittently rather than in a steady stream.

Now, as promised, the online tools: Websites like CalendarWiz.com, huddle.com, eyeOS.com, Keep&Share (keepandshare.com) and applications such as Microsoft Outlook (free) and Google+ (free) are specifically designed to permit principals and members of the learning community to share calendars and to-do lists, by invitation only.

Additionally, bulletin board messages can be posted at any time and read at one's leisure. Individuals can take as much time as needed to respond to certain activities. For example, viewing videos linked to professional development via online software is an asynchronous activity. There are key advantages to asynchronous collaboration tools:

- They are flexible;
- They save time;
- Individuals receive information when it is most convenient for them;
- There's less pressure to immediately act on the information;
- Individuals have time to digest the information and make considered decisions; and
- They can be used for day-to-day corroboration, especially when an urgent response/decision is not needed.

Using real-time chat, instant messaging, electronic whiteboarding, and other such tools is an effective means of communication and actually serves as a supplement to asynchronous communication and/or collaboration (University of Wisconsin–Madison Teaching Academy, 2014).

Time Management Tricks of the Trade

- Handle routine questions, concerns, or problems by interacting with teachers and students during daily walkthroughs.
- Be visible and engage in conversations with others. This is a real time saver (see final bullet), and more important, it serves to reveal a leader's genuine interest in the school community.
- Tour the building more than four times a day, giving teachers regular opportunities to have quick and meaningful discussions.
- Be visible and accessible, thus preventing the escalation of more unneeded and unwarranted problems.
- Understand that across-campus visibility solves the time management issue of having lines of faculty and students waiting in the office before, during, and after the school day.

Use these time savers or let me create havoc by stealing even more valuable time!

—The Silent Time Thief

Other Time Management Tips

Yukl (2012) relates that collaboration is a most proactive influential tactic and moreover, it is a means by which a principal can gain power—legitimately, appropriately, and positively. How can a principal offer to provide relevant resources, materials, and assistance to faculty and staff in a time-saving manner? First, collaborate (remember: "I'm here to work with you!"), and second—manage the paperwork! Paperwork (hard-copy or electronic) is the number one time-consuming administrative task that interferes most with principal and faculty collaboration. How can a leader manage paperwork?

1. Schedule unencumbered time during the day to do deskwork. This time may be before or after school (both excellent considerations) or during the school day. If the work must be conducted during school hours, it is essential that the principal and secretary understand there will be no visitors and no telephone calls accepted except in the case of emergency. This in-school time block should never exceed 30 to 60 minutes.

2. Use the TRAF system. This is an essential paper-bearing conveyor belt built right in the principal's office! More important, it is probably one of the best time management systems ever created, and it is easy to

incorporate. TRAF requires leaders to do only one of four things with paper that is in their hands or peering up from a desk:

Toss, Refer, Act, or File

Quickly examine the piece of paper. Decide if it is worth spending a finite time working on or even looking at.

- If the answer is no—*toss* it in File 13—the wastepaper basket!
- If the answer is yes—*refer* the piece of paper to someone else. Delegate this responsibility for action to a secretary, clerk, assistant principal, or some other subordinate.
- If the answer is yes, and it can't be referred to another individual—*act* on the issue presented. Take action and make the effort as seamless and prompt as possible. Either "do this" or "do that," and quickly rid the desk of the paper-related concern.
- If the paper and related topic needs to be accessible—*file* it in a project file and return to it later, at a more convenient time, for completion.

Properly and effectively managing paperwork provides time for more important collaborations—with faculty, students, parents, and community members.

COLLABORATING WITH STUDENTS, PARENTS, AND COMMUNITY MEMBERS

The best principals collaborate with all stakeholders, including students, parents, and community members. Collaboration is an essential strategy for benefitting the individual as well as the organization; for listening to the faculty voice; for making team decisions; for benefitting all stakeholders—most notably students; for determining what really matters; and for creating a supportive leading, teaching, and learning environment.

Amazingly, in many schools, the most overlooked group in collaborative planning is the group who can benefit most—students. There are three reasons for collaborating with students:

1. They know more than you may think, and they're willing to tell you what they think. Just ask them and learn lots!

2. Students can provide a valuable perspective and dimension to any planning process. Don't think for a minute that students are too young and/or immature to appropriately and effectively contribute to curricular and instructional discussions. Students provide excellent ideas that can lead to effective educational experiences.

3. Students involved in planning can be elevated by their involvement. In other words, when given a voice, students develop a sense of ownership. This increased ownership leads to an increase in learner responsibility.

Time-on-Task Learning Activities

Maximizing time-on-task learning is more than serious business at North Star Academy in Newark, New Jersey. It is a laser-like focus that optimizes every minute of instructional time. Principal Michael Mann points to some highly distinguished numbers as well as a strong emphasis on team collaboration.

First, the numbers: North Star Academy serves students in grades 9–12; has a 76% free and reduced-price lunch population; has high scores on state exams (students on average get 92% correct on the state's ELA test and 100% correct on its math test); maintains an average attendance rate of 95%; has a 100% college acceptance rate for its high-poverty student population; and requires additional instructional time, compared to surrounding districts, of 70 more minutes per day and 11 more days per year.

Now, collaboration: Teachers and administrators collaborate, maximizing time on task and working together as an instructional team, emphasizing lesson planning, lesson structure, and six core components to student learning: (1) *Do Now* (a quick exercise to initiating student thinking); (2) *Oral Drill* (a review of previous material, vocabulary, or essential facts and information); (3) *Heart of the Lesson I* (first 20–25 minutes of time-on-task optimal learning); (4) *Heart of the Lesson II* (second 20–25 minutes of time-on-task optimal learning); (5) *Homework* (nightly); and (6) *Exit Ticket* (brief concluding assessment to check for understanding).

The teaching and instructional teams collaboratively develop classroom management plans, plan all lessons to maximize time-on-task learning; minimize noninstructional time; and emphasize attendance.

Time spent interacting and collaborating with students is time well spent. Again, as a reminder, students know a lot—just ask them!

Parents Aren't Annoyances

For many years parents were, in some instances, intentionally described as being an "annoyance" to educators, and as a result, were often purposefully prevented from "interfering" with school-related decisions. Research has and continues to reveal that involving parents in curricular and instructional matters produces significantly higher levels of student achievement (Comer & Haynes, 1991; Epstein, 2001, 2005; Herman & Yeh,

1983; Lee & Bowen, 2006; Noel, Stark, Redford, & Zukerberg, 2013; Sanders & Lewis, 2005; Sheldon & Epstein, 2005). Here's what we know:

- School age children spend 70% of their waking hours with parents or guardians. These people are our students' first and most important teachers. Educators must involve parents/guardians and sometimes educate them as well—as a means of further increasing student achievement.
- Earlier parental involvement equates to more powerful student growth and development as related to the following:
  - Higher grades;
  - Increased school attendance;
  - Better self-esteem;
  - Lower rates of suspension;
  - Decreased use of drugs and alcohol; and
  - Fewer instances of violent behavior.
- Parental involvement is the most important way to improve schools.
- Lack of parental involvement is a serious problem facing public schools.
- The most consistent predictor of student academic achievement is parental involvement and expectations.
- Schools that encourage students to practice reading at home with parents best ensure students make significant gains in reading achievement.
- The single most important factor in parental involvement is school and district leadership.

The National Network of Partnership Schools (NNPS) has been described in the research literature (Epstein, 2001; Sanders, 1999, 2001; Sheldon, 2005; Van Voorhis & Sheldon, 2004) as a means to assist schools, districts, states, and organizations in sustaining strong programs of partnerships to better ensure student academic success. School principals are central to developing and improving partnerships by regularly meeting with a range of stakeholders to plan, implement, and evaluate their efforts to increase family engagement (Epstein, Galindo, & Sheldon, 2011).

The NNPS incorporates six "keys" that lead administrators and teachers in developing strong programs of school, family, and community partnerships for student excellence in schools. These keys are as follows:

- **Parenting.** Principals and faculty must assist parents with parenting and child-development skills and work to develop homes that support children as students.
- **Communicating.** Principals and faculty must communicate with parents about school, school programs, and student progress.

- **Volunteering.** Principals and faculty must recruit and involve parents as volunteers and audiences at school.
- **Learning at Home.** Principals and faculty must engage parents with their children in learning activities at home, to include working with their children completing homework.
- **Decision Making.** Principals and faculty must include parents in participative decisions and governance at school through PTAs/PTOs, site-based decision-making teams, committees, action research teams, and other parent-related initiatives.
- **Collaborating.** Principals and faculty must coordinate resources and services for students, parents, and families with outside agencies and other service providers.

Campus and district administrators must recognize that there are many reasons for parental collaboration. However, the most important reason is aiding students to succeed today and later in life (Noel et al., 2013).

Community Leaders Can Help

Who are community leaders? These are individuals who interact with or collaborate with the administration, faculty, and staff. Community leaders can come from business, have religious affiliations, be politicians or have political connections, or work for or with service agencies or other organizations such as United Way, Habitat for Humanity, Community Food Bank, Caring Hospice Services, Boys & Girls Clubs, Big Brothers Big Sisters, Ronald McDonald House, Special Olympics, Women in Need, Susan G. Komen foundation, American Heart Association, Girl and Boy Scouts, Homefirst Interfaith Housing & Family Services, Literacy Volunteers of America, 4-H, Salvation Army, American Red Cross, Children's Hunger Fund, Amnesty International, American Cancer Society, Points of Light Foundation, and Youth Serve America, to name a few.

Community involvement to increase student achievement and develop better schools and school systems can be realized through the following four means or methods:

1. **Communication.** Principals must collaborate with business and community leaders, detailing school programs, initiatives, pilot programs, and other instructionally oriented activities. Principals must also seek and actively listen to the "outsider" message. Such messages can very well provide important and relevant advice and information. As noted previously, this type of collaboration provides another set of eyes that permits principals to better understand concerns or issues that normally might not be observed.

2. **Volunteering.** Principals must recruit and organize community help and support. Volunteers help, rather than hinder, instructional

programs and curricular initiatives, and more important, aid in increasing student achievement. (See the section entitled *Introducing Lens 4: Collaboration and Time* in Chapter 1, "Time Management and Your Leadership.")

3. **Decision Making.** Community leaders must be encouraged to participate in the site-based decision-making process. They provide differing and frequently essential perspectives that can improve schools and increase the academic success of students.

4. **Collaboration.** Principals would be wise to identify and integrate resources and services from the community to strengthen school programs and to provide for family services (health, cultural, recreational, and social support) to improve student learning and development.

THE INFORMED SCHOOL COMMUNITY

An extensive base of research confirms what every school principal must understand: The utility of active family and community involvement is a significant contributor to student achievement and school success. However, while administrative knowledge and experience, policy directives, and educational research endorse the advantages of collaborating with family and community, to do so can be challenging!

Source: Ralph and Alice cartoon by Alex Carruth.

Establishing Long-Term Relationships

Epstein (2001) stipulates that three spheres of influence strongly contribute to student achievement—school, home, and community. The closer the interactions among these three, the greater the opportunity for students to understand the importance of education, and the more significant a student's commitment to schooling. To ensure the collaborative overlapping nature of the three spheres (school, home, and community), a principal must make time to work with the learning community to develop a comprehensive plan and program. Such is the basis for collaborative partnerships to, again, help increase student achievement and further ensure that the learning community is successful.

Developing a Comprehensive Plan and Program

A comprehensive plan or program for establishing long-term relationships with community must include seven disciplines (Chadwick, 2004) to best ensure the presence of family, school, and community partnerships:

1. **Parenting.** Families must be encouraged (and sometimes taught) to develop a safe and healthy home environment in which students can learn and advance not only academically, but socially and behaviorally.

2. **Communicating.** School principals must provide families with information about instructional and curricular programs, along with other aspects of the learning community that can foster student learning and achievement.

3. **Volunteering.** Principals and faculty must recognize that involving parents at school as volunteers is a research-based, student-centered best practice. Accommodating parent volunteers (and business or corporate volunteers) can increase student academic achievement.

4. **Learning.** School principals must recognize how essential, if not critical, learning at home can be. Parents who supervise their children at home with homework and other school-related activities better ensure their children will succeed in school and in life. Frequently, a principal and team will have to train parents how to help their children learn at home.

5. **Decision Making.** Families must be involved in the decision-making processes at school. Such is ingrained in the research literature. When parents are part of a school's site-based decision-making team, they are involved, they provide new and different perspectives, and their involvement helps not only the school but, more important, their children—academically, socially, and behaviorally (Fullan, 2014; Heller, 1999; Henderson & Mapp, 2002; Ubben, Hughes, & Norris, 2015).

6. **Problem Solving.** Principals can better solve student-oriented problems and issues when parents are engaged in problem solving. If a student misbehaves, there are compelling reasons for the misbehavior. Parents must be involved in aiding principals, counselors, and teachers in discovering the source of a problem. Students + parents + learning community + collaboration = problem solved!

7. **Collaboration.** Interactive partnerships with families result in relationship alliances and greater cooperation. Mobilizing families will improve not only schools, but students, parents, and community life.

FINDING TIME—MAKING A DIFFERENCE!

Time is of the essence! Nothing distinguishes exceptional principals more than their alertness to time. Recall this time adage: "Ordinary leaders think merely of spending time. Great leaders think of using it!" Now consider the following: "If not now, when?" Don't be one of those principals who state, "I'm too busy to find the time to get organized!" Forty-three percent of Americans describe themselves as disorganized, and 21% miss crucial deadlines. These individuals can't find the time. Principals can ill afford to fit into this category!

I Don't Have Time Because I Have Too Much to Do!

Sylvia Sidney, principal at Meadowbrook School, is faced with a difficult issue that has serious implications for the students she serves as well as the entire school community. Test scores must increase if Ms. Sidney and faculty wish to meet the Annual Yearly Progress requirement of the No Child Left Behind Act. However, Sylvia is uncertain whether she should focus on students near the proficiency threshold (on the bubble) or those with more serious academic concerns. Sylvia recently confided to a colleague, "I don't have time because I have too much to do!" What's this principal to do?

Pause and Consider

- How might Principal Sidney reflect upon Chadwick's (2004) seven disciplines as means to create a response that will not leave any child academically behind?
- How might Principal Sidney better collaborate with and engage families and community to best benefit the students at Meadowbrook School?
- Should Principal Sidney and team concentrate on those students on the bubble, or those with a greater chance of failing the state exam? How might collaboration be initiated relative to this process?

- Could another discipline, not already noted, be implemented? What would this discipline be, and how would this additional dimension serve as a means of collaboration, and thus help the students at Meadowbrook School?
- How might Principal Sidney better utilize her time to accomplish her noted objective?

You were asked to consider how Sylvia Sidney, principal at Meadowbrook School, might better utilize her time to accomplish her detailed objectives. If you are not certain as to how, consider the following examples that principals can incorporate:

- **Clear your desk.** Perfect Order Professional Organizing (2014) notes that leaders waste six weeks per year seeking lost documents. Desk clutter accounts for 80% of office time wasted (Von Bergen, 2006). At the conclusion of every day, prior to departure, take care of your desk—inspect it, clear it, organize it, and appreciate it. It will look great and make you look great!
- **Develop a morning ritual.** Come into the office prior to the arrival of faculty and students and "work" your inbox, outbox, and "pending" box. Get organized before the events of the day create disorganization and exhaust valuable time!
- **Go digital.** Get rid of the stacks of paper that clutter the office desk, round table, file cabinets, and floor. Let technology be a time-saving servant. Don't be a servant to paper and hard-copy files that cover the office!
- **Use your calendar wisely.** Make appointments, complete all tasks that must be done each day, and insert important items that you need to know about or be aware of each day.
- **Plan weekly.** Planning daily equates to too much to do! Principals who plan daily end up listing three weeks' worth of stuff to do each day. Impossible! Carefully consider and list in a planning calendar those things that need to be accomplished this week. Then, began to develop a daily calendar.
- **Meet with staff, but plan meetings thoughtfully and carefully.** Meetings, meetings, meetings! Will they never cease? "Death by Meeting" is actually a book title (Lencioni, 2007), and this choice of title describes the frequent mental anguish of meeting attendees. Principals spend at least half of their work week in meetings. Fully 90% of principals squander their time, and the time of others, in meetings (MTN Universal, 2014). Meetings must be interactive, not passive; structured with an agenda that is followed closely; strategic, tactical, and consensus building; and, most important, brief! Advice for the school principal: If you call a meeting, be certain that

the meeting is essential and nontrivial, and that it starts promptly and ends on time. Know instruction, because if you don't, you are wasting personal time and faculty time, and they know it and don't appreciate it!

- **Delegate and beat deadlines.** Why do it all yourself, especially when in-house talent exists? These talented individuals can complete certain tasks better than many principals. Hand over the work and beat the dreaded deadline. When principals do, everyone looks good!

DIVERSITY ENRICHES THE LEARNING COMMUNITY

Diversity in schools today is almost commonplace. Diversity includes differences in age, gender, sexual orientation, political beliefs, socioeconomic status, religion, physical and mental ability, language, and ethnicity. All, working collaboratively, can shape and enrich the learning community. School principals and team must

a. Recognize and accept diversity as a positive aspect of the learning community,

b. Have an understanding or knowledge of diversity and how it can improve the climate and culture of a school, and

c. Take action to best benefit a diversified student population.

Why Diversity?

To acknowledge that diversity is a positive aspect of the learning community, a principal and team must first recognize and accept diversity. A significant increase among nonwhite populations is projected over the next 25 years. This change, this diversification in population in the United States, is rapidly occurring. For example, dramatic increases in the number of Hispanic students in schools are common in many locales across the United States. Those who think this ethnic group can be found only on the United States–Mexico border are clearly misinformed. The greatest increase in student population, nationwide, since 1990, has been the Hispanic student (US Census Bureau, 2014). One of the authors of this text resides in the largest US city on the United States/Mexico border. This city is a cosmopolitan urban center with numerous elements of diversity and cultural identity. Such cultural and diverse identities are not concentrated in El Paso, Texas, alone. What are the elements of diversity and cultural identity that make up your city or town and school today? How can these elements enrich the learning community?

Making Diversity Work in Schools

What are the best things principals can do to ensure that diversity is a positive element of the learning community? First, recognize that cultural transitions must occur, and, as leaders, facilitate this process. Listed below are five approaches to cultural transition as described by Adler (1975). This dated material is as relevant today as it was 40 years ago.

1. **Initiate contact.** Bring the new, the diverse, and the accustomed together. Contact overcomes differences and breeds familiarity and positive interaction.

2. **Disintegrate the familiar.** Break down the old norms and understandings, relating what must be.

3. **Reintegrate with new cues.** Inform faculty, students, parents, and community members about students from any new cultural background who will be enrolling in the school, and inform them how this new group is an essential contributor to school success.

4. **Identify with the new and diverse culture.** Interact, engage, and collaborate with members of the new culture. Establish opportunities for people to come together and to recognize how much they actually have in common. The authors have found that one of the best methods of bringing diverse groups together at school is through programs (PTA meetings, student performances, athletics, band and choral performances) and the provision of food. We all like to eat! Bring people together by having the district food service department prepare foods that are new and, of course, tasty!

5. **Incorporate biculturalism.** Maintaining an immigrant culture can be an asset to schools and can actually lead to increases in student achievement (Feliciano, 2001). Americanization can actually undermine student success. Educational success, as related to biculturalism, can be the result of a strong immigrant and cultural ethic characterized by high aspirations, a belief that effort will be rewarded, and a respect for authority; these all make for a better community (Alexandrowicz, 1999; DeMatthews, 2016; Feliciano, 2001).

Remember, people's perceptions, emotional ranges, behaviors, and levels of tolerance and acceptance change depending on where a school is in a cultural transition. It is human nature to respond to change and to new settings and cultures with initial shock, then subtle interest, then overt curiosity, then excitement, and finally, total acceptance. How can acceptance be accomplished in the collaborative setting of a school?

A school's curricular and instructional programs must be enhanced or even renewed to address diversity and allow for greater collaborations. Listed below are seven approaches (some positive, some negative), as identified by Cordeiro and Cunningham (2012), Cunningham and Cordeiro (2006), DeMatthews, (2015a, 2015b), and Sorenson, Goldsmith, Méndez, and Maxwell (2011) that principals and teams must be aware of. They must ensure that negative approaches do not interfere with or impede students' education; they must ensure the more positive approaches are implemented:

- **Cultural Deficiency.** (Negative). A student's language is considered an academic deficiency—an impairment, because it is not the dominant language used at school. A student's learning style is considered deficient and thus an impediment to academic socialization and to the culturally dominant norms of the school. The student's family is perceived to be a barrier to the student's academic success, as they are deficient in relation to the norms associated with other parents. This approach is not only deficient and negative, it is wrong!
- **Cultural Difference.** (Negative). The student's language is different from the dominant school language and thus problematic to the student's academic success. The student's learning style is a hindrance to learning. The student's family is not regarded as a key player in the student's education. Again, a deficient and terribly wrong approach!
- **Human Relations.** (Positive). All students must develop positive attitudes toward those students who are different racially, culturally, and in terms of gender. Cooperative learning is a key instructional method for helping students achieve this approach.
- **Single-Group Studies.** (Positive). A single-group focus might be a course in Hispanic studies or literature or women's studies or literature. The goal of this approach is to raise the significance of the intended group.
- **Multicultural Education.** (Positive). This curricular/instructional approach provides for educational equity, student empowerment, cultural diversity, harmony in the classroom, expanded understanding of various cultural and ethnic groups, and the development of more positive student, teacher, and parent perspectives about new and different cultures or ethnicities.
- **Social Justice Education.** (Positive). This curricular/instructional approach addresses oppression and inequality based on race, social class, gender, and disability.
- **Bilingual Education.** (Positive). It is essential for principals to determine what type of a bilingual instructional approach is most

appropriate for those students who are proficient as either mono-lingual (speaking, for example, Spanish only) or bilingual (speaking, for example, Spanish as a home language, and English as a second language). Programs for this approach include English as a Second Language (ESL), Sheltered English, Transitional Bilingual Education, Two-Way Bilingual Education, Maintenance Bilingual Education, and Structured Immersion.

FINAL THOUGHTS

Exceptional principals collaborate, first and foremost. They take a "How can I work with you?" approach to leading, seeking insights from individuals with differing perspectives, developing a culture of collective and equal power and worth.

Exceptional principals utilize both asynchronous and synchronous collaboration as a means of managing and saving time. Asynchronous collaboration is more flexible and allows for the receiving of information in a convenient, time-saving manner. Synchronous collaboration is face-to-face in orientation and ideal when interactions must be interactive with all parties present.

Exceptional principals manage their time effectively and efficiently. They schedule unencumbered time to complete desk work. They use the TRAF (Toss, Refer, Act, or File) system.

Exceptional principals recognize students are essential in any collaborative process, as students must have a voice. These principals also understand that parents are collaborative partners, not annoyances. Parents bring a different perspective, which helps ensure organizational success. Additionally, exceptional principals know community leaders and effectively communicate and collaborate with them. Leaders seek volunteers from the community to help with decision making and problem solving.

Exceptional principals keep the school community well informed, establishing long-term relationships and developing a comprehensive plan or program to ensure effective collaboration and family, school, and community partnerships.

Exceptional principals realize that diversity in schools enriches the learning community. These leaders make diversity work by incorporating positive curricular approaches such as single-group studies, multicultural education, social justice education, and bilingual education.

Exceptional principals collaborate. They meet as equals, lead as equals, decide as equals, and resolve as equals. Are you an exceptional principal—a lead learner among equals? Do you collaborate by understanding and incorporating the age-old adage, "All of us are smarter than any one of us?"

DISCUSSION QUESTIONS

1. Why is collaboration a "first and foremost" principal skill? Explain. Who benefits most from collaborative leadership—students, faculty, or community leaders and members? Why?

2. How does parental and community involvement actually serve to increase student achievement? Explain. Of the seven disciplines essential to developing a comprehensive plan or program, which are the most essential to developing long-term relationships relative to engaging and involving parents and community?

3. You are a principal or prospective principal. Examine the seven time-saving examples listed in the chapter section *Finding Time—Making a Difference!* Which of the seven do you believe is critical to managing time more effectively and efficiently? Why?

4. In the *Finding Time—Making a Difference!* section of this chapter, one of the time-saving examples is headed "Go digital." Give examples of how you personally allow technology to be your servant. How do you better manage your time with the incorporation of technology? Be specific in your answer and provide examples.

5. Diversity enriches the learning community. Adler (1975) detailed five approaches to cultural transitions, which are identified in the chapter. Which of the five transitions do you believe would best serve a principal, faculty, and students in relation to making diversity work in a school? Explain.

SELF-REFLECTION ON LENS 4: COLLABORATION AND TIME

Return to Chapter 1, "Time Management and Your Leadership," and reflect on the *Time Management Self-Assessment Instrument* (TMSI). In this chapter, you examined Lens 4: Collaboration and Time. Review your responses on the TMSI Scoring Template for Lens 4. Think about the material examined within this chapter and how it relates to Lens 4. Which of your beliefs were reinforced? Which items are you now reconsidering? Why? Would you change your score on any of the items? If you would, why? How does this chapter relate to your use and understanding of time in relation with the PSEL 2015 standards? Explain.

CASE STUDY APPLICATION

IF ALL FEEDBACK IS SO POSITIVE . . .?

Jenda Milner serves as principal at Lyndon B. Johnson (LBJ) School. She possesses a gift—the ability to collaborate with faculty and staff. This gift is essential to exceptional school leadership and success. She encourages her faculty to be open and honest by revealing that she values their opinions and is always willing to listen to them. She frequently conducts informal conversations along the hallways of LBJ, and she makes it clear that even negative feedback is a positive opportunity for school improvement. She never intimidates others, but she asserts and maintains the highest of expectations. Students deserve the best, and the best is what Ms. Milner expects from everyone on campus!

For several weeks in the spring semester, Jenda and the site-based decision-making team (SBDM) at LBJ have been collaboratively attempting to resolve a curricular/instructional/diversity issue. Time is critical, because any incorporation of new initiatives or programs must coincide with the campus improvement plan analysis and budget development processes. Campus demographics have changed significantly—almost overnight. With the arrival of a major overseas company, employees and families have transferred in from places such as Spain, China, the Philippines, Cambodia, and Thailand. The children and spouses of these white-collar employees usually speak their home languages—Spanish, Hmong, Cantonese, Filipino, Cambodian, and Thai—and the new students speak little English. Teachers are at a loss as to how to instruct these new and diverse students. One of Jenda's assistant principals, Bob Sessions, has told the teachers to sit the kids in class and "they'll eventually learn what we speak!" Principal Milner was aghast at such a statement and promptly but respectfully noted, "We can find much better methods to meet the language, instructional, and social needs of these new and diverse students!"

However, the SBDM team members continue providing feedback to Ms. Milner that is positive, noting that the issue is under control and that Ms. Milner is doing a wonderful job of leading during this transitional period. Jenda thinks to herself, "Yes, we are all collaborating trying to solve the problem, but if all the feedback is so positive, why do I think I'm not being told the whole truth?" She decides to delve more deeply into the problem—not only the issue of the newly arrived English language learners, but why the team is not telling her everything. Jenda contemplates, "I just wish I had more time to do my regular work plus the work of digging deeper for ways to teach students who don't speak English!"

(Continued)

(Continued)

APPLICATION QUESTIONS

1. Principal Milner could better collaborate, relative to the issue at hand, by seeking insights from people with differing perspectives. Who are these people, and how could they assist Ms. Milner in incorporating ideas into a problem-solving consensus?

2. In the chapter section *Faculty Have a Vested Interest,* seven secrets of collaborative practice are listed. Which of these could Ms. Milner and team incorporate? Is Number 7 a potential solution? Why or why not? Would asynchronous collaboration better assist Principal Milner? Why or why not?

3. Which guides identified in the chapter section *Other Time Management Tips* could help Ms. Milner save time and solve the curricular/instructional/diversity issue? Explain.

4. Which collaborators—faculty, students, parents, or community leaders—might aid Principal Milner in resolving the curricular/instructional/diversity issue? Explain.

5. Examine the *Why Diversity?* section of the chapter. Determine how Ms. Milner could find help to address the differences between the new student cultures and the dominant school culture. Provide examples.

6. To make diversity work at LBJ School, what approaches must Principal Milner use: Cultural Deficiency, Cultural Difference, Human Relations, Single-Group Studies, Multicultural Education, Social Justice Education, or Bilingual Education? Provide detailed analysis and explanation.

7. Student diversity in schools extends beyond the scenario presented in the previous case study. Skiba, Horner, Karega Raush, May, and Tobin (2011) exposed a persistent historical discipline gap between African American students and White students, and a gap between students with disabilities and White students without disabilities. This gap places both the African American students and students with disabilities at risk of being suspended or expelled despite evidence that suggests neither group is more likely to engage in misconduct than their White and nondisabled peers. A national investigation of student discipline referrals highlighted that African American students were 3.78 times more likely to be referred to the administrative office than were their White peers, and they were more likely than their White peers to receive expulsion or out-of-school suspension as a consequence for the same or similar disciplinary behavior.

Point. While disciplinary management of students is surely needed in some situations, the trends—as noted above—are undeniable: Students of color are far more likely to be removed from class for misbehavior than their White peers, and this trend grows sharper when students with disabilities and/or English-language learners are factored into the equation.

Question 1. Think about the implications as related to a student at your school, or consider your own child relative to the point above. How can you protect a student from such disparities in treatment? Explain.

Question 2. While disciplinary guidelines may be fairly written, will they be fairly applied? Your thoughts? Why or why not?

The Last Laugh

Lexophile is a term used to describe individuals who have a love for words, such as those who appreciate the phrase "To write with a broken pencil is pointless." Listed below are a couple of time-sensitive lexical expressions, and one additional example for all school principals to consider. Remember, a good laugh is timeless!

- When a clock is hungry, it goes back four seconds!
- A thief who stole a calendar got twelve months!
- Those principals who get too big for their pants will be totally exposed in the end!

6

Ethics, Integrity, and Time

If I am not for myself, who will be for me?

When I am only for myself, what am I?

If not now, when?

—Hillel, 1st century Jerusalem sage (*Pirkei Avot 1:14*)

SHAPING A SCHOOL

Ethics. Integrity. Two words that frequently appear in leadership literature. Two words we struggle to define sans a dictionary, yet in our own minds we believe we know their meaning. Plato's *Apology, Crito,* and *Republic;* Spinoza's *The Ethics,* and Bonhoeffer's *Ethics* readily point toward the importance of ethics and integrity within ourselves and our interactions with others. Ethics and integrity are not limited to individuals. Organizations demonstrate ethics and integrity as well; thus the school leader's responsibilities include establishing and maintaining a culture that encourages ethical behavior. While ethics and integrity are not defined by time, they are influenced by it. Branson and Gross (2014) caution that leadership is like a double-edged sword. In the midst of "doing good," principals must not be tempted to advance their own agenda at the expense of others.

The opening quote from the *Pirkei Avot* or *Ethics of Our Fathers* establishes the tone for examining ethics, integrity, and time. Hillel's first century questions coupled with the writings of Plato, Spinoza, and Bonhoeffer assist principals in realizing that ethics, integrity, and time are far from new topics for humanity. Hillel's almost 2,000-year-old advice provides comfort in knowing that school leaders are never alone in this age-old struggle, demonstrating integrity and ethical behavior.

The positional power inherent in the school leadership role provides an opportunity for a principal to shape a school's ethics and strengthen relationships with all stakeholders (DeMatthews, Edwards, & Rincones, in press). Failing to use this power judiciously creates a potentially challenging legal and/or moral situation (Koestenbaum, 2002). An integrity-based approach combines a concern for law with an emphasis on ethical behavior (Paine, 1994). When principals act unethically and lack integrity, school stakeholders lose confidence in them (Ross, 2009). If decisions are made to benefit the few, other school stakeholders lose trust and confidence, resulting in a negative impact on academic achievement. A high level of trust is essential for academic success (Tschannen-Moran, 2014). The public expects all educators to do the right thing. And doing so promotes a rich and effective learning environment. Following school policies and expecting others to do the same demonstrates ethical management and personal commitment to ethical behavior (Paine, 1994).

Principals live active, hectic lives. Many, if not most, school principals are addicted to busyness. Smith and Smith (2011) caution busyness can cause principals to lose focus on life's purpose. A supermajority of educators are hardworking and dedicated, spending time and money on aspects of schooling considered important and meaningful. Effective educators never do things halfway. From the moment principals wake up, they review their daily obligations to students, colleagues, and themselves. They try to juggle their time but still "drop the ball." When school leaders do so, they experience a sense of failure.

The to-do list is too long. Smith and Smith (2011) suggest narrowing the list to the one item that must be done *now*, requiring careful prioritization. The to-do list never goes away. It requires continual prioritization and management.

Reviewing how a principal spends time helps the school leader discover what matters most. When a principal falls victim to busyness, a loss of the vision and mission of private and professional living occurs. Finally, if a principal cannot find time to address others' concerns, it signals to others that their concerns are not important. Principals must ask themselves, "How do I manage my time while maintaining my ethics and integrity?"

Moral responsibility is often ignored or, at best, given slight consideration in education preparation programs for teachers and administrators (Senge, Cambron-McCabe, Lucas, Smith, Dutton, & Kleiner, 2012). Ignoring moral education and focusing primarily on pedagogical and leadership skills primes educators for failure, because these skills, while important, are not sufficient for educating the general population. Ethics, morality, trust, and integrity are vital to success. Senge and colleagues (2012) further assert that high values are expected in public schools. Ethical educators purposefully reflect on the long-range influence of their decisions on colleagues, students, parents, and the wider community. Twenty-five years ago, progressive John Goodlad (1990) identified concern for American cultural values as a key consideration leading to the creation of the public education system.

Ethics and integrity are associated with values, morals, trust, and meaning. Homer-Dixon (2006) divided values into three broad categories: (1) utilitarian values, our likes and dislikes; (2) existential values, those things that that add significance to our lives; and (3) moral values, which define our sense of fairness and justice and are particularly centered on opportunity, power, and wealth. Homer-Dixon (2006) asserts that society's inability to address existential or moral values reduces us to using our utilitarian values—our personal likes and dislikes.

The National Policy Board for Educational Administration (NPBEA) recently rewrote the former Interstate School Leaders Licensure Consortium (ISLLC) standards, producing the Professional Standards for Educational Leadership (PSEL). This rewrite recasts the standards "with a stronger, clearer emphasis on students and student learning, outlining foundational principles of leadership" (NPBEA, 2015, p. 2). PSEL Standard 2, Ethical and Professional Norms, addresses the ethics and professional norms for educational leaders. PSEL Standard 2 contains six elements that elaborate on the work and actions required to fulfill this standard.

PSEL STANDARD 2: ETHICS AND PROFESSIONAL NORMS

PSEL Standard 2, Ethics and Professional Norms, calls on educational leaders to "act ethically and according to professional norms to promote *each* student's academic success and well-being (NPBEA, 2015, p. 10). The defining elements of this standard provide greater clarity to this standard:

Effective leaders

a. Act ethically and professionally in personal conduct, relationships with others, decision making, stewardship of the school's resources, and all aspects of school leadership.

b. Act according to and promote the professional norms of integrity, fairness, transparency, trust, collaboration, perseverance, learning, and continuous improvement.

c. Place children at the center of education and accept responsibility for each student's academic success and well-being.

d. Safeguard and promote the values of democracy, individual freedom and responsibility, equity, social justice, community, and diversity.

e. Lead with interpersonal and communication skill, social-emotional insight, and understanding of all students' and staff members' backgrounds and cultures.

f. Provide moral direction for the school and promote ethical and professional behavior. (NPBEA, 2015, p.10)

The Sorenson-Goldsmith Integrated Budget Model (see Figure 6.1) illustrates how PSEL Standard 2, Ethics and Professional Norms, and its six elements are manifested in the field.

Figure 6.2, The PSEL Elements Manifested in the Sorenson-Goldsmith Integrated Budget Model, illustrates how each of the budget model elements connects to the 2015 PSEL Standards. The elements are abridged in this table for clarity. The solid alignment of the Sorenson-Goldsmith Integrated Budget Model with the 2015 PSEL standards and their

Figure 6.1   Sorenson-Goldsmith Integrated Budget Model

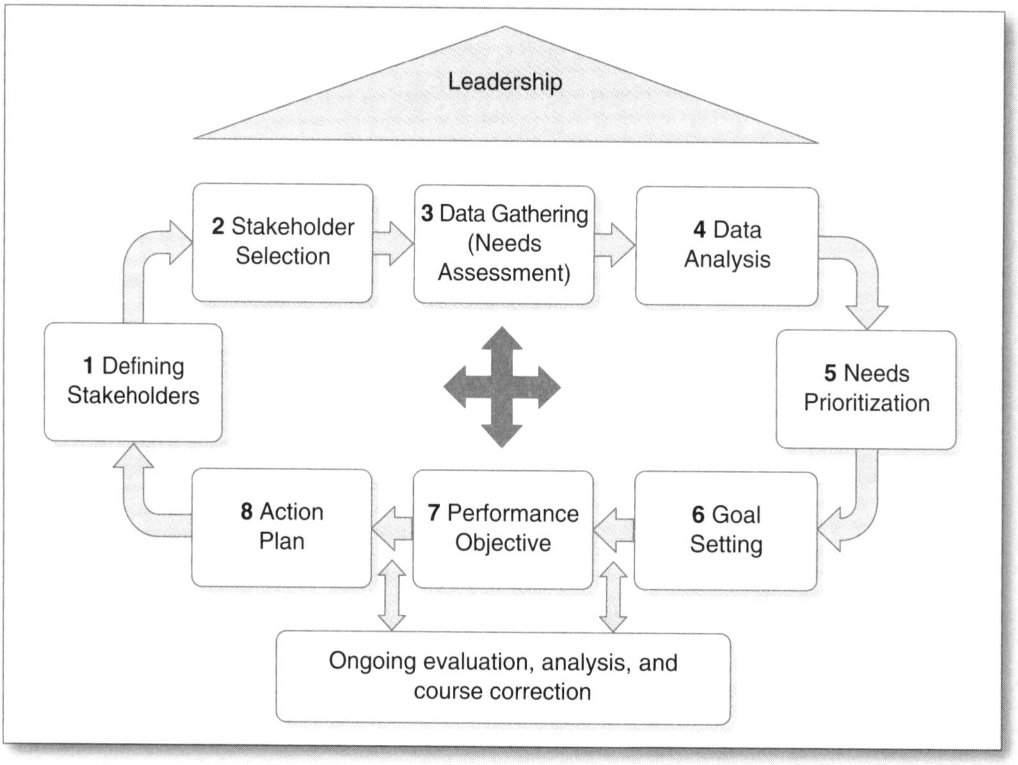

Source: Sorenson & Goldsmith, 2013, p. 81.

Figure 6.2   The PSEL Elements Manifested in the Sorenson-Goldsmith Integrated Budget Model

Sorenson-Goldsmith Integrated Budget Model Components	PSEL Standard 2 Elements (Abridged)
1. Defining Stakeholders	(a) safeguard and promote the values of equity, community, and diversity
2. Stakeholder Selection	(d) safeguard and promote the values of democracy (e) social-emotional insight and understanding of all students' and staff members' backgrounds and cultures
3. Data Gathering	(a) decision making
4. Data Analysis	(a) act ethically and professionally in personal conduct
5. Needs Prioritization	(a) decision making (b) place children at the center of education
6. Goal Setting	(e) lead with interpersonal and communication skill, socio-emotional insight into and understanding of all students' and staff members' backgrounds and cultures (f) provide moral direction for the school
7. Performance Objective	(c) place children at the center of education and accept responsibility for each student's academic success and well-being
8. Action Plan	(a) stewardship of the school's resources (b) act according to and promote the professional norms of integrity, fairness, transparency, trust, collaboration, perseverance, learning, and continuous improvement

accompanying elements provides schools with a strong framework for quality moral leadership in a professional and productive environment.

When principals communicate with stakeholders, they must be ethical if they are to be trusted, accepted, and valued. When any ethical qualities are missing, some stakeholders—if not most—will become hostile, defensive, or distressed or feel misunderstood. The tongue when not tamed can cause immense problems.

Green (2013) reminds school leaders their tongues can cause problems when they (1) participate in inappropriate conversations, (2) don't protect confidential information, (3) make a promise about something over which they know they have no control, or (4) provoke a defensive climate. Most if not all of us have trouble taming our tongues. For example, we might begin a conversation with "Don't tell anyone this, but . . ." There is a strong likelihood that the conversation will be passed along and probably embellished in the process. Having such a conversation violates PSEL Standard 2, Section A.

The Concerned Parents Meeting Vignette

Principal Steve Monroe loves working at Mission Santa Fe School (MSS), a large school of 2,500 students. MSS has a diverse population consisting of 55% Hispanic, 28% White, 12% Asian, and 5% African American students. While the vast majority of the student population qualifies for the free and reduced-price lunch program, approximately 10% of the population is very wealthy; this group is composed of children of doctors, lawyers, federal judges, and other professionals. These parents possess lofty expectations for their children's education and future. Having their children graduate in the top 10% of their classes and score well above average on the SAT is just the beginning of these parents' dreams and expectations. While having lunch with Mr. Monroe at the exclusive Oil Man's Club, one father said, "Mr. Monroe, I have one expectation of you. I need my daughter to attend college at either Princeton or Stanford. I've done my part by contributing millions of dollars to each university; now it is time for you to do yours."

Tuesday morning, Mr. Monroe received a phone call from Mrs. Godoy, wife of the local bank president. She said that she and several other parents wanted to visit with him at lunch. Mr. Monroe accepted the invitation, offering to provide lunch from a local deli.

As the parents and Principal Monroe enjoyed their lunch, Mrs. Godoy began. "Mr. Monroe, we have concerns regarding the honors and Advanced Placement classes. We think you are allowing too many of *those* students into the classes and *those* students might not be able to keep up."

Mr. Monroe swallowed hard and began to think about why he liked working at MSS.

Pause and Consider

- Place yourself in Principal Steve Monroe's chair. He has influential parents, parents with power and prestige in the community, parents with connections to community leadership. How would you treat all the people involved fairly, equitably, and with dignity and respect, including the students whose parents have little to no connection to community leadership?
- What role, if any, does PSEL Standard 2 play in addressing this vignette?
- What can Principal Monroe do to enhance the educational program for the students whose parents have no influence, who are marginalized in the community?
- How was Principal's Monroe time impacted?
- How were other school stakeholders impacted, time-wise, by this meeting?

All school leaders, to include Principal Steve Monroe, would do well to consider Homer-Dixon's three broad value categories. Leaders must ensure that their personal likes and dislikes do not interfere with the organization's vision and mission, since the school belongs to everyone—not just the leader or the leadership team. For example, if a principal favors a particular instructional strategy, she must not allow this to influence her assessment of students, parents, or even a teacher who, for example, meets with academic success while using other instructional strategies.

Likewise principals must be aware of their existential values—those things in their lives that provide significant personal meaning—and not allow those things to distract from the school's mission and vision. Principals must be receptive to other school stakeholders' existential values, thus fostering an inclusive environment. Finally, principals must be sensitive to moral values and personal understandings of fairness and justice in all interactions with various stakeholders. Principals must ensure that their conduct does not deprive others of opportunity. Nor should principals allow power and wealth to influence their leadership role, especially as it relates to those served. Fullan's (2008) six secrets of change emphasize both good values and results. By choosing good values and "moral purpose, striving to develop oneself, and mak[ing] a meaningful contribution through one's work and life" (Fullan, 2008, p. 44), principals increase their ability to effect positive change.

A SCHOOL LEADER'S THOUGHTS ON ETHICS, INTEGRITY, AND TIME

A conversation between Lloyd Goldsmith and Steve Waddell, superintendent of Lewisville Independent School District (Lewisville ISD) located in the Dallas/Fort Worth metroplex, provides a practitioner's

Ralph and Alice share the cynicism that far too many people have concerning the integrity and ethics of political leaders. They also remind us of the importance of being sure our words and actions as school leaders are bathed with integrity and ethics.

Source: Ralph and Alice cartoon by Alex Carruth.

view of how integrity, ethics, and time impact and inform a district's day-to-day interactions.

Lewisville ISD comprises approximately 52,700 students, with five high schools and five campuses for ninth and tenth grade. The student ethnic distribution is approximately 48% White, 28% Hispanic, 12% Asian, and 9% African American. Thirty-one percent of the students are economically disadvantaged (Texas Education Agency, n.d.).

A Voice From the Field—Part II

Lloyd: When an educator fails to adhere to ethical principles and professional norms, how does it impact a school or school district?

Steve: It is imperative that educators act with integrity using ethical principles. This high ground begins with doing things that are best for students. When you think in terms of integrity and ethical behavior, you must begin by thinking about your students. Educators must be about students first and foremost. We must examine this from an ethical and professional perspective. We must also consider it from the standpoint of the students.

Lloyd: If you are dishonest as an educator, does it hurt students?

Steve: It has to. If we as school leaders are unethical with the way we use money, does it harm students? How could it not? If we treat people poorly or use people or are uncaring, does that hurt students? Of course it does! When we treat people that way, they are not doing to their jobs as well. Resentment builds.

Lloyd: Steve, you seem to be pointing toward acting with integrity toward all.

Steve: Yes. In every action we take as educators, we must ask ourselves, "Is this best for our students?" When you start with this question, I don't think you can *not* come up with the right answer, one that upholds your integrity. As leaders we must behave ethically and with integrity. Our behavior impacts everyone in the school system.

Lloyd: We never know who is watching us and looking toward us for examples of integrity and ethical behavior.

Steve: That is correct. I had a teenage student who looked up to me as a model. As an educator, I can't think of a greater compliment. I can't think of a greater example to illustrate how important we are to our students. If someone is looking up to us and admiring us and we behave badly, it hurts that person. We must remember students are looking up to us whether we are teachers, principals, superintendents, or custodians or hold any other position within the school or district.

Lloyd: Educators are to act as a moral compass for the school district. When they do, what benefits does that have for the district?

Steve: People want to feel proud of their school or school district. The superintendent is the face of the district. The principal is the face of the campus, and the teacher is the face of the classroom. All must behave impeccably. However, as humans we all have our frailties. We must strive to behave properly at all times.

Lloyd: Educators are supposed to maintain visibility and be approachable by all stakeholders. How does this benefit the school?

Steve: When I was a high school principal, I was always in the hallways. I told my assistant principals that I always wanted them in the hallways and the cafeteria. When that bell rings for a class change you are in the hall. The only reason you are not to be in the hall is if there is an emergency, and I get to decide what an emergency is. It's amazing what a difference that makes.

Lloyd: I can't help but smile, Steve. I had a superintendent who told me the same thing when I got my first administrative job as a junior high assistant principal.

Steve: Lloyd, I went to every ball game whether at home or away. It was some time later when people started commenting to me how they were always seeing me. I thought that was odd, because I thought that was what I was supposed to do. I expected the same from my principals. As superintendent, I have people always commenting they see me all the time, everywhere.

Lloyd: As a superintendent, do you visit campuses?

Steve: Yes. As a superintendent, I think I need to be in more places. I realized from the community perspective and for the teachers' sake I need to. Teachers say, "You come to our school all the time." Coaches say, "I see you at ball games." Kids want to take pictures with me. It means a lot to people. It makes people feel valued and connected to you. When you are in a leadership role, your presence means a lot. It makes people feel valued. I tell young administrators, you don't have to have a college degree to show up and be visible. It will make one of the biggest differences.

Lloyd: You invest a lot of time being visible throughout the district. Why do you do this?

Steve: School leaders who hide away and do not get out and about find their jobs that much tougher.

(Continued)

(Continued)

Lloyd: Saying that reminds me that I got my arm twisted to work in an inner city ministry working with alcoholics, drug users, and the homeless. Doing so required investing a lot of my time in this work—time I was hesitant to surrender. This past week the father of a homeless person with whom I worked died. I went to the funeral home to attend the wake. It gave me a lot of "street cred" to do so. Trust increased, as did a sense of community. I invested time and displayed integrity. I invested capital in them and our relationship.

Steve: Yes, genuine capital too—not fake capital.

Lloyd: I see similarities in working with inner city missions and being a principal or superintendent. The same caring attitude and people skills are required. It's all about life.

Steve: It's one of the most important things you can do in life. You don't have to do any research. It's the simplest thing in the world. If you invest your time, it means everything.

Lloyd: Steve, I have one final question. As a successful superintendent in a large district, do you have any time management tips? How did you manage all the people pulling on you, wanting your time?

Steve: The bigger the district, the more important time management becomes. You have to prioritize things that really matter and know what they are. You must discern the things that really count and focus on those things. The ability to delegate comes from having a good organizational structure. I reorganized for efficiency, reducing from 13 assistant superintendents to 5 assistant superintendents. It made a big difference even just in managing the number of people I worked with directly. I gave them jobs to do and let them do their jobs. We met every week to touch base, which allowed everyone to know what each of the others was doing. I had a strong executive assistant whom I could trust to do things. I gave up my calendar and let my executive assistant manage it. You need to be certain the time you spend on work is targeted to make a difference. We dabbled with various time management ideas. Our strengths are a good executive assistant, a logical leadership team, delegating, focusing on priorities, and working hard.

Lloyd: Thank you for investing your time with us, Steve.

For school leaders like Steve Waddell, interacting ethically with the school and district stakeholders transcends all PSEL standards. Steve reinforces the district's shared vision and mission each time he interacts with students, parents, and other district patrons. This cultivates a caring school community. As Steve goes about the district, be it in the classroom or an athletic event, he is cultivating a caring school community. He invests his time and resources to build and encourage teachers and other staff. Effective principals like Steve understand the positive impact of time well invested within a context of moral and ethical actions.

The New Principal: A Story of Ethics, Integrity, and Time

A school had three principal changes in four years. The first two principals employed a top-down leadership style. Each of these two principals utilized intimidating e-mails and memorandums ordering changes. Teachers and paraprofessionals were on edge waiting for the next stringent decree. The last of the three principals resigned three weeks before school began at the request of the superintendent.

A new principal was assigned to the campus two weeks before school began. The superintendent informed the new and relatively inexperienced principal that the campus was "wounded" and needed a lot of assistance. The superintendent shared his expectation that the new principal would "turn the ship around." The tone of the superintendent's voice was warm and comforting. While this was a daunting expectation, the new principal sensed that the superintendent would be supportive.

The new principal scheduled appointments with all the faculty and staff members to get to know them personally and to hear their thoughts or concerns about the school. The principal did a lot of listening and not much talking. After visiting with all faculty and staff, the new principal invited them and their families to a cookout at his home shortly before school began.

During the first week of school the new principal circulated about the campus visiting students, staff, and faculty. Gradually the new principal began walking through classrooms. Much—if not most—of the faculty was on edge with these walkthroughs. Later, when the faculty checked their mailboxes, they discovered kind notes acknowledging something positive that the new principal observed in their classrooms.

The new principal began randomly taking over teaching lessons and would send the teacher to the break room for coffee or a soft drink. Teachers became more and more comfortable with the new principal's walkthroughs. No longer were they perceived to be "gotchas," something they had experienced in previous years. With time, the new principal became the accepted principal, as he had established a new and open culture, and a positive climate had been established.

This story oozes ethics, integrity, and time. The principal's behavior toward the faculty and staff began changing their perception of the school, the principal, and themselves. They were being treated as equals with respect and honor. Ethics, integrity, and time started transforming this campus's culture.

How to Thwart the *Silent Time Thief*

How does one thwart a time thief when it comes to ethics and integrity?

Allow us to spell out how the *Silent Time Thief* is thwarted when it comes to ethics and integrity.

1. *Trust* must be a cornerstone in all our actions.

2. *Integrity* is part of our world.

3. *TiMe* is valued and respected.

4. *ValuEs* are used in decision making.

5. *STandards* guide our policies.

6. *EtHics* are core to our decision making.

7. *DIspositions* must be driven by our ethics.

8. *LEadership* values ethics and integrity.

9. *Fairness* is valued.

TRUST
INTEGRITY
TI**M**E
VALU**E**S

STANDARDS
ET**H**ICS
DISPOSITIONS
LEADERSHIP
FAIRNESS

—The Silent Time Thief

FINAL THOUGHTS

Ethics. Integrity. Time. Let's return to where the chapter began. Twenty centuries of time have passed since Hillel asked his questions. The authors believe the reader should pen the final thoughts of this chapter. After all, ethics and integrity are highly personal matters that are manifested in a highly public forum. Some scaffolding is provided for this unorthodox chapter conclusion.

In Chapter 2, "Vision, Mission, and Time," we cited Horng, Klasik, and Loeb (2010), who presented 41 exceptional principals' tasks in six categories: administration, organization management, day-to-day instruction, instructional program, internal relations, and external relations. Revisit the six exceptional principal task categories from an ethics, integrity, and time perspective. Wearing an ethics and integrity lens, review the six exceptional principal task categories (see Figure 6.3, Principal Task Categories), and make connections between the descriptors, the task categories, ethics, integrity, and time. Doing so provides you, the reader, the freedom and responsibility to develop your personal understanding of ethics, integrity, and time.

DISCUSSION QUESTIONS

1. Conduct a time use audit of your work calendar for the previous four weeks using Figure 6.3, Principal Task Categories. Which category contained the most items from your professional calendar? Which category contained the fewest items? What, if any, changes should you consider in how you budget your time?

2. Homer-Dixon (2006) divided values into three broad categories: utilitarian, existential, and moral. Reflect on these three value categories. Provide three personal illustrations for each value category.

3. Tschannen-Moran (2014) asserts that it is the principal who is responsible for touting the school's vision in a trustworthy manner to all stakeholders. How have you seen this manifested in your career? Identify two unique ways to tout your school's vision to all stakeholders.

4. Hall and Hord (2001) remind principals not to underestimate the impact of teacher commitment and effectiveness on students and other stakeholders. How can principals model learning while leading and building a school culture that supports students, teachers, and the community?

5. Figure 6.1, the Sorenson-Goldsmith Integrated Budget Model, was used to illustrate how PSEL Standard 2, Ethics and Professional Norms, could be effectively implemented. Explain how this model supports PSEL Standard 2 from an ethics, integrity, and time perspective.

6. Ethics, integrity, and time were discussed in Lloyd Goldsmith's interview with Steve Waddell. Name two insights you gained from this interview. What question would you ask Superintendent Steve Waddell that wasn't asked? Why would you ask that question?

7. The story of the new principal's ethics, integrity, and time is based on a true experience. What personal or professional experience serves as your own story about ethics, integrity, and time? Why?

Figure 6.3 Principal Task Categories

• Fulfilling compliance • Managing school schedules • Managing student discipline • Managing student services • Managing student attendance • Preparing and implementing standardized tests • Supervising students • Fulfilling Special Education requirements	• Managing budgets, resources • Hiring personnel • Dealing with concerns from teachers • Managing non-instructional staff • Networking with other principals • Managing personal schedule • Maintaining campus facilities • Developing and monitoring a safe school environment	• Informally coaching teachers to improve instruction • Formally evaluating teachers • Conducting classroom observations • Implementing required professional development • Using data to inform instruction • Teaching students	• Developing educational program across the school • Evaluating curriculum • Using assessment results for program evaluation and development • Planning professional development for teachers • Planning professional development for prospective principals • Releasing or counseling out teachers • Planning or directing supplementary or after-school instruction • Utilizing school meetings	• Developing relationships with students • Communicating with parents • Interacting socially with staff about non-school related topic • Interacting socially with staff about school-related topics • Attending school activities • Counseling staff • Counseling student and/or parents • Informally talking to teachers about students, not related to instruction	• Working with local community members or organizations • Fundraising • Communicating with the district office to obtain resources (initiated by principal) • Utilizing district office communications (initiated by district)

Source: Horng, Klasik, & Loeb, 2010. Used with permission.

8. The codes of ethics of the American Association of School Administrators, the National Association of Elementary School Principals, and the National Association of Secondary School contain ten items in common (Zirkel, 2015):

   1. Students first
   2. Honesty and integrity
   3. Due process and civil rights
   4. Obeying the laws
   5. Implementing school board policies
   6. Pursuing correction of educationally unsound laws/policies
   7. Avoiding using position for personal gain
   8. Degrees/certification from accredited institutions
   9. Research and professional development
   10. Honoring all contracts until fulfillment or release

   What connections exist between these three organizations' codes of ethics and PSEL Standard 2?

SELF-REFLECTION ON LENS 5: ETHICS, INTEGRITY, AND TIME

In Chapter 1, "Time Management and Your Leadership," you completed the *Time Management Self-Assessment Instrument* (TMSI) designed to prompt your thinking on six time management lenses. In this chapter we examined TMSI Lens 5: Ethics, Integrity, and Time. It is time for self-reflection. Review your responses on the TMSI Scoring Template for Lens 5. Consider the material from this chapter and its association with the items from Lens 5. What beliefs were reinforced? What items are you reconsidering? Why? Would you change your score on any of the items? If so, why?

CASE STUDY APPLICATION

THE TEXTING COACH

Jose de la Torres, assistant principal at Mission Santa Fe School, was busy finishing up paperwork after another long day at work. At about 5:00 p.m., he heard someone enter the main office. Jose arose from his desk and walked to the reception area to greet two individuals. He recognized the student, Maria Cruz, immediately. She appeared to be accompanied by her mother. After welcoming them to his office and inviting them to have a seat, Jose asked how he could help them.

Mrs. Cruz began by saying that Maria had some information pertinent to an impropriety on the part of a teacher. Maria started telling a rather lengthy story about a teacher-coach, Coach Vladimir, who was texting her on a regular basis. She also indicated that the coach had asked her to stay after class today, whereupon he kissed her. Maria opened a manila folder she was carrying and handed Jose copies of numerous text messages between herself and the teacher-coach.

As Jose asked questions regarding the text messages documented in the copies in front of him, Maria told a story about running into the coach at Pete's Pizzeria located in a nearby community. Maria reported she saw the coach in the pizzeria's arcade one Saturday and thought nothing of it. Coach Vladimir was there with his family celebrating his oldest child's fourth birthday. Soon afterward, however, the coach asked Maria for her cell phone number; he began texting her about schoolwork and her participation in the school's dance team. Coach Vladimir began asking her if she would be performing at the football game's halftime show. He told her he wished he could see her dance. He also told Maria she looked "hot."

Before long, Coach Vladimir began texting Maria during football games and on weekends. Maria said she did not think much of it and that she was a little flattered he would spend time communicating with her. However, today he kissed her after school. She knew this crossed the line. After all, she thought, the coach was married and had two small children.

After listening to this story for approximately an hour, Jose excused himself and called his superintendent, Dr. Abe de Zavala. Dr. de Zavala was working late completing some work for the next school board meeting. Dr. de Zavala listened quietly to Jose's story and advised him to immediately contact the principal and inform him of the situation. De Zavala also advised that Coach Vladimir would be placed on administrative leave with pay pending the conclusion of an investigation.

The following morning, Principal Steve Monroe reported to campus and called Superintendent de Zavala objecting to the recommendation placing Coach Vladimir on administrative leave pending the conclusion of the investigation. Principal Monroe felt that this was tantamount to finding a person guilty without a trial. "His reputation will be ruined if we suspend him," pleaded Principal Monroe. Dr. de Zavala quickly reminded Principal Monroe that the school has an overwhelming obligation to keep children safe. If the allegations turn out to be false, "we will apologize to Coach Vladimir," responded de Zavala. "But we have not denied him a property right by taking this action."

Hanging up the phone, Principal Monroe and Assistant Principal de la Torres prepared to meet with Coach Vladimir to send him home and begin the investigation. Principal Monroe asked one of the female assistant principals to also assist him in the investigation. As the facts began to roll in, Principal Monroe went from dismay to shock to disappointment to anger. The evidence supported the girl's statement that the coach did text her numerous times, even from the sidelines during football games. He also texted her from the field house during football staff meetings conducted on Sunday afternoons.

Later in the afternoon, Principal Monroe met with Superintendent de Zavala and delivered his initial findings. It seemed that now they had more questions to answer than before.

- Who else needed to be interviewed?
- How much did the girl's friends know? Some of the texting occurred during football games while she was sitting in the stands with the dance team.
- Coach Vladimir was texting the student while he was on the sidelines and in Sunday afternoon meetings. How much did the coaching staff know?
- Were any other students involved with the coach?
- Did any other faculty or staff members know about the situation?
- Did other parents and/or community members know about the situation?

APPLICATION QUESTIONS

1. What systems, policies, and expectations should be in place to protect students and teachers from abusing technology, social media, and chat messaging services?

2. Although no system or policy is foolproof when it comes to teacher integrity or the lack thereof, what types of trainings and supervision should be in place to protect students from sexual misconduct by their teachers?

3. All school staff must be required to report incidents of sexual misconduct or other incidents associated with student health and safety. What are the key components of mandatory reporting, and what situations require staff to report incidents of abuse to the appropriate authorities?

4. The school community, including other teachers, students, and parents, may learn about the allegations and pending case against Coach Vladimir. When questions arise, how should the principal respond to each stakeholder group? What information can and cannot be communicated, from ethical, moral, and legal perspectives?

(Continued)

(Continued)

5. When sexual misconduct allegations arise, what school district, law enforcement, and governmental personnel should be contacted? If principals have questions or concerns about how to proceed, who can they reach out to for assistance?

6. Unethical, immoral, and illegal acts at school or with school students can impact time. Explain how, by what means.

7

The 21st Century Education System

Improvement, Time, and Technology

Change will not come if we wait for some other person, or if we wait for some other time. We are the ones we've been waiting for. We are the change that we seek.

—Barack Obama,
44th president of the United States

THE EDUCATION SYSTEM TODAY AND CONTINUOUS SCHOOL IMPROVEMENT

Any scrutiny of the 21st century education system would be incomplete without a further examination of research-based and innovative leading, teaching, and learning practices, to include technology enhancements and time considerations. Each is essential to a vibrant and student-centered instructional program. Collectively, they are critical in the 21st century to increasing student achievement, especially as related to changing and more diverse student demographics. So, it's a given: School improvement takes time. However, principals can never say: "There's still time, or maybe next time." Why? There's a concept that cannot be ignored—"It's too late!" To paraphrase the previously quoted words of President Obama and use them in an educational context, we cannot wait for others to find the time to improve our schools. We are the ones who must make the essential changes. We must be the ones who find the time to bring positive change!

Earlier in the text, Chapter 3, "Leading, Teaching, Learning, and Time," began this investigative process by recommending progressive leading, teaching, and learning approaches, and principals and teachers were strongly advised to support and incorporate recommended 21st century teaching and learning models that can lead to continuous school improvement. Yet, as already noted in this chapter, all too frequently, nothing in education changes but the date on the calendar. In other words, archaic teaching techniques, strategies, skills, models, and approaches often remain in place in our schools. Why? Typical responses include these: "It is how we were taught." "It's prescribed by policy and/or procedure." "It's the way we've always done it." In truth, the archaic is frequently perceived to be better than something new or different or change oriented. Frequently, principals and teachers fear making changes or taking instructional risks, particularly in today's high-stakes testing and accountability era. Such thinking can be attributed to this mentality: "Why overturn the apple cart with something new when we can continue to use what helps us maintain our own private agendas and personal securities?" The reader may scoff at this statement as being trivial, ridiculous, or even untrue. However, this assessment relates to far too many teachers and principals! Madeline Hunter, an influential American educator, once noted, "If you want to feel safe and secure, continue to do what you have always done" (Tomlinson & Imbeau, 2010, p. 114). School improvement requires time, a change-oriented mentality, and risk taking!

Initiating Systemwide Change

Taking and advancing the recommendations from Chapter 3, "Leading, Teaching, Learning, and Time," principals and teachers must be prepared for and willing to accept proven change, innovation, and research-based practices that will maximize the impact of leading, teaching, and learning, thus increasing academic success rates for all students and continuously improving the instructional setting. John Hattie (2012), in his best-selling text, *Visible Learning for Teachers*, examines the initiating of such systemwide changes. Hattie links significant (the greatest to date) meta-analysis research on teaching techniques and strategies with practical instructional implementation in a step-by-step guide that details lesson preparation, learning interpretation, instructional feedback to students during lessons, and postlesson directions. Noted below are five critical aspects of leading, teaching, learning, and overall school improvement, as identified by Lemov (2015), Hattie (2012), and Sorenson, Goldsmith,

Méndez, and Maxwell (2011). Principals and teachers taking these actions can expect students to achieve and succeed beyond what standardized testing results disclose.

1. Teaching ability varies greatly among teachers; and therefore associated student learning varies greatly as well.

2. Principals, teachers, parents, and even students must place significantly higher value on the precept that research-based teaching and learning effects are essential to student achievement.

3. Principals must be vigilant regarding the establishment of instructional expertise and expectations critical to achieving positive effects for *all* students.

4. Convincing evidence (data) must reveal that teachers are passionate and inspired to promote student learning and achievement. Those teachers and principals who fail to produce must be professionally trained. If no "convincing evidence" is then produced, these same individuals *must* be replaced!

5. Inspired, passionate, and positive teaching is preceded by inspired, passionate, positive, and leader-driven professional development that

    o Ensures an in-depth teacher understanding of subject area(s).
    o Supports student learning correlated with data-based decision making. (In other words, an effective and pronounced analysis of data as related to teacher instruction and classroom interactions with students must occur.)
    o Aids teachers in understanding how to provide exceptional instruction and effective student feedback.
    o Develops principals into exceptional instructional leaders—not just sideline participants—in teaching, learning, professional development, and leading processes.

Hattie (2012) also details how time must be established to train teachers and principals in the art and science of (a) preparing exceptional lessons, (b) initiating exceptional lessons, (c) ensuring exceptional lesson flow through learning and feedback, and (d) concluding lessons—each as a safeguard that *all* students learn and achieve.

Preparing Exceptional Lessons— A Means of Promoting Accountability

Preparing exceptional lessons isn't happenstance. Anyone who has ever taught—at a public school, private school, or Sunday school; or even presented at an educational conference or provided professional development at a school—understands teaching is hard work. Preparing to teach an exceptional lesson takes serious concentration, extensive knowledge of the subject area, an innate set of skills, time, and a love for and understanding of students. Such is also applicable to leading. Principals must be, first and foremost, teachers! In other words, principals are not only lead learners, they are lead teachers. Madeline Hunter, more than three decades ago, stated, "Show me an exceptional principal and I'll show you an exceptional teacher!" (Folkart, 1994). These same words are most appropriate and applicable today. Lemov (2015), Hattie (2012), and Sorenson, Goldsmith, Méndez, and Maxwell (2011) offer five steps principals must initiate to ensure exceptional teaching and learning.

FIVE STEPS TO EXCEPTIONAL TEACHING AND LEARNING

Step 1: Principals must ensure teachers know and understand their students.

This sounds simple, yet it is probably the single most important aspect of developing any exceptional lesson, and furthermore, it readily correlates with being an exceptional teacher. To know and understand students, the best teachers recognize that students must believe in their ability to learn (self-efficacy). Exceptional teachers, as they plan and prepare lessons, seek key materials, techniques, and strategies that are student centered and student oriented. In other words, lessons are prepared with this in mind—students must see the difficult task of learning as a positive challenge, not a personal threat.

In knowing and understanding students, the exceptional teacher recognizes students will frequently encounter impediments or obstacles to their own performance and achievement (Hattie, 2012). These include procrastination, failing to practice to achieve, cultural misunderstandings, and strategically reducing individual effort. Such can be overcome when a teacher takes *time* to develop effective and efficient teaching methods that will better ensure all students positively succeed in their learning efforts.

The Top 11 Time-Saving Tips for Effective and Efficient Teaching

Teaching is a challenging career. Teachers, like principals, think and do a lot each school day—from planning and developing lessons to understanding core curriculum and to interacting with students, parents, colleagues, and administrators. One more thing! The teacher's plate is always full—so much so, teachers must develop time-saving methods to work smarter, not harder. Here are the 11 top time-saving tips to effective and efficient teaching. Most of these tips also apply to the school principalship, and exceptional principals guide teachers in mastering these time-saving tips.

11. Go Digital

Utilized appropriately and effectively, technology makes teaching easier. Learning management tools like Moodle (moodle.com, which is free) and Blackboard (blackboard.com, which is pricey but often adopted by school districts) streamline the teaching process. Teachers at any level can incorporate technology to assign, submit, discuss, and grade student work online. Digital tools can enhance face-to-face classroom experiences. New technologies such as McGraw-Hill Education's *LearnSmart Achieve* adaptive learning program can assist English language learners. Going digital ensures all students will be actively engaged in class assignments and learning activities, as programs are typically interactive and multimodal. Finally, going digital provides, more than ever before, a plethora of online data, information, and resources.

One more consideration: Twitter! Believe it or not, Twitter can be a powerful educational tool. Noted below are ten Twitter uses in education.

1. **Tweet about upcoming due dates, assignments, and/or events.** Twitter enables principals and faculty to message students and stakeholders.

2. **Coordinate assignments.** Students can use Twitter to collaborate on different projects and maintain a quick reference related to changes.

3. **Connect with community and engage parents.**

4. **Connect classrooms.** Teachers and students from around the world can collaborate on project via Twitter.

5. **Facilitate research.** Typing key words into Twitter's search engine provides an excellent method for students to research ideas and events as they occur.

6. **Facilitate discussions.**

7. **Post videos.** Use Twiddeo to post clips of in-class skits, travel experiences, and other relevant and timely applications to student lessons.

8. **Network with other educators.**

9. **Use hashtags to organize discussions.** Be specific with a hashtag to connect with and engage stakeholders relative to a common theme, interest, event, or idea.

10. **Summarize learning.** It's quick and amazing how class learning can be summarized in Twitter's 140-character posts.

(Continued)

(Continued)

10. Clear Up the Desktop

Not the physical desktop, the virtual desktop! Organize your e-teaching by clearing up your laptop's desktop. More than 50% of all technology users spend 30 minutes or more each week searching for lost or missing files. Bundle your files into folders. Organize the folders by topic, theme, or dates. Numerous organizational apps are available; a highly rated version is Teacher Kit (https://itunes.apple.com/us/app/teacherkit-class-organizer/id389584618?mt=8). Teacher Kit does more than organize desktop files. It's a class organizer, teacher planner, gradebook, assignment list retainer, attendance keeper, and student grader.

9. Make Learning Enjoyable

Become innovative and save instructional time by reducing student disinterest and disruptions with a change in lessons. Make learning anything but plain and boring. Incorporate relevant and student-centered learning activities or interesting minigames. While *fun* is an F-word, it's the F-word that creates a great learning environment, as well as a cool teacher! (Want to learn more about making learning fun? Read Number 8.)

8. Incorporate Digital Blended Learning

Blended learning is nothing new, unless you enhance this teaching strategy with technology. Teachers who utilize digital blended learning introduce subject area topics via videos, discussion boards, tutorials, and real-life learning in apps such as Edmodo (edmodo.com). Digital blended learning allows teachers to use efficient and timely interactive learning sessions as introductory activities, and its more in-depth modes of instruction turn classrooms into creative and constructive learning environments.

7. Know Your Students

Every student is different. Knowing individual quirks, characteristics, traits, insecurities, fears, and misconceptions can save a teacher a significant amount of time when trying to get through to a child. Students respond more quickly and appropriately if they think a teacher understands them, cares about them, and knows their names.

6. Communicate With Parents

A great timesaver is talking to parents. Want to get to the root of an instructional problem? Talk to a parent. A student is disruptive? Talk to a parent. Sense a social or anxiety issue with a student? Talk to a parent. Instruction is all about ensuring students learn. If a problem exists and is impeding instruction and student learning, a visit with parents frequently saves a teacher time in trying to determine what the problem is.

5. Stay After School

All of the authors of this text were once public school teachers. Two of the authors have children of their own who are teachers. The authors and their children will readily share one time-saving tidbit: To be the best teacher, stay after school a little later at least one, two, or more days a week. This time actually saves time by allowing teachers to get caught up, to get ready for the next week, to get organized, to have the next day's lesson framed and ready, and hopefully to avoid taking work home on the weekend or returning to the school on the weekend. One of the authors taught history at the middle school level. He stayed every afternoon, Monday through Thursday, 45 minutes after everyone had gone home. Why? Staying after class for three hours each week saved him six hours on Friday or Saturday or Sunday.

4. Multitask

When students are doing independent seat work, it's time to do teacher work. File, update lesson plans, check for additional digital resources, grade papers, enter grades into the grading system, text a parent, et cetera. Recall the phrase, "Multitasking 101: How to get a lot of stuff done in not a lot of time!"

3. Develop Long-Term Planning

Long-term planning takes time, but in actuality, it saves time. Plan ahead at least two weeks. Even better, plan units in advance, saving lots of evening time for family. One of the authors of this text actually spent a week each summer, prior to the start of the school year, planning his entire instructional year. To this day, some 30 years after teaching his final history lesson, the author has on file his yearly plans! This long-term planning saved weeknights and weekends for family, fun, and festivities.

2. Get Organized

Set boundaries—professional and personal. Establish guidelines as to when to be at work and when to be at home. Don't blur the two. Get further organized and save time by saying no when saying yes interferes with your time. Save time by relaxing. Relaxation reduces stress, improves health, and keeps you well, out of the doctor's office, and thus saves you valuable time. Minimize student grading, get your desk and classroom in order and keep both in order, delegate by empowering students to take on tasks that should be student responsibilities, and finally, automate. You live in the digital age. Make the digital age work for you and save time!

1. Use To-Do Lists

Throughout the chapters of this book, the authors have repeatedly pronounced the great benefits of utilizing to-do lists. Set priorities in writing, check them off as completed, and stay on task and on time.

Sources: Crean, 2014; Daniels, 2014; Haas, 2014; Miller, n.d.; Wilson, 2015.

Student learning success can be achieved by reducing student anxiety and uncertainty, by learning cultural characteristics of students and their families, and by showing students how they can develop greater self-esteem and become more effective monitors of their own learning and academic success. How? By motivation—both intrinsic and extrinsic!

Alfie Kohn, perhaps one of the nation's most outspoken critics of education's fixation on test scores, reveals in his classic text, *Beyond Discipline: From Compliance to Community* (2006), that the greatest impediment to student success and achievement is us—educators! Nothing denies a child (of any age) the opportunity to succeed, or promotes inappropriate student behaviors, more than a teacher who doesn't care, doesn't understand the subject matter, doesn't understand the students, doesn't effectively prepare lessons, isn't positive and uplifting, and/or can't control the students (often because of failing to overcome one or all of these motivational killers). Students must also be self-motivated (Hattie, 2012). Students must recognize the learning to be imparted is of relevance and interest to them. In many schools, students don't always see or understand the big picture. Students ask, "Why do I need to learn algebra or history when I intend to be an exercise physiologist, or work with my father roofing homes?" Students frequently think or verbalize, "This stuff is a complete waste of my time!" Guess what? They're probably right, because they are not motivated to learn what is actually very important!

Exceptional principals direct teachers to effectively plan for such student thoughts and questions, and anticipate and ensure all students understand the need and reasons for learning the subject matter and associated learning. Exceptional principals provide relevant, research-based professional development so teachers can prepare exceptional lessons that take time to reveal within the lesson why the learning is important to all students, thus helping students to become more motivated. Ralph Waldo Emerson (1841), American essayist, poet, and philosopher, wrote, "There is no teaching until the pupil is brought into the same state or principle in which you are; a transfusion takes place; he is you, and you are he; and by no unfriendly chance or bad company can he ever lose the benefit." Even modern film recognizes the critical impact of learning—"All knowledge is learning and therefore good" (Wincer, 1985).

Exceptional principals guide teachers to better understand their students by modeling for faculty methods to establish lesson and learning goals and objectives. These goals must be oriented to student mastery (the ability to grow and develop by effort), performance (competence as measured by accomplishment), cultural norms (social, behavioral, ethnic, and educational customs), and social-being (learning by working with others).

Exceptional principals ensure that teachers help their students overcome. Overcoming (conversely defined as learning material that seems at first to be overwhelming and/or incapacitating) is critical to learning and is an exceptional teaching and leading skill that aids students in their own achievement.

Hattie (2012) further proposes that principals and teachers help students overcome self-dependence (esteem and success is not correlated to adult directives only), overcome self-discounting or distortion (dismissing praise or feedback as less than valuable, accurate, or worthwhile), overcome self-perfectionism (self-standards that cannot be met, with failure being the result), overcome hopelessness (believing achievement gains will never occur), and overcome social and cultural comparison (related to low self-esteem, this ever-present classroom ill produces negative effects and readily reduces learning, achievement, and overall school improvement).

Step 2: Principals must ensure that teachers collaboratively plan lessons and extract feedback from each other about the impact of their teaching.

Impact or targeted leading and learning, as defined by Hattie (2012), Lemov (2015) and Sorenson, Goldsmith, Méndez, and Maxwell (2011), involves principals helping teachers recognize the appropriate direction of any lesson, collaboratively defining said direction, and ensuring that students are actively engaged in the lesson direction. Such can be acquired via the collaborative development of learning goals. (Return to the section on goal writing in Chapter 2, "Vision, Mission, and Time.") Effective goal development ensures students will recognize when they have achieved a learning competency or lesson mastery level. Students must know when they have attained the established goals; otherwise, their learning efforts have been in vain. Exceptional principals expect teachers to take time to plan collaboratively and determine appropriate and challenging goals and teaching expectations, and then develop lessons in which the students will achieve the desired goals and, moreover, recognize their learning efforts have tangible and positive results.

Let it be noted, possibly as a form of disclaimer, that the information detailed in Step 2, Principals must ensure that teachers collaboratively plan lessons and extract feedback from each other about the impact of their teaching, must not be misconstrued or misinterpreted as encouraging faculty to teach to the test (state accountability exam). Suggesting the use of an accountability exam as a "one only" or total authentic measure of academic achievement is by no means the author's intention. Principals and teachers should never label students and their achievement (or lack thereof) based on a single test score, or use a student's test score as a motivator to greater achievement. Goal development in this section is all about fostering unique, individually tailored goals and objectives to promote better teaching structure and thus increase student learning. An example would be a student collaboratively developing, with the teacher, weekly goals reflective of the instruction to be presented over a period of, let's say, one or three or possibly six weeks (all depending on the student's developmental level). These developed goals and objectives would be evaluated to determine student mastery of lesson content, i.e., learning, and just as important, for the teacher to gain more insight relative to the instructional processes, methods, and strategies implemented to better provide for increased student engagement, direction, and focus—thus optimizing learning opportunities. Again, neither this example nor Step 2 is ever to be interpreted as a means for tracking competency mastery relative to state accountability standards and/or exams.

By collaborating in goal development as part of preparing any lesson, teachers and students are able to create goals that are learning focused and achievement oriented. Collaborative goal development allows for principal and teacher recognition of the following:

- When students know and understand the lesson goals, there is a greater likelihood of achieving academic success.

- Differentiated learning is an absolute! Not all students are at the same intellectual level, begin at the same place of knowledge attainment, or work at the same learning pace (Lemov, 2015). As each individual's fingerprints are different, so is each student's ability to learn. The old adage, "all students can learn," is true, but it is the principal's expectation that teachers know individual student strengths, weaknesses, and capacities, and most important, each student's ability to achieve identified and established learning goals.

- Learning is neither linear nor neatly organized, as curriculum guides and scope and sequence charts frequently are. If learning were measured, dispensed, and acquired in absolutely the same way for all people, which sadly is a frequent method of teaching/learning in schools, the world would be a much better place! Every individual would be a model, if not a perfect citizen. There would be no human-related problems. All would be wonderful, and peace on earth would have long ago been attained. However, Fantasy Land does not exist in education or in leading, teaching, and learning. Learning, again, is different for every student and thus, principals must provide professional development so every teacher understands that preparation for lessons and learning must take into account the fact that children are diverse, and so are their styles and means of learning. Can a principal or teacher guarantee that differentiated learning will lead to a perfect world? Certainly not! Can a principal or teacher expect students exposed to differentiated learning will more aptly acquire and utilize important knowledge for the better benefit of themselves and others? One would trust!

- Learning can be achieved by the incorporation of multiple activities. If students learn differently, principals must direct teachers to develop different learning activities. This concept is actually quite simple. The complexity lies in the development of numerous learning activities per lesson goal. Can it be done? Yes! Do all teachers want to do it? Well, the authors suspect you already know the answer to that query! Must it be done? Absolutely, if principals and teachers expect all students to learn! Does it take time? Of course! Do principals and teachers have time? Never! Must principals and teachers make time? Always! Every minute matters, and principals and teachers must work the clock.

Does Time Really Matter?

Adriana Sanchez, principal at W. S. Holland School, was meeting with one of her teaching teams, discussing a recent book study and its implications relative to instructional techniques and strategies. Adriana looked at the team members and stated, "Our greatest resource, as educators, is time. How you measure and manage time is crucial because it ultimately shapes both your own and your students' success in the classroom." The teachers looked puzzled, so Adriana realized further explanation was required. She noted "We've been focused on our study of the book, *Teaching Techniques for Successful Student Learning* by Dinah Moe. However, I've been reading a book by Doug Lemov entitled *Teach Like a Champion 2.0*. I really like this text and I'll tell you why. While the Moe book provides us with details as to which teaching strategies to implement, Lemov goes a step further and includes information about using time to better ensure teaching and student learning is measured strategically, intentionally, and visibly as a means of positively impacting academic achievement." Team expressions remained puzzled and were becoming more quizzical. Principal Sanchez trudged forward. "Folks, this is what I've gleaned from the Lemov text. Exceptional teaching produces exceptional learning and here's how!" Adriana passed to the teaching team a handout that included the following time management tips as related to exceptional instruction and learning:

- Show the clock
- Use specific, odd increments
- Set time goals
- Use countdowns
- Every minute counts

Principal Sanchez asked the teaching team a rhetorical question: "Does time really matter in the instructional setting? Before you answer, pause and consider the items on your handout. We'll talk later." Adriana observed those same quizzical looks in the team members' faces. She knew in her heart that she had the

(Continued)

(Continued)

teaching team thinking, and just as important, she had—in a timely manner—gained their undivided attention!

Pause and Consider

- How would you answer the question posed by Principal Adriana Sanchez, "Does time really matter in the instructional setting?" Explain your answer.
- How do you think principals should help teachers make the most of allotted instructional time?

Not certain as to how principals help teachers make the most of allotted instructional time? How they train teachers to "work the clock"? The authors of this text recommend that the five previously noted Lemov (2015) principles be purposefully followed:

Principle 1: Show the clock. Lemov (2015) highly recommends teachers learn to make time more visible to their students. This means using projectable LCD clocks, or wall clocks, or stopwatches to pace student time in learning activities. For example, a teacher plans 10 minutes for an activity, but time slips away (isn't this always the case?); 20 minutes of time is unintentionally spent, and valuable instructional time is lost. Worse, some aspect of instruction is foregone, as it is now time to move to another subject area, or the bell sounds and students must move on to another class. Remember, time is of the essence!

Principle 2: Use specific, odd increments. Years ago, prior to her retirement in the 1980s, and certainly ahead of her time, Mrs. Melva Sebesta—a Texas high school choir teacher—would tell students to arrive for practice, or for a live performance at odd, yet specific times such as 6:58 p.m. Why this time? What happened to 7:00 p.m.? Certainly, 7:00 p.m. would be a better and more normal time, right? Here's why Mrs. Sebesta used odd time increments: Lemov (2015) tells us that round numbers imply "about" a time. In class, exceptional teachers will state, "Work in your groups for 13 minutes, and then we will discuss your findings." Specificity in a learning activity timeframe equates to time-on-task precision and a genuine concern for timely instruction and learning.

Principle 3: Set time goals. Proper time management can provide for efficiency in teaching and learning! Lemov (2015) recommends letting students understand certain time-oriented goals must be established for every learning activity. In a history class, for example, students have been working on a composition related to presidents of the United States. The teacher states on a Friday afternoon prior to the end of the school day, "We have 25 minutes remaining in class today. Spend this time working on a high-quality first draft paper. Begin!" A specific goal has been established within a very specific timeframe. Just as important, no class time has been wasted. Remember this time-honored but instructionally unsound teacher instruction: "We have just a few minutes left today. Check your desk for loose papers and toss any trash in the wastepaper basket. Get your books together, sit quietly, and don't forget to work this weekend on your first draft." This statement reminds us that time on task to the end of class, in this particular setting, will never occur!

Principle 4: Use countdowns. NASA for decades has used countdowns for a very important and specific reason—time is of the essence, because liftoff will occur only after crucial initiatives have been completed prior to those final voiced 10 seconds! Numerous critical initiatives happen each instructional day. They must occur for exceptional instruction to be imparted and for exceptional learning to be attained. Countdowns require attention—"I need your eyes focused on me in five, four, three, two, one . . . okay, our multiplication drill begins now!" Countdowns work most effectively, as time would otherwise be wasted. Time for wrap-ups or transitions, for example, is frequently lost when countdowns are omitted.

Principle 5: Every minute counts. Norma Garza is an amazing teacher. The son of one of the authors of this text was once a third-grade "at-risk" student under the tutelage of Ms. Garza. Norma, as a master teacher, never missed a chance to instruct! Here's what Norma did: She did not permit a minute to get away. Every instructional opportunity was a possibility for learning, whether on the playground, in the hallway, during lunch in the cafeteria, during before- or after-school tutoring, or in the parking lot while students waited for their buses or parents. She challenged students with learning questions and activities, some she seemed to pull out of thin air! If you were in the presence of Ms. Garza, no time was wasted—learning was happening!

Step 3: Principals must ensure that teachers recognize and utilize the "Five Cs" of visible learning.

The "Five Cs" have been defined by Hattie (2012) and Sorenson, Goldsmith, Méndez, and Maxwell (2011) and can positively impact student academic achievement. The Five Cs are *challenge, commitment, confidence, correlation,* and *conceptualization.* Each plays a crucial role in preparing an exceptional lesson.

1. **Challenge the learner.** Challenge as related to learning is understanding that a student must possess 90% of what is essential to mastering and ultimately enjoying the learning goal and associated task. Here's a home-related example: David and Lloyd join Rick to assemble a home office bookcase. All three men will be pleased with the challenge of

assembling the bookcase, as each can read and understand 95% to 99% of the directions. Their chances of successfully assembling the bookcase are quite high. While the task before them is a challenge, it is doable, and once the task is completed, the three men will sit down and admire their assembled work. In fact, they will find joy in at least two areas—(1) their collaborative effort and (2) their achievement in a timely task completion. The same is true of student learners.

2. **Commit students to the learning.** Students will be determined to reach a learning goal if they perceive their commitment will result in better performance. Principals and teachers must remember commitment to learning must be challenging but cannot be associated with busy work. Busy work never equates to learning. Moreover, when teachers add commitment to challenge, these two most powerful Cs in planning and learning result in a greater opportunity for students to achieve. Students are more apt to commit when teachers help them gain a reputation, among peers, as good learners.

3. **Confidence aids in learning attainment.** Confidence breeds success! Students must feel confident that they can achieve learning goals. Confidence is teacher related (quality teaching = quality learning), student related (past, present, and future success = confidence), task related (appropriate scaffolding = successful academic ascent), peer related (sharing = caring), and principal related (confident actions and behaviors = strong leadership). Recall the adage, "Confidence doesn't come when you have all the answers. Confidence comes when you are ready to face all the questions."

4. **Correlate student expectations with learning achievement.** Students' own predictions of achievement, especially for students of color, are often inaccurate. These students often overestimate their achievement simply because learning expectations were not appropriate—in most cases, expectations were too low. So, what are principals and teachers to do? The answer is a difficult one. Low expectations do not make for student academic success. They may paint a pretty picture initially. However, once low expectations become an established norm in one classroom and not in another, the confidence of students is automatically decreased by an increase in feelings of helplessness. This is when students, especially at the adolescent age, choose to drop out either physically or mentally or both! Principals must direct teachers to pursue a three-pronged approach: (1) Make learning expectations and achievement standards very transparent; (2) establish high, but appropriate and attainable, expectations; and (3) provide feedback at all levels of teaching and learning. 1 + 2 + 3 = "4 Student Achievement"!

5. **Conceptualize student learning with academic success.** The abstract or theoretical nature of learning (the conceptual side of the coin),

as correlated with student achievement, has its place in education. However, principals and teachers must recognize that any real, concrete, and/or practical application of new learning better ensures students will take an interest, find relevancy in the learning, and gain the desired knowledge. Thus, academic achievement occurs.

Step 4: Principals must ensure that teachers know curriculum.

John Dewey prescribed "curriculum making" in his definitive text, *Democracy and Education*, published in 1916. However, the first known and recorded effort in "curriculum making" and usage in a school system occurred in Los Angeles in 1922 (Hencley, McCleary, & McGrath, 1970). Some 90-plus years ago, curriculum understanding, development, and renewal was a new and comprehensive process involving teams of teachers. In 1960, McNally and Passow conducted a study that provided conclusive evidence reflecting that continuity, unity, and balance in teaching and learning are best achieved when faculty and principals work together and focus their time and efforts on behalf of students. Collaboration is most meaningful to teachers and absolutely beneficial to students and their learning/achievement. For teachers to know, understand, and apply curriculum, they must obviously become experts in curriculum. What is done today in schools is no different than what was espoused and conducted in 1916 and 1922 and 1960. Collaboration as curricular experts is crucial to successful leading, teaching, and learning!

Teacher isolation will void any steps to develop a schoolwide teaching/ learning purpose and community (Sorenson, Goldsmith, Méndez, & Maxwell, 2011). The understanding or knowledge of curriculum dictates a partnership between teaching teams, leadership teams, and curriculum experts. When teachers work in isolation (which can be the case in schools), morale worsens, teachers focus on students from a negative perspective, and very little time is spent in planning sessions on issues related to effective teaching practices and increased student learning. Recognition: When principals permit teachers to assume a private or isolated approach to curriculum knowledge, development, renewal, and practice, mediocrity prevails.

To best determine what must be taught and learned, along with the appropriate complexity, as well as the incorporation of mandated local, state, and national standards in the curriculum, principals and teachers must recognize that curriculum in the 21st century is oriented to test outcomes rather than to what should be taught to develop a better life and greater society. Understanding and appropriately developing and renewing curriculum makes for a difficult proposition. How? By what means? Contemplate this: Many would contend that the best desktop resource and book study text on the market today, relative to developing knowledge and understanding of curriculum and to curriculum development and renewal processes, is *The Principal's Guide to Curriculum Leadership* (Sorenson, Goldsmith, Méndez, & Maxwell, 2011).

Janice Joplin (n.d.) wrote, "Now that I'm here, where am I?" The previously noted text reveals the "where am I" in connection with attaining curriculum knowledge. While titled *The Principal's Guide to Curriculum Leadership,* this text is meant to be used in collaboration with teachers in professional development sessions, as it effectively defines curriculum, establishes appropriate expectations relative to investigating curriculum, details the importance of curriculum change and innovation, brings curriculum to the forefront of school-site action, defines systematic integration of curriculum, and describes step-by-step processes critical to exceptional curricular professional development, all in a timely fashion. A read of *The Principal's Guide to Curriculum Leadership* allows principals and teachers the opportunity to join the text character Will Wonkermann, principal of Childers School, in a chapter-by-chapter journey as he and his team develop their knowledge base and become curriculum experts!

Step 5: Principals must ensure that teachers incorporate technology as part of the instructional program.

Technology is a timesaver, and some of the greatest time management advances ever known to mankind have evolved with the coming of the 21st century digital age. Thus, principals must be responsible for creating a digital-age learning culture and environment. They must inspire and lead in the development and training of teachers, developing a culture of systemic transformation, excellence in professional practice, and technology integration by visioning and modeling expected teacher and student digital competencies. For many principals, that's a tough pill to swallow. In order to reach such goals, principals as lead learners must examine their own digital track record. More specifically, principals must recognize the following:

- They must consider how to effectively implement and utilize technology in the curriculum, teaching, learning, and leading.
- Essential human, material, and fiscal resources are necessary to accomplish campus-generated technological goals;
- They must consider how technology will support opportunities for teachers to better instruct, for students to learn better, and for the principal to lead.
- The digital era is now! Students and teachers require digital workstations and handheld devices.
- State-of-the-art digital devices, programs, applications (apps), and supportive technologies are required in order for proper curricular and instructional management to occur.

- Appropriate professional development is needed to ensure that technological competencies are acquired.
- Funding sources for technological acquisitions need to be identified and encumbered; and
- A digital-age learning culture extends into the following technological advancements:

  - Websites (school, principal, and teacher)
  - E-mail communication
  - Telephone message delivery systems
  - Texting
  - Instant messaging
  - Teaching and learning videos (found on YouTube, for example)
  - Virtual coplanning and shared lesson development
  - School survey tools

    - Survey Monkey
    - Permission to Use
    - Qualtric
    - Kaboom
    - Smartphone applications such as lesson plan ideas, teachers' planners, and ClassDOJO (www.classdojo.com)
    - Other applications downloaded on smartphones for purposes of exit ticketing to check for understanding or for voting or polling, and for rapidly gathering information from students, teachers, parents, and/or community members, and for research and journal article applications

  - Social media and network systems, including Facebook and Twitter
  - Professional network systems

    - Calendars
    - File management
    - Clinic records
    - Report generation (student, teacher, disciplinary, test proficiency, achievement mastery, scheduling, student records, report cards, et cetera)

  - Management systems

    - Coursework
    - Teacher supervision
    - Financial accounting
    - Security

  - Administrator blogs
  - Podcasts
  - Smartphones and tablets

A Continuation of the Five Steps
to Exceptional Teaching and Learning

Recall how you read previously (prior to the *Does Time Really Matter?* vignette) that collaborative goal development provides for better instruction. Taking principal leadership and student instruction a stride further, consider how the precept of collaborative goal development provides teachers with a better understanding and recognition of how unintended consequences and extracted feedback further affect opportunities for increased student achievement.

  • Unintended consequences (both good and bad) can affect the very best of learning intentions. One of the authors was raised near the Nueces River, where it flows southeast toward the Texas coastline. The author's father would frequently share with his son, who loved to traverse the outdoors—"Be careful! Your best intention is to put one foot forward in a most positive direction. However, when you do so, remember, the other foot can very well be bit by the ever-present cottonmouth water moccasin. So, watch out!" Good advice in all aspects of life, but most certainly relatable to teaching and learning. Know your intentions, relative to instructional processes and to the learners. Just as important, think through the possible unintended consequences and the subsequent impact on student learning! This applies to leading as well.

  • Conclude every lesson by extracting feedback from the students about the impact of the intended teaching and the desired learning. One of the authors of this text concludes every class session with the following question: "Any questions or comments for the good of the group?" Feedback from students is critical, and the same can be said of fellow teachers. Did the lesson/learning reach the targeted audience? Did the lesson/learning positively impact the targeted audience? Did the targeted audience learn, and what did they learn? If they did not achieve all desired learning, why not? Collaboration—teacher-to-teacher, and feedback—teacher-to-student and student-to-teacher, are essential if successful teaching and learning is to occur! Collaboration is also an essential aspect of principal leadership.

Leading, teaching, and learning must relate to today's digital era. Principal-led schools must integrate and utilize digital and technological applications (computers, laptops, tablets, cell phones, smartphones, digital surveying, student blogging, professional development applications, dashboard indicators, and analyses)—all for purposes of curricular, instructional, leadership, and student achievement advances. Plus, digital and technological applications assist with appropriate time management. Those principals who fail to lead, technologically—in the digital era—will be out of time and left behind. More important, the students in these schools will also be out of time and left behind, and that's not right!

Source: *Ralph and Alice* cartoon by Alex Carruth.

The Right Professional Development at the Right Time

Lifelong learning is a most pressing issue in our schools today.

How do we find time to train others to grow professionally?

—Cornelia Rayburn, Principal,
Grant Avenue Grammar School

Why make time for professional development? First, principals must understand the importance of providing training to faculty and staff. Consider the late Tom Landry, legendary football coach of the Dallas Cowboys. Coach Landry would share with his players that his job was to teach grown men how to do what they didn't want to do in order for them to become what they always desired to become. So it is in professional development. People learn best by training,

(Continued)

(Continued)

by seeing and doing (Osborne, 2010). This proven fact collides with need and time. Principal Rayburn is correct in the opening quote: Principals and teachers need training. Both will tell you they simply don't have the time. So, how has professional development evolved over the last couple of decades, from a time perspective? First, training sessions were held after school hours ("I'm dog tired and brain dead"), then on weekends ("I need time for family"), then during the workday ("I really need to be in class with my students"), then during the summer after contractual days ("there goes my vacation"), and in more recent years, via online coursework ("I really don't have time for this"). So, we're back to square one: "Why make time for professional development?" Might a second question be added? "How can time be found for professional development?" Simple questions—complex answers!

   First, you don't have time. Second, you still don't have time! What's a principal to do? What's a teacher or staff member to do? Here are seven strategies, with hints, that will help make professional development a lifelong activity and a timely priority, and most important, will assist in the development of expert power.

Strategy 1: Recognize Impediments

Developing a schedule for new learning can be troublesome. Professional development is time consuming. Time is something educators can't spare.

Hint: Identify barriers to allotting time for professional development. If, for example, time for lifelong learning is scheduled following school hours and online, and you wish to complete the professional development session at home and your children shout they are ready to play, consider promising them play time as soon as you have finished your "home" work. Explain that you need some study time, and then find a quiet place to think and work alone. Later, give the kids the play time they desire and deserve.

Strategy 2: Learn in Phases

Schedule your time for professional development in short phases. Small blocks of time can be very effective in helping process new learning, especially if it is online.

Hint: Use your smartphone to learn, especially when you are on the move and have 10 minutes to spare for a short span of concentration. Learning in small phases can maximize comprehension and minimize distractions.

Strategy 3: Form Habits

New learning must become a habit, a routine of living. Developing habits takes self-discipline and time. Habits are developed through consistency. Examine your schedule, and determine when you can work in the time for new learning.

Hint: Get up an hour earlier, or learn during a lunch break or after everyone has gone to bed. To keep the learning habit intact, reward yourself, after seven days, with something that motivates you to continue your lifelong learning habit.

Strategy 4: Establish Objectives

Recognize what needs to be learned. Set goals that assist you in visualizing what must be learned. Establishing learning objectives helps you overcome an always tempting desire to bypass professional development because you are pressed for time, or lack energy, or have something else you would rather do.

Hint: Identify what you wish to gain from learning and why you must make time for learning. Then, establish SMART objectives: specific, measurable, achievable, realistic, and timebound objectives to ensure learning is achieved.

Strategy 5: Timing Is Everything

Many professional development sessions are scheduled at the conclusion of a school day or on a weekend—times when individuals are exhausted. Energy levels come with differing peaks and valleys—all depending on the individual.

Hint: Principals should try to offer professional development sessions at least twice during the day—consider a morning session, and then later, an afternoon session. A third session, previously recorded, could be replayed in the evening hours for those night owl participants. Teachers: Know your energy peak—your best time of day for learning—and schedule professional development to your own personal thinking advantage.

Hint: See Strategy 7, Utilize Digital Technology, a different kind of time manager and saver!

Strategy 6: Collaborate Regularly

As previously noted in Chapter 5, "Collaboration and Time," working together significantly improves any learning situation. Professional development sessions are substantially improved and learning is significantly enhanced when participants are able to seek help or advice from others. Collaboration in professional development equates to accountability in learning. Learning becomes a priority when others are depending on you and you are depending on others.

Hint: Networking is a tremendous method of learning, as related to professional development. Networking can be accomplished via LinkedIn, Twitter, and other digital, interactive forums, as well as via online alumni networks and local college and university online forums and seminars.

(Continued)

(Continued)

Hint: Exceptional instructionally oriented professional development institutes are available. These institutes provide excellent forums for teachers and principals to interact, network, and collaborate. The Teacher College Summer Institutes (The Reading and Writing Project) is a perfect example. For 30 years, educators have come together for these sessions on the teaching of reading and writing. Collaboratively, they study methods and plan curricula, revitalize their thinking, and in the process, learn how to better encourage students to lead rich and literate lives. The institute engages teachers and principals in professional development sessions with some of the world's most renowned authors, consultants, and experts. For more information, go to http://readingandwritingproject.com/institutes/tc-summer-institutes.

Strategy 7: Utilize Digital Technology

Learning-centered, teacher-focused, principal-led, flexible, research-based professional development is designed to support educators in using digital resources to enhance student achievement. Digital technology, when utilized to promote professional development, must be collaboratively designed with professional learning plans providing continuous improvement in teachers' skill development, addressing the professional learning needs of teachers and administrators, and providing relevant and practical web-based learning experiences. Numerous digital professional development programs offer academies or learning sessions related to leadership, literacy, mathematics, and STEM teaching and learning.

Hint: Explore online professional development opportunities. Teachers and principals must maximize their available time—especially after school hours. Online professional development allows for learning that is more relaxed, with a self-set pace. The Wake County Public School System, the largest in North Carolina—serving more than 150,000 students in 170 schools, recently made a large-scale shift to a digitally oriented, state standards–based professional development program focusing on equipping teachers with the best tools and training at the best time to integrate technology into student learning.

Hint: Other online professional development courses include these:

- ASCD online courses for teachers—www.ascd.org/professional-development/pd-online.aspx
- PBS Teacherline—www.pbs.org/teacherline
- Scholastic U—http://teacher.scholastic.com/products/ScholasticU/
- Intel Teach Elements—www.intel.com/content/www/us/en/education/k12/teach-elements.html
- Khan Academy—www.khanacademy.org

Finding Time to Manage a Different Type of Time

There comes a time early in the career of a school principal when she or he is called upon to "fish or cut bait," when a school principal is required to "put up or shut up." This is a time of commitment—there is no time for vacillation or spinelessness. This time is a different kind of time management—a time to step forward and manage the way for the wavering, to strengthen the knees of the unsteady, and to lead the uncertain away from the broad paths of doubt, hesitation, and indecision. This is a time to lead others into the narrow lanes of steadfastness. This is a time for wholehearted commitment!

Principals know that divided loyalties make for halfhearted commitments, which in turn produce shallow convictions and eventually lead to defeat. Principals frequently find themselves entering an educational era when individuals of measurable fortitude and steadfast character are needed. This is not the time, nor the place, for the fainthearted. This is the time and place for outstanding leadership.

Of course, this is a time when I prefer to see leaders stumble, waste time, and mismanage!

—The Silent Time Thief

TWO ESSENTIAL PRINCIPAL RESOURCES FOR CONTINUOUS SCHOOL IMPROVEMENT

Today, principals work in a more fluid and expanding context than at any other time in history. Pressures are ever-increasing from a variety of challenges. In response to these challenges, effective leaders seek opportunities, they seek resources, they do the right things, and just as important, they do things right. The leadership ground rules of yesteryear are now obsolete. The best leaders work intelligently. To do so, principals must be sensitive to two essential resources—time and technology. The two interact to advance instruction and increase student achievement, and thus improve schools.

Resource 1: Time Sensitivity

Time management and sensitivity, relative to appropriate and effective instructional purposes, is a force impacting education today—often negatively. Time-sensitive instructional practices can end up being derailed for a multitude of reasons despite the best intentions and efforts of the most diligent principals. Potential curricular or instructional project killers frequently relate to inattentive or uninterested team members, faculty sabotage, administrative lack of knowledge or expertise (especially as related to technology and to data analysis/scrutiny), scope creep—whereby school districts continue adding more components and requirements to a district initiative, and unrealistic time lines. Each "time-killer" can doom any change process. As a result, principals must work to ensure the proper management of project-oriented time.

Naturally, there are steps that principals can incorporate to ensure that instructional projects do not disappear into a time-loss abyss. Principals must spend time

- Building a common vision (see Chapter 2, "Vision, Mission, and Time").
- Developing a sufficiently detailed plan.
- Bringing in team members for brainstorming and buy-in sessions (see Chapter 5, "Collaboration and Time").
- Establishing time lines and major milestones by developing time-sensitive metrics and ensuring that the process schedule is realistic. Unrealistic due dates and goal attainment dates can ruin timely project completion.
- Creating a culture of collaboration and commitment (see Chapter 5, "Collaboration and Time").
- Changing attitudes and mindsets.
- Recognizing a lack of support from district administration can destroy any potential school-site improvement.
- Seeking appropriate and effective experts of practice relative to professional development.
- Understanding that curricular and instructional projects are inherently uncertain, and uncertainty breeds contempt. Thus, decisions must be made with transparency, and principals must ensure early/timely dissemination of sufficient information. Informed faculty are more likely to be engaged and involved.
- Accepting that many faculty members have an inability to see reality, accept reality, and deal with reality. People problems are time- and project-killers.
- Reassuring faculty that slowing down can be speeding up! Here's what we mean:
  - When a curricular or instructional change or project begins to fail, the natural response is to take time to do more. However, think of a freeway—adding more cars only slows down an already clogged route leading to a final destination. So, much time is wasted. To speed up the route, reduce the number of cars, incorporate a mass-transit system, and thus, reduce wasted time. The same is true of any school project, initiative, or activity. To speed up the process and thus better manage time, reduce multidimensional tasks by focusing on the one critical dimension of the process that seems to be dooming the project. This is time well spent!

A recent study conducted by Lifsey and Associates of Nashville, Tennessee, found in a survey of 1,500 principals that a mere 40% of curricular and instructional projects were completed on time (Zarbo, 2014). To quote Lao-Tzu (n.d.), "Time is a created thing. To say 'I don't have time' is like saying 'I don't want to.'" Principals may not have time, but they must find time. To fail to find time suggests (actually screams), "There's no need or reason to complete the task at hand!"

The Top Three Time-Killers for School Administrators

- **Red-Tape/Bureaucracy:** Defined as a school district's over-reaching hand being everywhere, this time-killer is often thick and layered and can permeate a campus in the form of district policy, mandates, and regulations that are likely to be oppressively complex and time consuming. District bureaucrats frequently defend their own entrenched interests rather than act to benefit the school system. These "red-tape" bureaucrats take pride in their craft, resist changes in established routines, and sadly, prefer to ignore special campus-level circumstances that can bring about time-saving, cost-efficient, and important instructional improvements.
- **Meetings:** Consider the following adage: "The only thing that comes out of meetings is people." Principals can spend up to two to three hours a day sitting at a conference table listing to someone rambling and wasting valuable time. Return to the Chapter 3 case study, Death by Meeting!, for how-to indicators as related to conducting appropriate and effective meetings.
- **Procrastination:** Twenty percent of school administrators procrastinate at least one hour per day, often more. Procrastination can be related to fear of failure or even fear of success. Procrastinators may be concerned with what others think of them, thinking they lack effort, ability, or expertise. Procrastination destroys teamwork and the benefits it provides for time management, decision making, task completion, and ability to lead.

Listen to me! Time is the scarcest resource, and unless you manage it properly, I'll gladly mismanage it for you!

—The Silent Time Thief

Resource 2: Technological Sensitivity

The future is already here. It's just not evenly distributed.

—William Gibson (2003)

The digital age with its technology advancements and utilizations in our schools is upon us; in actuality, it has been with us for some time. Has the digital age brought the best to how we live and work? William Gibson—a fiction novelist and essayist who coined the term *cyberspace* and established the conceptual foundations for the World Wide Web— certainly thought so. The authors of this text do as well, and they are old enough (dare they reveal) to vividly acknowledge how, over time, technology has brought numerous and necessary changes to leading, teaching, and learning, although these changes are though not evenly distributed. The authors recall three of technological advances that greeted them in the very early years of their careers as public school educators—(1) the electric typewriter (that's right; there were no word processors, let alone desktop computers, in the 1970s), (2) the mimeograph machine (right again, there were no desktop printers or office-housed digital copiers, and (3) the over-head projector (you're right again—a technological innovation long since replaced by expanding electronic images powered by software such as Microsoft's PowerPoint). How far have we come since the 1970s? Well, a long way, folks. And, believe us, for the better!

Today, new technological and digital advancements influence all aspects of education, including curricular decisions, methods of instruction and student learning, and communication with faculty, students, parents, and community members. The use of electronic or digital media is now a time-saving and preferred mode for acquiring information and has huge implications for curriculum decisions, instructional models, student and teacher evaluations, and the acquisition of vast databases for instant and empirical research findings. And, all are available for schools, classrooms, and student use.

Consider the following: Anyone who is age 15 to 35 (The Millennials) is probably more technologically competent than members of any older generation, including Generation X (ages 35–50) and the Baby Boomers (ages 50–70). Children ages 3–15 (Generation Z) are very adept at using handheld digital devices and even more technologically oriented with digital equipment and programming. Now, recognize the average age of a school principal is 49 years (making the average principal a Generation Xer), and sadly, far too many principals of this age/generation are anything but adept with digitalization (NCES, 2013). This trending, average age (49 years) of principal-leaders has remained constant in surveys dating back to 2007 (NCES, 2013). What does it mean?

First, it means school systems and the general public should be concerned, very concerned. Why? Recent research reveals that having principals serve as technological leaders in today's digital age equates, sadly, to the image of a bumpy road. Not a pretty sight nor a pathway to opportunity that is easily traversed. In other words, consider the following: A decade ago, Brockmeier, Sermon, and Hope (2005) revealed that principals were not prepared to facilitate the attainment of technology's promise in leading, teaching, and learning. At the time, this was a field of emerging research.

Today, the verdict remains less than promising. Five years after the release of the Brockmeier, Sermon, and Hope study, Wang (2010) revealed that too many principals did not have a vision of technology integration relative to leading, teaching, and learning. In the Wang study, it was found that principals not only lacked a digital vision and commitment, they frequently failed to provide essential digital resources for their faculty and students, and moreover, they neglected empowering others to digitally lead in teaching and learning. One year later, Chang (2011) found the following:

1. It remains a real and serious concern whether principals, in this digital era, can become competent technological leaders;

2. Principals must understand that their role has changed from that of a school administrator, or even an instructional leader, to that of a multifaceted digital and technological curricular leader; and

3. Principals must recognize that one of the more important tasks of a principal is to determine how to become an appropriate, time-saving technological leader.

What about today? Surely, the empirical research and accompanying evidence provide a better image of the principal as the technological expert in leading, teaching, and learning. Right? Don't hold your breath! Abilock (2012) posits that a 21st century challenge in education continues to be assessing the curricular and technological competence of principals in a manner that is both systematic and sustained. What does this assessment reveal? Whitehead, Jensen, and Boschee, in their text *Planning for Technology* (2013), assert that technological change for principals can be career threatening, especially if principals fail to find time for new digital approaches for delivering education to students. Such approaches require advanced knowledge and expertise as well as ability to successfully lead technological initiatives. Currently, technological leadership in many schools is simply average; more often, it is mediocre, and thus fails to deliver timely, digitally oriented direction to 21st century learners; further frustrates technologically competent teachers; and fails to provide the business community with what they most desire—the best, brightest, and most technologically proficient employees that a school system can educate. Why? Principals simply continue to maintain the status quo, failing to transform teaching and learning by providing a more advanced and student-centered digital/technological academic culture and learning environment. Thus, in far too many instances, nothing has changed in principal leadership/sensitivity in relation to technological expertise except the date on the calendar. Again, why?

There are four main barriers to seriously consider:

1. **Awareness.** Many principals simply don't know about Square or Expensify or Google Scholar or Google Now, or the purpose of Bluetooth

connectivity to school devices such as printers, smartboards, and other technologies. They haven't seen or used these products because they're too busy running their schools, treading water—trying to remain afloat in the sea of overwhelming administrative duties.

2. **Complexity.** True story: A principal, known to one of the authors of this text, is quite brilliant and, in fact, an audiophile. His son-in-law (a Millennial) recently set up a Sonos speaker system in his father-in-law's living room, along with a music system that included Pandora and Rdio, a Roku media player, and a Vizio sound bar. Then he introduced his father-in-law to a Harmony 700 advanced home automation remote, along with numerous other musical devices and digital media services. Later, as a refresher, the principal's son-in-law walked him through the setup step-by-step over the telephone, and judging from both the principal's and son-in-law's narratives, the experience revealed a realization of how challenging technology can be for principals who are not digital natives.

3. **Cost.** New technologies cost money. With time and advances in manufacturing or cloud computing, newer technologies become more efficient to produce and deliver, but in school systems, funding will always be a barrier to adoption.

4. **Perceived Value.** The benefits of newer technologies are not always appreciated. Either the cost/benefit analysis isn't strong enough, or the need for certain technologies in a school or classrooms is not yet apparent to principals.

Considering the barriers, what is the implication for practice in relation to technology sensitivity and leading, teaching, and learning in the digital age? Straightforward answer: Principals who embrace the ever-changing role of digital leader, and become competent technological leaders, are those who will effectively prepare their students for the challenges facing them as current learners and future citizens and ultimate 21st century employees. This type of leadership requires principals to

- Analyze and update the technological infrastructure of their school;
- Support student and teacher technological needs;
- Combine technology and digital innovation with teaching, learning, and leading;
- Provide digital expertise through active involvement in and promotion of technological professional development and planning; and
- Ensure sound digital financial management (Whitehead, Jensen, & Boschee, 2013).

To sum up, Eric Schmidt, executive chairman of Google, said it best: "We are what we tweet" (Schmidt & Cohen, 2013, p. 114). Are you tweeting?

Are you leading—digitally? Are you appropriately, effectively, and efficiently managing instructional and administrative time?

FINAL THOUGHTS

Exceptional principals value and manage time. They understand that time is an important aspect to improving schools. The best principals think of time in terms of "if not now, when?" They also appreciate three critical aspects of life that cannot be recovered: (1) the *word* after it is said, (2) the *moment* after it is missed, and (3) the *time* after it is gone. Exceptional principals appreciate and are motivated by two adages: "With time, the trouble is, you think you have it," and "Use time and never waste it!" These leaders know that lost time is an abomination. Why? It's never recovered. With lost time, everyone loses—most notably, students!

Exceptional principals understand there is a clarion call for the improvement of public schools. These leaders initiate systemwide change by placing a high value on research-based teaching and learning effects, by establishing high instructional expectations, by inspiring passionate and positive teaching approaches, by supporting student learning as correlated with data-based decision making, by using time to help teachers understand how to provide excellent instruction and seek student feedback, and by being active leaders in teaching, learning, and professional development.

Exceptional principals ensure that teachers know and understand their students. These leaders make time to coach their teachers how to work collaboratively in planning lessons and in extracting feedback from colleagues about the impact of their teaching. These same leaders are cognizant of and use time wisely, expecting their teachers to show the clock, set time goals, and make every instructional minute count.

Exceptional principals expect teachers to know the curriculum and incorporate technology into the instructional program. These leaders provide relevant and time-oriented professional development to faculty and staff. As leaders of professional development, exceptional principals recognize impediments to effective professional development and provide opportunities for their teachers to overcome such barriers by forming new learning habits, learning in phases, and establishing schoolwide and personal objectives relative to what must be learned. Exceptional principals grasp the significance of collaborating and use technology to efficiently advance professional development.

Exceptional principals possess an awareness of new technological developments, advance technology, comprehend barriers to technological implementation, understand the complexities of technology expansion, fight for additional funding for technological innovations, and perceive the timeliness, great value, and benefit of technology.

DISCUSSION QUESTIONS

1. In the chapter section *Initiating Systemwide Change*, five steps are identified that *principals must ensure* are taken relative to exceptional leading, teaching, and learning. Of the five, which one do you perceive to be the very best approach to ensuring continuous school improvement? Consider the step you selected, and determine how time and management of time will be a factor in formulating and applying the step to practice. Provide examples to support your answers.

2. Reflect upon the resources Time Sensitivity and Technological Sensitivity. Explain the manner in which principals must dedicate themselves to time and technology to ensure school improvement that will positively impact the instructional program. Be specific in your answers.

3. Barriers exist that make principals reluctant to initiate or fearful of initiating the use of technology as a means of school improvement. Do you agree that the identified barriers exist? Why or why not? Can you think of a barrier not identified in the chapter? Does time management factor into your answers to this question?

4. Chapter 5, "Collaboration and Time," identifies time management tips critical to a principal's success as an instructional leader. Determine at least one time management technique that is essential to school improvement for 21st century leading, teaching, and learning.

5. Hattie (2012), Lemov (2015), and Sorenson, Goldsmith, Méndez, and Maxwell (2011) are cited within this chapter regarding exceptional leading, teaching, and learning. Specifically, these authors recommend that principals initiate five actions (see pages 150–164) to better increase student academic achievement. Which of these actions might take considerable time for a principal to implement? Why? How is time management a critical key to instructional program improvement and student success? Be specific in your answers.

SELF-REFLECTION ON LENS 6: THE 21ST CENTURY EDUCATION SYSTEM AND TIME

Return to Chapter 1, "Time Management and Your Leadership," and reflect on the *Time Management Self-Assessment Instrument* (TMSI). In this chapter, you examined Lens 6: The 21st Century Education System and Time. Review your responses on the TMSI Scoring Template for Lens 6. Think about the material analyzed within this chapter and how it relates to Lens 6. Which of your beliefs were reinforced? Which items are you now reassessing? Why? Would you change your score on any of the items? If you would, why? How does this chapter relate to your use and understanding of time in relation to the PSEL national leadership standards? Explain.

CASE STUDY APPLICATION

HAS OUR SCHOOL EVOLVED?

Jennifer Raye, principal at Cullen School, finally found time at the conclusion of the school day to sit down and visit with her administrative team. Present in the principal's office that late afternoon were assistant principals Suzan Rowman and Lalo Garcia. Jennifer looked across the desk at Suzan and Lalo and said, "Folks, I'm all tuckered out, but I'm not so tired that I can't think. In fact, I've been thinking about how we are always putting out one fire after another, never slowing down, and never having the time to get caught up!" The two assistants raised their fatigued eyes to face Principal Raye and slowly nodded in agreement. Jennifer smiled and said, "You two look as worn out as I am, but you both understand we've got to talk this through. How do we find more time to work smarter, not harder, and work with less stress and weariness?"

Lalo again looked up and said with conviction, "Does either of you know the name Mark Zuckerberg?"

Jennifer and Suzan looked at one another and then back at Lalo and in unison said, "No."

Lalo went on: "Well, Mark Zuckerberg launched Facebook—ever heard of it?"

Both ladies laughed, and Principal Raye said, "Yes, Lalo, who hasn't? Even my parents—who don't even own a computer—know the name Facebook, although they have no idea what it is other than what I've shown them on my tablet—mostly photos of my kids and our vacation trips."

Lalo went on: "Here's my point. Facebook revolutionized the way we navigate the web and connect with others. Today, we should be doing what Zuckerberg did a decade ago and what Sony did half a century earlier with the way we listen to music!"

Suzan spoke up, exclaiming, "Good to know, Lalo, but what do Facebook and Sony have to do with us, with time, with instruction, and with the fact that I'm dead tired? I don't see a connection."

Jennifer and Lalo both laughed at Suzan's comment, and then Lalo proclaimed, "Okay, just listen a minute. We must eVolve." He wrote the term *eVolve* on the office marker board, stating, "My assertion is all about time, technology, and relevancy—about unleashing our fullest potential in a way that will improve, simplify, and ease the way we work! We must talk about incredible, timely, groundbreaking digital enhancements to be initiated here at Cullen School!"

Jennifer and Suzan curiously looked at each other and then back to Lalo. Jennifer said, "Okay, Lalo, now that you've got our attention, what's your plan?"

"Yeah," said Suzan, "What is your plan? Because I can better utilize my time doing other work if you're simply giving us a digital history lesson!"

(Continued)

(Continued)

Lalo laughed and said, "What we each need is what I call a digital toolbox. It provides us with group share technology, a team manager, a communication edge, professional website capability, and a time enhancement system! The time enhancement system is important because we need time, and just as important, we need to save time."

"Okay, Lalo," stated Jennifer. "You're beginning to get out of my league."

"Yeah, Lalo," said Suzan, "as far as I'm concerned, you're coming at us from left field!"

Again, Lalo laughed and said, "Ease up, ladies! I know it's been a long day, but I've got a plan to help us eVolve so leading, teaching, and learning can be timely, easier, and significantly improved. Don't we want our school, our students, our teachers, and our lives to better eVolve, and to improve? We don't want to work in the past, do we? We want to save time, right?"

The late afternoon conversation did eVolve into several additional administrative staff meetings and even more faculty meetings. The administrative team, faculty, and staff worked collaboratively to eVolve toward cutting-edge technology, recognizing the benefits of kicking into overdrive the school's instructional program, and discovering along the way a few digital age DOs and DON'Ts. To improve teaching and learning in the 21st century, the Cullen School team collaboratively led themselves and their students away from an era best described as progressing at the "speed of dark"—moving forward into the new and improved "speed of light" digital age! Read and learn what they did together!

Group Share Technology

This is the centerpiece of the school's leading, teaching, and learning efforts in the digital age. Group share technology is interactive, with time-saving interfacing tools that allow principals and teachers to utilize a school website that is private, for educators only. With an interface located on the school's web page, group share technology provides direct links to all data tracking systems (IEPs, attendance, academic performance, student discipline, et cetera).

Part of group share technology is a live school calendar, a professional development portal whereby teachers can upload their own lessons, but also a place where there are links to websites that provide teacher training and learning. Living documents—such as a school's strategic plan, goals, mission and vision statements, et cetera—can all be uploaded for easy access and utilization. Group share technology makes available, in timely, friendly formats that are easy to navigate digitally, important documents and school-related information. A perfect example, on the market today, is HipChat. HipChat is a group and private chat, file-sharing, and integration system. It allows a principal and educators to take the office with them wherever they may go. It permits individuals to stay in the know with notifications, application program interfaces (APIs), and integrations for JIRA, Bitbucket, GitHub, Heroku, Zendesk, MailChimp, et cetera.

Group share technology can be enhanced with the use of smartphones, tablets, and private cloud computing. Additionally, Eamonn O'Donovan, former principal and assistant superintendent of human resources at a school system in southern California, shares four guidelines to be used by school leaders when evaluating potential adoptions for group share:

1. Talk to early adopters and learn from them.

2. Avoid the first generation of new devices, software, and apps.

3. Any contemplated device or app must enhance group share productivity and save time.

4. Cost must be directly proportional to the device's productivity and time savings (O'Donovan, 2012).

Team Manager

Principals can manage the instructional team, teaching and learning faster and more easily. Principals and team members can upload key documents, projects, instructional resources, agendas for future meetings and related discussions, and other relevant information to the group share technology location. Principals can develop blogs and discussion boards related to pertinent topics that require in-depth discussion. This makes face-to-face meeting time much more efficient. Sharing edited Microsoft Word documents in DropBox or Google Docs can be a simple and timely method of initiating the process. Principals can also consider reviewing their district's technology software and applications (apps) to determine what types of digital meeting spaces have been purchased by their districts and which can be accessible to teachers and staff. Custom reports can be made available in seconds, and real-time data are at the fingertips.

Communication Edge

Connectivity with instructional team members, students, and parents is frequent and timely. Collaboration is common. Goal development, planning, data analysis, and curriculum development and renewal are all time manageable and initiated with ease through group share technology. Social media play an important role in managing and saving time for educators. Facebook, Twitter, and Instagram—for example—aid in the development of community. Parents, business members, and community leaders are informed and invited to events, discussions, and forums held at the school site and online. Why? Consider this quotation from *My Grandfather's Blessing* (2001) by Rachel Naomi Remen, MD: "We seem to have forgotten one of the basic laws of survival: Strength lies in community"

(Continued)

(Continued)

(p. 114). Communication is connection. Connection is time saved. Schools and principals should be a point of connection, engaging and involving community. When people are connected within a learning community, they can participate, learn, be advised, and develop strong relationships. Technological communication helps bridge the connect/disconnect schism. Effective communication skills and technologies equate to time well spent and saved! A simple truth: A successful learning community connection is a timely investment that contributes to a school's overall improvement and student success.

Time Enhancement System

This is the ultimate tool necessary for tracking what is occurring in and across the school, in the classrooms with teachers, and with students. The enhanced time system permits the school principal and teachers to view important data, such as student attendance data, from a PC, laptop, tablet, or smartphone. Information is stored in a software or application database, where administrators and faculty can access it easily and immediately. Real-time access to data enables administration and faculty to examine differing schedules, for example, without time-consuming face-to-face meetings.

From a student attendance perspective, applications (apps) can be configured to recognize district and school policies and to send alert messages ensuring that attendance trackers are notified when a student is close to exceeding the number of absences allowed by the district/campus attendance policy. Such a system not only improves attendance, it accurately records data, thus saving time and reducing human error. The time enhancement system has an easy-to-navigate dashboard and tools that are intuitive to use, requiring minimal employee training.

A time enhancement system aids principals in better managing time to best benefit leading, teaching, and learning, and assures principals that the following are readily accessible:

- Data on student mastery and learning,
- Data on attendance,
- Data on teacher planning and lesson constructs,
- Data on teacher appraisals and evaluations,
- Data to plan for student success, and
- Data to pace teaching and learning (recall, work the clock, and remember, every minute counts).

Professional Websites

This digital era instructional tool places aspects of curriculum, teaching, and learning front and center and features enhanced customization. Professional websites are designed to provide information about subjects of interest, such as tutorials, online classes, instructional materials, homework sites, blogs, and reference and research sources.

It is essential that district leaders and campus administrators establish exact purposes of and specific guidelines for the use of professional websites. For example, is the website designated to attract parents to the school? Is the website to provide information to students or to the general public or both? Is the website to raise funds for the school? Knowing and sharing—with faculty, students, parents, and the general public—the true purpose of the website is an absolute.

Finally, listed below are a few technology-oriented DOs and DON'Ts that are essential, effective, and efficient time savers:

The DOs

- Always encourage students and faculty to utilize and share technologies.
- Always incorporate technology that is strategic, preserves time, and increases efficiency.
- Always set time-bound technological goals.
- Always be prepared to embrace change, recognizing, however, that not all change is good. Good or effective change is more strategic, time focused, and student centered than the status quo.
- Always make change personal.
- Always ensure change is in the best interest of students. Principals must ask themselves and their teachers a very important question: "How will the change proposed best benefit students?"

The DON'Ts

- Never cross the line. Understand the stark realities of virtually connecting teachers and students. You know what we're talking about—sexual misconduct, spamming practices, sharing information, sexting, videos, or sharing ideas that are not age-appropriate. Word of advice: Keep everything G-rated!
- If an individual is to remain an effective principal or teacher, there are ethical practices and moral behaviors that must be followed. The same is true and relatable to the proper use of the digital tools and technologies. (Recall from Chapter 6, "Ethics, Integrity, and Time," the case study The Texting Coach.)
- Never use or share outdated information and/or data. Principals must ensure that they and teachers understand what data and information can and cannot be shared with the general public. Confidentiality is the key!
- Never ignore social media. However, recognize the "cons" associated with social media, and share with faculty both benefits and detriments.
- Never assume that all teachers are technologically competent.

(Continued)

(Continued)

APPLICATION QUESTIONS

1. **Fact:** How principals manage their time is an important key to improving schools, specifically related to instruction and student achievement. Research sponsored by The Wallace Foundation reveals the following with respect to how principals apportion their time in doing their jobs: (1) Principals spend the least amount of time working instructionally with students, (2) few principals articulate a vision of what an instructional leader does or which instructional activities should be the highest of priorities, (3) principals spend significantly less time providing feedback to teachers than on other tasks, and (4) principals seldom interact with working teacher groups, and thus are not involved with grade-level or departmental instructional discussions/decisions (Turnbull, Haslam, Arcaira, Riley, Sinclair, & Coleman, 2009).

   Question A: From what you've ascertained from your readings in all of the chapters of this text, how can the Cullen School administrative team become better as instructional leaders, avoiding the weaknesses revealed in the Wallace Foundation's study?

   Question B: Considering Question A and your answer(s), how do your recommendations make principals better managers of time? Be specific in your answers.

2. **Fact:** Smartphones save time. The convenience of smartphones and applications will save principals significant time, according to a study of 2,120 participants conducted by Harris Interactive for ClickSoftware (2013a). App usage on the smartphone saves principals 88 minutes of time each day, or the equivalent of 22 working days each year. Researchers also concluded that, as much time as the smartphones save, the use of this mobile technology innovation has only scratched the surface of its potential to propel professional time-saving success.

   Question: Assume the role of devil's advocate, and describe how smartphones and other cutting-edge technology actually waste time for a principal. If such "waste-time" exists, what is the root of the problem, and how might it be solved, and not from the perspective of a Luddite or technophobe?

3. How can the Cullen School administrative team and faculty effectively and appropriately improve their school, utilizing group share technology as an instructional tool?

4. Which of the Five Cs identified in the chapter (see pages 159–161) could help Principal Jennifer Raye and her assistant principals address curricular/instructional issues related to school improvement? Explain. Related to eVolving, what technologies described in the chapter could aid the Cullen School administrative team in saving time?

5. In the eVolve scenario, Assistant Principal Lalo Garcia noted, "I've got a plan to help us eVolve so leading, teaching, and learning can be timely, easier, and significantly improved." Which of the following "ideas" best enhance what Mr. Garcia proposes? Group share technology, team manager, communication edge, time enhancement system, professional website, and/or the DOs and DON'Ts of technology? Explain how and by what means.

6. In the chapter, it is recommended that *principals ensure that teachers incorporate technology as part of the instructional program.* Of the numerous examples provided on pages 162–163, which could assist the Cullen School administrative team and faculty to improve instruction, increase student achievement, and save time? Be specific in your answers.

Fantasy to Reality: How to Save Time and Improve Instruction, Digitally!

The previous case study, Has Our School eVolved?, while based on a composite of schools and administrative leader experiences, is in fact, fictional—an essay in fantasy. Reality, however, sets in with more in-depth probing, as related to a series of questions we suspect you, the reader, have already conjured: (1) "Can a school really eVolve?" (2) "Do real programs actually exist that provide group share technology, team managers, communication edges, time enhancement systems, and professional websites?" (3) "Will digital systems in schools actually save time?" (4) "Will teaching and instruction improve?" and (5) "Can student achievement increase?" The answer to these queries is a resounding *yes!* Listed below is a sampling of some nationally renowned and marketed digital systems and programs related in varying forms and degrees to each of the five fictional eVolve components; there is also a brief review of a book about 12 educators who are using digital innovations in college classrooms. Are there downsides to any of the following digital systems? Of course, but read on.

Eduphoria

This is a digital system of integrated apps designed to assist districts, campus administrators, and teachers with lesson planning, monitoring student progress, and streamlining time-consuming administrative and instructional duties.

Eduphoria is designed to develop complete curricula and enhanced instructional programs and lesson activities—all integrated with district and campus instructional goals and expectations as well as national and state standards.

(Continued)

(Continued)

Eduphoria provides professional development management focusing on teacher and principal growth by integrating evaluation, goal setting, and collaborative learning processes. This system also provides for test construction as well as timely analysis of student data through multiple indicators with the click of a mouse.

Aware

Eduphoria SchoolObjects: Aware is a subcategory of the Eduphoria digital system and features school-specific digital tabs related to analyzing student test scores and related data, reviewing student information reports, managing student assessment processes, monitoring student growth and development, and developing reading/math/science assessments. These time-saving components provide detailed and critical data and information to enhance teaching, leading, and learning.

PowerUp

Another time-saving digital system, PowerUp WHAT WORKS, offers customizable resources to improve teaching and learning for struggling students and those with disabilities. This product integrates four essential areas (noted below) designed to save time, improve instruction, and enhance the use of technology.

1. **Evidence-Based Practices.** Technology-enhanced, evidence-based practices focusing on the content areas of reading, writing, and math are selected for district/campus implementation.

2. **Common Core State Standards.** All material correlates with the Common Core State Standards, focusing on English language arts and mathematics. A broad range of customizable materials and resources—incorporating technology—prepare teachers, administrators, and professional development facilitators for developing instructional programs focusing on college and career readiness.

3. **Technology Implementation.** Research-based digital processes effectively and efficiently improve student outcomes, saving time.

4. **Personalization of Learning Through UDL and Differentiated Instruction.** Universal design for learning (UDL) is a set of guidelines for developing a curriculum that provides all students with equal opportunities to achieve. UDL and differentiated instruction serve as time-centered, focused blueprints to aid principals and teachers in identifying learning goals, developing evidence-based instructional practices, incorporating digital tools for enhanced student achievement, and constructing assessments correlated with high expectations, skill development, and increased achievement standards for struggling students.

Knewton (Flipped)

The flipped classroom is "a new method of teaching that is turning the traditional classroom on its head" ("Flipped Classroom," n.d.). Programs from Knewton (www.knewton.com) facilitate the use of this method, allowing teachers to create lessons that students can view at home at their own pace, and to communicate with peers and teachers via online discussions. Then, concept engagement takes place in the classroom with students working collaboratively with teachers monitoring student progress and providing individual support, or in lab settings, or via interactive instructional activities that illustrate the learning concepts previously presented online.

Twelve Innovators (12 Tech)

Rebooting the Campus: 12 Tech Innovators Who Are Transforming Campuses is an e-book published by *The Chronicle of Higher Education.* The work of these innovators has applications that reach far into the K–12 domain. They are transforming schools with new teaching approaches using digital tools. Additionally, they are making use of the following innovative practices, to name a few, to increase instructional time and technology application by

- Sharing instructional materials online;
- Improving learning through social networking;
- Making information systems more time efficient;
- Using Twitter to make classroom learning better;
- Encouraging online student-centric collaboration;
- Integrating mobile devices into learning situations;
- Enhancing classroom learning with digital tools; and
- Transforming teaching and learning with social media.

Now, you may ask: "Which digital system/program is best?" As the authors tell the students and principals with whom they work, "Make the best of your time and seek the very best answers by digging deep, examining the empirical research, gathering and analyzing critical data and information, and making student-centered decisions!"

Ladies and gentlemen, start your search engines!

8

Technology

Staying a Step Ahead of the Silent Time Thief

The number one benefit of information technology is that it empowers people to do what they want to do. It lets people be creative. It lets people be productive. It lets people learn things they didn't think they could learn before, and so in a sense it is all about potential.

—Steve Ballmer (*AACIS Unlimited Potential Grant Announcement,* 2005)

THOUGHTFUL AND SELECTIVE TECHNOLOGY INTEGRATION

Steve Ballmer's quote highlights how technology must be viewed as a tool to empower people to be more creative and productive. Technology must be used to expand one's potential to change the world. Yet, not all emergent technological innovations will be useful for principals, teachers, students, and parents, because such innovations are not always appropriate, relevant, or applicable to the classroom or to the management of a school. School leadership is vital in integrating technology in schools (Anderson & Dexter, 2005).

Effective principals must be thoughtful and selective when integrating technology into their schools. On one hand, principals cannot ignore the rapid integration of technology into all facets of life and learning. This necessitates that schools adopt technological innovations to increase their ability and potential to communicate with parents, connect students with new information, and increase the distribution of information and ideas across the school and its faculty. On the other hand, principals must not be overly consumed with technological gizmos and gadgets that may turn out to be fads wasting time, resources, and energy. Adopting new technologies requires time and an implementation curve. Principals, with the help of other stakeholders, must consider, "Will this technological innovation enable us to be more efficient, effective, and creative?" If the answer is no, then the technology should not be adopted. If the answer is yes, the school must move forward in vetting new technologies for possible adoption.

Adopting technology for the sake of having technology is a time thief!

—The Silent Time Thief

The preceding chapters emphasize the necessity of a clear vision and mission that instructionally focuses change, innovation, communication, and an efficient use of time. This emphasis is well supported in empirical research focused on effective school leadership (Leithwood & Sun, 2012; Marzano, Waters, & McNulty, 2005). At this point, the authors have established the need for principals to be reflective, thoughtful, and flexible when making decisions. These points are stressed because no specific set of technological innovations fully protects a school from the *Silent Time Thief* and inefficiency. Instead, principals must save time and maximize resources through the adoption of technology.

Effective and efficient principals take strategic actions to engage all stakeholders with technology. They promote creativity, foster real-world learning opportunities, and increase communication among teachers, leaders, families, and communities. With a common vision for technology, schools move away from having teachers utilize random software or devices and move toward a seamless integration of technology relevant to 21st century skills students need to be successful. Instruction is well planned, so students and teachers continue to enhance their technological skills year after year.

Principals must consider the following recommendations as potential adoptions. The innovations integrated throughout the chapter are highlighted to demonstrate how they can be meaningfully integrated in a school's instructional culture. Some innovations are commonplace on campuses across the country (e.g., smartphones, tablets, Microsoft Outlook, Google Docs), but, based on informal conversations with principals, it is clear that many principals as well as teachers have not entered the digital age. Principals must thoughtfully consider these innovations and seek out others through ongoing discussions with relevant stakeholders. Technology adoption must be thoughtful, strategic, and aligned to teacher and student needs. What works best for one school may not work best for another.

DIGITAL ORGANIZATION: TIME MANAGEMENT 101

A large portion of campus leadership is dictated by a range of additional administrative responsibilities that include parent conferences, district meetings, disciplinary hearings, teacher evaluations and conferences, cafeteria duty, managing the budget, and an ongoing list of reports and plans due throughout the school year (Horng, Klasik, & Loeb, 2010). Principals must be organized, efficient, and prepared for each day. The demands of the principalship continue to increase. Unfortunately, many principals remain glued to outdated resources, skill sets, habits, and technologies. For some principals, using a paper-based calendar or jotting down notes from a teacher evaluation on paper or on a school district–provided form is common. These principals would find more time if they adopted technology to assist them in their leadership obligations. Three technology-enriched time management tips to assist principals are the following:

1. **Prioritize.** Effective principals prioritize their time and efforts (Leithwood, Harris, & Hopkins, 2008). Principals must be instructional leaders, but administrative paperwork pushes them from this role. Principals make decisions about what is important. They focus on school vision, mission, goals, and curricular/instructional initiatives. This means prioritizing instructionally centered efforts such as attending grade-level team meetings, subject area meetings, professional learning community meetings, and data analysis sessions. Blocking out time to conduct classroom walkthroughs and provide meaningful feedback to teachers is a priority. Regardless of what a principal prioritizes, it is important to create priorities and stick to them. Technology is a tremendous tool for prioritization and keeping a principal focused.

    - Discard the paper-based notepad and calendar. Use a tablet, iPad, or smartphone to create a prioritized to-do list for each day. As each task is completed, cross it off. Monitor progress throughout the day. Use smartphone applications like Wunderlist, Remember the Milk, or MyLifeOrganized (MLO) to develop lists that provide reminders and track progress over the course of each day, week, and school year.

- Use a tablet, iPad, or smartphone to enhance focus rather than serve as a distraction. Use smartphone applications like Focus Booster to allocate time, track time on task, and measure productivity.
- Consider switching the smartphone to airplane mode or turning the Wi-Fi off on the laptop when attending top priority meetings. Doing so unplugs you from the Internet and distracting e-mails, enabling you better to concentrate on the task at hand while still receiving messages. Remember, technology should enhance your efficiency potential—not distract.

2. **Increase Visibility.** Principals who are visible in classrooms, hallways, and meetings have a greater impact on student achievement and teacher practice than those who are not (Nettles & Herrington, 2007). Unfortunately, principals often get bogged down with paperwork and tethered to their offices. When principals are actively engaged in their schools, they develop a clearer understanding of what is occurring and can proactively address potential problems. Laptops, tablets, smartphones, and their applications increase a principal's visibility and ability to monitor what is happening on campus, and they enable a principal to provide meaningful support to teachers and staff.

- Laptops are light and easy to carry for a reason. Effective principals take advantage of mobile devices. Consider completing routine office tasks in a common area, in a professional development session, or during extracurricular events. Mobility allows principals to multitask while being visible to the school's stakeholders. These principals communicate to others while they are completing administrative tasks and ensure they are not burying their heads in a laptop or smartphone, ignoring teachers or students. Effective principals notify staff when they are working in a particular area to provide additional support if needed.
- Extended meetings before or after school can be physically and emotionally exhausting. Technology is useful for creating opportunities to meet, collaborate, and share information. Effective principals use their laptops, tablets, or smartphones to schedule meetings and communicate via Skype, Google Hangouts, or other web-conferencing tools. Web-based meetings provide opportunities for principals and teachers to meet virtually about instructional practices, managerial logistics, professional development, and other pending business.

3. **Distribute Leadership.** Scholarship in the field of educational leadership increasingly emphasizes the importance of developing teacher

leaders (DeMatthews, 2014a, 2015b; Spillane, Halverson, & Diamond, 2001). As noted in Chapter 3, "Leading, Teaching, Learning, and Time," and Chapter 5, "Collaboration and Time: Two Keys to Instructional Success," developing additional leaders in the school is not simply delegating work to others. Rather, it is about increasing a school's organizational capacity. When principals develop leadership capacity in others, they increase the school's overall organizational effectiveness and efficiency. Technology can increase a principal's ability to enhance teacher leadership.

- Technology allows principals to monitor the progress of teacher-led work groups, communities of practice, and grade-level teams. Google Docs and DropBox are effective tools to use to share and review meeting agendas; assess and edit working documents from teacher groups; and store important data, policy documents, or research articles connecting teachers and staff with information needed to make decisions. For the more sophisticated principals, applications like Mind42, Toggl, and Evernote can be useful in storing/sharing information, tracking group progress, and creating a database of valuable information that can be quickly accessed.

- Setting goals, journaling, and providing feedback to emerging teacher leaders are key attributes of an effective principal. It's naïve to assume that work and leadership responsibilities can simply be delegated. Less experienced principals often struggle with organization, a sense of legitimacy, and more challenging and dynamic leadership activities. Effective principals are reflective about their own practice and discover ways to cope and improve. The website and application Day One (www.dayone-app.com) provides an on-the-go journaling experience that allows principals to reflect on their leadership experiences, and the app provides a "when, where, and what" via an automatic time stamp. This application and similar journaling and blogging applications provide reminders via smartphones, and entries can be archived as well as shared via Twitter or e-mail. These tools provide principals with the time and opportunity to understand the leadership experiences of their teachers.

WORKING WITH DIGITAL TOOLS—
SAVING TIME AND MAKING HAY!

Most schools and districts have been slow to adopt new technologies (West, 2012). Even when systems and technologies are purchased and adopted, school districts and campuses rarely provide faculty, administrators, and staff with ongoing training to make full use of those technologies.

Consequently, a continuum of knowledge, expertise, and ability to fully utilize new technologies exists across schools. Some applications are straightforward and easy to use, and these serve as deterrents to the *Silent Time Thief*. In the sections to follow, we consider some recent and useful systems, applications, and technologies that allow school administrators to stay connected, manage their busy schedules, and access information in a quick and flexible way. Most of these technologies are available in schools or free via the Internet. Each company and product website provides guides and information to utilize these resources, and many include free support.

Microsoft Outlook

Microsoft Outlook is software principals can use to access, view, and organize their e-mail, calendar, contact information, and activities. Principals should be aware of key features of Microsoft Outlook that will increase their time efficiency and management. First, Outlook can be utilized on almost any device, including iPads, iPhones, Android devices, and via Internet-connected PCs and Macs. Outlook can be installed on smartphones and tablets or accessed via www.outlook.com as a free e-mail service. This enables employees to work from any device at any time.

Second, Outlook stores and connects users with their important contacts and helps quickly locate and organize new and existing e-mail messages.

Third, principals are able to share their calendars, schedule meetings, and invite others to meetings via Outlook's calendar system.

Finally, principals and staff can create multiple file folders and color code particular types of messages or events to help keep them organized. The following Microsoft Outlook tips help principals to avoid becoming victims of the *Silent Time Thief*.

- **E-Mail Folders.** *The Silent Time Thief* steals time whenever a principal is missing an important document, has to leave a meeting, puts a phone call on hold, or needs to ask for help locating information. The nature of the principalship in the 21st century means principals receive a large portion of their information via e-mail or other mobile applications. Principals often receive more than 100 e-mail messages a day. If they create individualized file folders for different stakeholders, areas of work, and projects, principals will be more apt to quickly access the valuable information needed. Additionally, Outlook allows a principal to search for e-mails using a variety of functions and provides a color-coding scheme and priority flag, so a principal can get back to the most important e-mails when time permits. Figure 8.1, Outlook E-mail Folders, shows multiple file folders (i.e., Parents, Professional Development (PD), School District, Student Discipline, and Teachers). Folders are easily created and organized, and e-mails can be sorted into different folders with a simple click and drag.

Figure 8.1   Outlook E-mail Folders

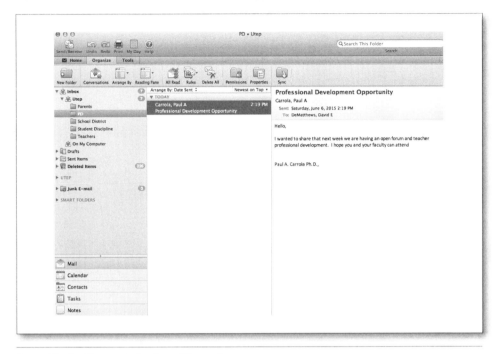

- **Calendar.** Outlook's calendar allows principals to track their meetings, but adds convenience in a number of ways. Reoccurring meetings can be scheduled in advance, and Outlook provides automatic reminders. For example, a principal can enter a reoccurring professional learning community meeting or a monthly parent engagement breakfast by inputting the meeting's frequency. Principals can color code their calendars based on meeting or activity type, and they can share their calendars with office staff or teachers to coordinate schedules. If a meeting must be cancelled, principals can send a quick cancellation notification to all participants. Figure 8.2, Outlook Calendar and Appointment Creator, shows the Outlook Calendar and the appointment creator that permits a principal to create an appointment, select date/time/reoccurrence, and invite other contacts.

- **Contacts.** The 21st century principal must communicate efficiently with others. Outlook's contacts can be synced to a school district's contact list database, providing easy access to all district personnel and staff. In addition, e-mail groups can be set up to send "blast" e-mail messages to a school's faculty, certain grade levels or departments, or even parents.

Figure 8.2 Outlook Calendar and Appointment Creator

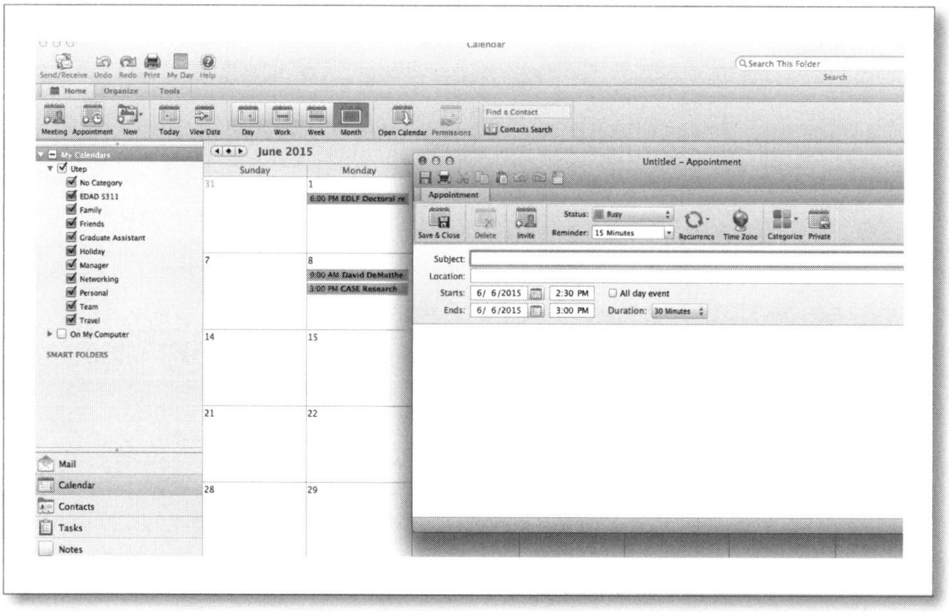

Source: Used with permission from Microsoft.

- **Tasks.** Outlook provides a task management tool that can be very helpful in organizing tasks and projects across teams. Principals can create a task or activity, categorize it to a certain aspect of their work, set a due date or label it as a reoccurring priority, and even forward the task on to another person via e-mail. Prioritizing time and tasks can be difficult in a busy work environment; Outlook's task function enables them to set reminders for priorities and time efficiency purposes.

For additional information about Microsoft Outlook and to learn more about its functionality, visit www.MicrosoftOutlook.com.

Google Apps for Work

Google provides a number of applications for work and business that can help principals improve time management and communication. Consider reviewing the range of products offered by Google at www.google.com/about/products, including Google Apps for Work. This app costs $5 per user per month, or $50 per user per year. It includes business e-mail, video and voice calls, integrated online calendars, 30GB of online storage and file syncing, online text documents, security, and phone and e-mail support. Some features of Google Apps for Work are available free of charge. Some of Google's products may not be necessary for principals. For example, many school districts have their own e-mail programs; thus Google e-mail accounts for faculty and staff are not necessary. To avoid the *Silent Time Thief*, consider utilizing Google Hangouts, Google Calendar, Google Drive, and Google Docs/Sheets/Forms/Slides/Sites. Below are a few applications principals should consider to enhance their visibility and time management skills.

- **Google Hangouts.** Google Hangouts allows principals to connect with others to text, voice, and videoconference. A principal can also conduct face-to-face conversations. Hangouts are limited to 15 participants and are encrypted to ensure a secure experience. Consider the possibilities for interacting with teachers, teacher leaders, parents, and students via this technology. For example, a busy parent can participate in an administrative team meeting or conference with a teacher about student behavior or academic performance. A principal can informally check in with a teacher about the day's lesson or connect the teacher to a colleague who may be able to give advice, mentoring, or support around a particular aspect of teaching practice. The opportunities for using Google Hangouts are limitless, especially when considering connecting teachers and staff with professional development professionals from across the country and the world.

- **Google Calendar.** Google Calendar is a shareable, integrated online calendar that integrates with e-mail accounts, contacts, Google Sites, and Google Hangouts. Google Calendars are a fantastic way to break away from printing the ever-problematic paper calendar. A Google Calendar can be published directly onto a Google Site or web page. Google Calendars are living documents that can be updated immediately. For example, imagine there is a plumbing issue in the school and Back-to-School Night must be postponed. The school must contact parents. After school personnel update the Google Calendar, parents can check online to view the new event date. If parents received an invitation for Back-to-School Night via Google Calendar, they will be notified if the event time, date, or place is modified. This mode of communicating event dates, times, and changes beats that old-fashioned "backpack method" of sending flyers home with students. Another interesting Google Calendar feature is its ability to create groups. Group calendars can be used for various groups (e.g., grade-level teams, professional learning communities, and parents). It is challenging for a principal to know everything happening on campus. When faculty and staff consistently utilize and share Google Calendars, everyone can be current on event schedules.

- **Google Drive.** Google Drive permits individuals and groups to file and secure work online in one place. Additionally, Google Drive allows users to access work whenever it is needed via laptop, tablet, or smartphone. The first 30GB are free, and if that is insufficient, additional storage can be purchased at a nominal fee. Consider the flexibility of syncing some or all files automatically and never having to worry about losing a document again. Also consider using other online systems such as DropBox to store your information. Figure 8.3, Google Drive Files, shows different folders for saving and sharing files and information.

Figure 8.3   Google Drive Files

- **Google Docs/Sheets/Forms/Slides.** Google docs, sheets, forms, and slides provide editable files that have no dedicated software (i.e., Google Docs does not require Microsoft Word or other word processing, spreadsheet, or slideshow software) and allow multiple people to work on files simultaneously. Imagine meeting in a Google Hangout with a workgroup to discuss an upcoming professional development activity. Individuals on and off campus can collaboratively—as if they were meeting in the same room—work on the documents, slides, or forms to be used in the activity. Google Docs allows principals to decide who has access to documents and files and permits users to grant individuals or groups the right to view and/or edit the files. The possibilities are limitless in schools for principals, teachers, students, and parents. Parents and teachers might collaborate on a recital, class trip, or out-of-school activity using Google Docs; or a group of teachers may codevelop a professional development activity. Similarly, Google Forms, Google Sheets, and Google Slides assist groups in developing surveys, school-based documents, and presentations. Figure 8.4, Working Documents in Google Docs, shows a group of files saved in a user's Google Docs account. A user has the ability to edit and share these documents with other users.

Figure 8.4   Working Documents in Google Docs

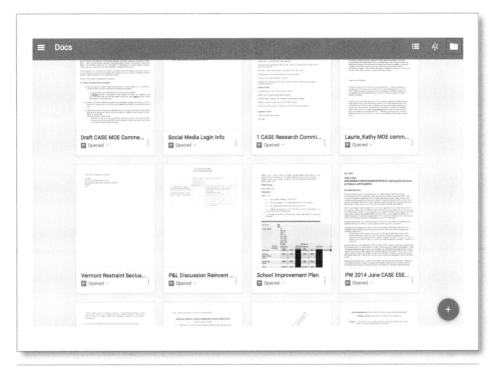

Source: © 2015 Google Inc. Used with permission. Google and the Google logo are registered trademarks of Google Inc.

- **Google Sites.** Google Sites provides an internal website that can be customized for any school. Creating a Google Site is almost as simple as editing a document. Google provides numerous supports and training videos to build skills. Google Sites allows faculty, staff, and parents to access key information or to learn about a particular issue related to the school. Google Sites also allows faculty and staff to embed Google Calendars, Docs, Forms, and Sheets, as well as other materials that are relevant to the school. As with everything else Google has to offer, users can manage which individuals and groups share access to view or edit files, and which have access simply to view the site. Users may make the site available to anyone on the web as well.

Navigating Google products is simple and straightforward. The Google products website (www.google.com/intx/en/work/apps/business/products) provides clear information about their products.

Tom's Planner

This application (www.tomsplanner.com) provides a web-based project planning space enabling the user to create, share, and easily manipulate project plans. It includes a Gantt chart (see Figure 8.5, Tom's Planner Gantt Chart), a type of chart that illustrates start and finish dates of projects across a calendar. Principals are able to publish Gantt charts, invite others to collaborate on projects and access the charts, add links to key documents and websites, and embed their project schedules into their own schedules. In addition, the Gantt chart is a live and editable document. This reduces the risk of having multiple versions of an outdated or incorrect project plan/chart as a result of uncoordinated efforts.

Increasingly, school leadership is project oriented, includes diverse groups and communities of practice, and works with standards, data, and other information sources (Drago-Severson, Blum-DeStefano, & Asghar, 2013). Tom's Planner and other project-planning applications provide a systematic framework for working on school-related processes, such as a review process for textbook adoption, an implementation plan for a new special education or bilingual coteaching model, or even an event tracker for a school fundraiser. The application's emphasis on organization and time lines helps a principal and staff better manage time and avoid being negatively impacted by the *Silent Time Thief*. Figure 8.5, Tom's Planner Gantt Chart, illustrates a time line and project options as well as different tools and settings that can be used in the application.

Figure 8.5   Tom's Planner Gantt Chart

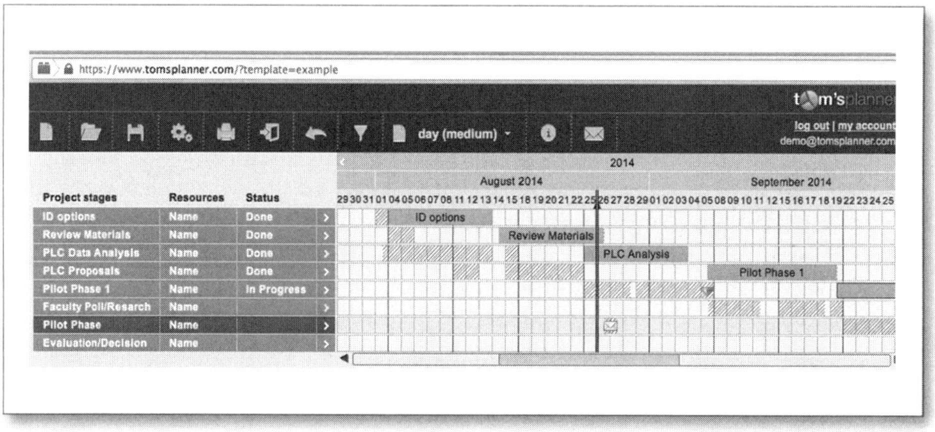

Source: Used with permission from Tom's Planner.

Facebook

Facebook has more than one billion active users a month. To ignore Facebook is to miss a tremendous opportunity to meaningfully engage families, students, teachers, and other stakeholders. Facebook can be a school's main advertising and information location; it can include contact information, a schedule of upcoming events, and access to important documents and websites. Facebook is great for connecting families, students, and teachers. A new generation of teachers is connected to Facebook and other forms of social media (e.g., Twitter, Instagram) throughout the day via their smartphones, computers, laptops, and tablets (Kist, 2013). Principals can share links to professional development articles, YouTube videos, lesson-planning websites, and other relevant information. Although Facebook and other forms of social media have many positive implications, principals must ensure the proper precautions are taken. Five recommended precautions are the following:

- Review district policies regarding social media, and adopt a school social media policy that outlines how teachers and staff should and should not interact with students and others via social media.
- Revisit school and district policies on privacy as related to photography. Faculty, staff, and students with smartphones can quickly and easily upload and share pictures via social media.
- Consider whether texting with students is appropriate, and if so, under what conditions. Parents should be engaged in this matter. A teacher sending a student a text with some clarity on a challenging homework assignment during business hours might be appropriate.
- Consider whether or not faculty should be allowed to engage with students on social media on a continuing basis. This might include "friending" or "following" the student on a social media platform.
- Consider similar policies for texting, cell phone communication, and other social media applications.

Wiggio

Wiggio (www.wiggio.com) is a free application that supports group work. Groups can include clubs, parent–teacher organizations, committees, learning communities, grade-level teams, social groups, or interdisciplinary groups tasked with a specific project. The application provides a suite of tools, including voicemail and text messaging for the group; a shared calendar of meetings, events, and deadlines; a virtual location for storing files; and conference-calling technology. In addition, users are able to send quick polls to members to plan meetings or test an idea with the group. For example, a principal wants a group of teachers to consider revising the master schedule to allow for additional planning and professional development time for grade-level and subject-matter teams and to include special education teachers. The principal uses Wiggio to poll teachers on schedule options and to identify the best time to meet to discuss the options. In addition, the principal is able to share planning documents and solicit input from teachers. Teacher leaders and grade-level teams can use Wiggio's tools and organizational structure to improve efficiency and communication. Figure 8.6, Wiggio's Project Management Tools, provides an example of a user's homepage and includes the user's current groups, folders for storing and sharing files, and a calendar. From this homepage, the user is able to send e-mails, poll group members, and create events.

Figure 8.6   Wiggio's Project Management Tools

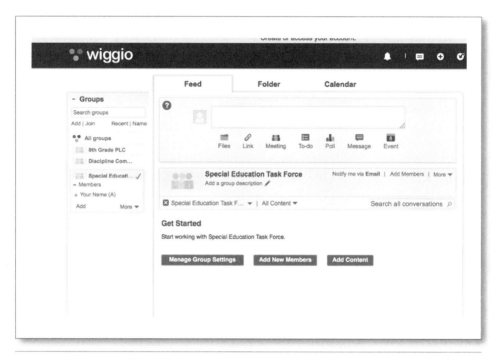

Source: Used with permission from Wiggio.

Evernote

Evernote (www.evernote.com) is a free application that consolidates your digital workspace, provides an area for you to maintain short lists and detailed agendas, and keeps you focused on priorities and deadlines. The application allows you to collect a range of materials, take photos and connect them to projects, and manage key articles. In addition, users are able to increase their organizational efficiency by using Evernote as a meeting tool, because Evernote can rapidly turn your notes into screen-friendly slides. Evernote can also be synced across phones and computers, scan and digitize business cards and handwritten notes, and easily connect to the Internet. Principals can use Evernote to scan and save handwritten notes from informal teacher evaluations, or student work samples that can later be used to highlight a teacher's ingenuity. Evernote is similar to some of the other applications that support principals and teachers in facilitating meetings and sharing information. Figure 8.7, Evernote's Homepage and Daily Agenda, provides an example of a user's main screen and includes daily agenda items and notes for those items. From this page, the user is able to create new items, store files, share information with other users, and utilize other aspects of Evernote.

Figure 8.7   Evernote's Homepage and Daily Agenda

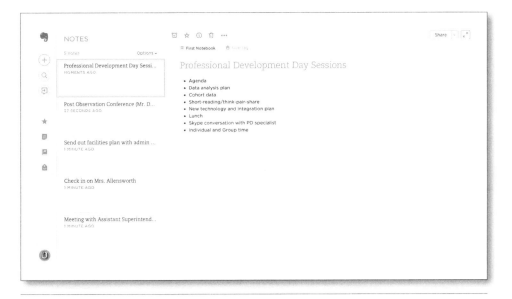

Source: Used with permission from Evernote.

WEB CONFERENCING—A TIMESAVER TO AVOID DEATH BY MEETING!

Principals often believe they must be omnipresent. However, an effective and efficient leader leads without micromanaging every meeting and interaction. Instead, effective principals focus on being visible, collaborative, and engaged. Web conferencing is a tool principals can employ to maximize their visibility while connecting the school with parents, experts, and other stakeholders.

Web conferencing must be used effectively. Web conferencing is a catchall phrase to describe various methods by which individuals and groups communicate via online collaborative programs and applications. Web conferencing includes webinars, streaming video via web cameras and digital cameras, chat sessions, screen and desktop sharing, and a combination of these options. Additionally, social media websites can be used to web conference. Products for each type of web-conferencing option include the following:

- **Streaming Video Conferences.** Google Hangouts, Skype, GoTo Meeting, Adobe Connect
- **Chat Sessions.** Google Hangouts, Skype, GoToMeeting, Adobe Connect
- **Desktop Sharing.** Google Chrome Remote Desktop, CrossLoop, ShowMyPC, Yugma SE (for Skype)
- **Social Media Websites.** Facebook, Twitter

These applications are constantly evolving, and newer applications are often added to the market.

Checking for updates on these applications is smart business and will save a principal valuable time. Of course, you can ignore this advice and I'll be delighted to waste your time!

—The Silent Time Thief

Skype

Web conferences are ideal for meetings or conversations with parents, teachers, or other stakeholders if done properly. Web conferencing is effective only with thoughtful advanced planning. Below are four steps to ensure all users are prepared to utilize web conferencing technology. Skype is used here to illustrate web conferencing, but principals should talk to teachers, parents, staff, and even students to learn about what web conference software is right for their school and audience. Skype also allows for connectivity with Microsoft Outlook and feeds directly into Facebook. Many parents use Facebook and are likely to conference via Skype.

Four Steps to Web Conferencing Success

- **Step 1: Learn the software and its tools.** Numerous web-conferencing applications exist. Make certain you are knowledgeable about the application you are using. Software must be up to date on your computer, and you must have all the necessary equipment (e.g., web camera, headphones, speakers, smartphones). Be knowledgeable about the application features and how they can be used. Skype allows for video calls, group video calls, voice-only calls, instant messaging, screen sharing, and file sharing. To learn more about Skype's features, visit www.skype.com/en/features/.

- **Step 2: Ensure others are familiar with the web-conferencing software.** Web conferencing will not run smoothly when others are not familiar with the application or are unprepared to meet. Consider providing professional development opportunities for teachers and staff in the use of Skype or other web conferencing applications prior to using them in a live web conference. Consider appointing someone knowledgeable in web conferencing to assist teachers and staff. When conferencing with parents or other stakeholders, schedule enough time in advance so that all users can be prepared. Consider drafting simple directions that include all necessary information to access the application (e.g., how to download Skype, usernames, and connectivity requirements).

- **Step 3: Prepare materials in advance.** Just because a meeting is virtual does not mean preparation is not required. Consider what would be needed if the group were meeting face to face. Refer back to the case study Death by Meeting! in Chapter 3. How would you present materials? How would you facilitate discussions? Would you provide documents, reading materials, and/or a meeting agenda? Skype allows you to share materials and provides multiple options for group video calls.

- **Step 4: Practice with a colleague, peer, or friend prior to hosting your meeting.** Finally, be aware that implementing an effective web conference has its challenges. Individuals must remain engaged, stay connected to vital information, and feel supported to share their ideas, opinions, and perspectives. This requires a skilled moderator who not only is knowledgeable about the content being discussed, but also pays close attention to who is and is not engaged. Excellent facilitators draw all participants into conversations. Those new to Skype or other web-conferencing applications should schedule meeting times with a colleague or friend to practice and improve everyone's skills.

 Hosting a web conference without the proper training is a great way to waste everyone's time.

—The Silent Time Thief

In addition to the four steps listed above, it is important to make a good impression through the use of appropriate web conference etiquette. Web conferencing can be a bit awkward at first. Maintain proper web etiquette and the conference will be successful.

- **Open web-conferencing sessions early.** If you are the facilitator of a web conference, log on at least 7 to 10 minutes prior to the meeting so other users can also log on, review the agenda, and ensure they are familiar with Skype and its interface tools. This will pay off later in the meeting, when everyone is on the same page and technical difficulties are minimized.

- **Introductions are essential.** Begin each session by introducing yourself, and feel comfortable restating your name when speaking to a large group. Remember, you are not physically being observed in a room, and participants might not immediately recognize your voice.
- **Pay close attention to your microphone.** Whether you are using a smartphone, web camera, or headset, mute your microphone when you are not speaking. This prevents other participants from hearing any background sounds or noises from your keyboard and computer.
- **Make eye contact.** If using video conferencing, make eye contact with the camera when you speak. If you are not using video conferencing, upload a clear and professional picture to your Skype profile, so people can see and connect with you.

FINAL THOUGHTS

This chapter described an array of tools and applications that can be applied by principals seeking to maximize their time while remaining visible, aware, and engaged in instructional leadership. Decisions of whether or not to adopt new technology must be based on a community dialogue that centers on one foundational question: Will this technological innovation increase potential to be more efficient, effective, and creative? The answer to this question is rooted deeply in a school's vision and mission as well as the needs of teachers, students, families and other stakeholders.

The need for efficient and effective leaders to prioritize their time and meaningfully distribute leadership through the empowerment and development of teacher leaders was established. Exceptional principals draw on skills, attributes, and orientations identified and embedded throughout this text. This is no easy task, but technology supports principals in exemplifying standards of practice in their daily work and routines. A number of useful applications and programs were identified that can be adapted to meet the needs of a school. Microsoft Outlook, Google Apps for Work, Wiggio, and Skype were highlighted because of their popularity, low cost, and the authors' own experiences working with these tools.

Investing in professional development and purchasing software and hardware allows these tools to be utilized and creates a 21st century school where teachers, students, and administrators are all working with state-of-the-art technology and practices. Exceptional principals actively engage in identifying and considering these products. Exceptional principals also search for additional products that might be more suitable for their contexts and circumstances. Remember, technology is constantly evolving; it is not sufficient to consider revisiting it only at the end of a five-year plan.

Keep in mind that a great deal of technology costs little to nothing when used on or downloaded from the Internet. In other words, do not blame your Stone Age technological know-how on your dwindling school budget. Exceptional principals engage faculty, staff, students, and families in discussions on how to best select and use technology to enhance learning and improve communication. Exceptional principals continually review new programs and options, read blogs, and follow interesting education technology websites that detail emerging innovations (e.g., *U.S. News and World Report's* Technology in the Classroom, www.usnews.com/education/technology-in-the-classroom, and *Education Week's* Technology Page, www.edweek.org/topics/technology/index.html?intc=thed). Finally, and most important, exceptional principals have fun experimenting and trying new technologies. Go ahead and try it yourself!

DISCUSSION QUESTIONS

1. Learning from peers and practices on other campuses is an important aspect of effective school leadership. Identify and share three applications that principals and teachers can use to improve their practices and three additional applications that might be used for web conferencing, data analysis, and/or sharing resources and information. Discuss the following: (1) How do these applications encourage creativity? (2) How do these applications maximize time usage? (3) What are some of the pros and cons of adopting these applications?

2. Identify five challenges principals confront when promoting technology integration on a campus. What strategies can you offer to support principals in overcoming these challenges?

3. Three practices to improve time management are (1) prioritizing, (2) increasing visibility, and (3) distributing leadership. How do these practices impact time management? Connect each of these practices to your school's mission and vision statements. How do these practices positively impact instructional programs?

4. Interview your principal to find out how he or she utilizes technology. What does the principal consider as his or her technology strengths? What does the principal identify as areas in which she or he needs to improve in the use of technology?

5. Review your campus and school district goals/plans in relation to students utilizing technology and being prepared for the 21st century. How are your school and district plans being implemented in your school and/or classroom? If plans are not being implemented, what would you do as a principal to move your campus to digitally modernize and be more willing to adopt innovative technologies?

6. Reflect on recent online conferences you have attended. How was web-conferencing technology utilized? How did the facilitator and participants practice web-conferencing etiquette? Create a cheat sheet for faculty, staff, and parents showcasing how to successfully engage in web conferencing.

CASE STUDY APPLICATION

A NEW LEADER, AN OLD PROBLEM: HOW TO INTEGRATE TECHNOLOGY INTO A SCHOOL'S CULTURE

Rod Hobbs served as a new assistant principal at Martin Luther King School. He was only 27 years old and had only five years of teaching experience. According to Principal Elke Chen, "Rod possesses a comprehensive knowledge related to data-driven instruction and technology…two things that are lacking in our school." As a teacher, Rod used Microsoft Excel spreadsheets to track student performance on a variety of state standards and shared these data with parents, using multiple means of communication. During his interview for the assistant principal position, Rod impressed the interview committee with his knowledge and expertise associated with data-driven instruction. However, one question caught him off guard: "It seems to me you know how to analyze data and communicate with teachers, but what schoolwide systems would you put in place for teachers who lack sufficient knowledge about data-driven instruction, spreadsheets, and technology?" Rod had not reflected on how he could take his effective teaching practices and translate them into schoolwide practices.

Rod spoke with teachers and staff over the summer about how they used data to guide their instruction, how they shared information with other teachers, and how they communicated with parents. Principal Chen had very little knowledge related to technology use and believed Rod's focus in the next school year should be to lead the school in a "technological overhaul." Rod quickly realized that the faculty had a continuum of skills. One teacher almost entirely refused to use e-mail, while another developed a webpage that provided access to class resources and materials for students and parents. One teacher said, "I'm paid to teach, not be on the Internet or Facebook." Other teachers reported using Skype or Google Hangouts to conduct face-to-face conferences with parents unable to come to the school to discuss their children's progress. The more technologically advanced teachers inquired whether they would be made to attend basic technology training. Rod recalled how boring professional development sessions were when one-size-fits-all sessions were conducted rather than sessions tailored to the unique needs of teachers.

Rod and Principal Chen decided to create a technology and data team consisting of five teachers and a parent. The team identified three specific goals: (1) learn how to organize and easily share data across the campus, (2) utilize social media and web-conferencing technology to more meaningfully engage parents and other stakeholders, and (3) support teachers who struggled with using technology in their classrooms and as a tool to engage in data analysis and communication. The group agreed professional development activities needed to be tailored to each teacher's individual needs and abilities.

The group recommended the following plan: (1) A train-the-trainer model would be used, where select teachers would learn about an area of technology or a data-driven approach and then share what they learned with other groups of teachers. (2) Model or lead teachers would be identified whom other teachers could reach out to for help and assistance. (3) The administrative team would be actively engaged in all training, either as lead trainers or as active participants. (4) Each grade-level team would collaborate on projects that would create an online storage space for student data and relevant lesson plans and materials; these teams would also use data analysis to identify key priorities for targeted instruction in the classroom and at home.

Rod believed the technology and data team had provided the school with its marching orders, but he thought to himself, "How can we make this broad plan actionable? What activities and applications can we use to really engage teachers and administrators and make them feel like this can benefit their work as educators? The team is optimistic about the future, although they recognize they need additional information and a bit more time to plan. This will be an ongoing activity over the course of the next three academic years."

APPLICATION QUESTIONS

1. Imagine you are Rod Hobbs, the new assistant principal assigned to Martin Luther King School. You are tasked by Principal Chen with ensuring that teachers are using technology in their classrooms for parent communication and for sharing information. What would be your initial steps? What questions might you ask teachers, students, and parents to learn more about their needs and current expertise? How would you begin planning for the upcoming school year?

2. In the chapter, a number of programs and applications were reviewed that schools can incorporate to increase time efficiency and effectiveness. Select one and develop a plan to support teachers at Martin Luther King School in adopting and utilizing this technology. Identify three potential obstacles, and describe how you would address each obstacle.

3. The practice of distributed leadership emphasizes the development of teacher leaders rather than the simple delegation of tasks, activities, and duties. How might Rod apply distributed leadership practices to increase Martin Luther King School's capacity to utilize technology?

4. In this case study application, Rod identified teachers and a parent to participate on the committee. Who else might Rod included in the committee? Explain why, and defend your choices.

5. Schools must have access to specific hardware and software in order to adopt innovative practices. What types of software and hardware do you have access to at your school? Which programs and applications could you utilize, given your technology needs? How might teachers at your school gain access to new software and hardware if the school's budget is insufficient to purchase any?

References and
Further Readings

Abelein, S. (2013). *How to build a connection between school culture and student achievement.* Retrieved from http://www.catapultlearning.com/connection-school-culture-student-achievement

Abilock, D. (2012). True—or not. *Reading: The Core Skill, 69*(6), 70–74.

Adams, C., Forsyth, P., & Mitchell, R. (2009). The formation of parent-school trust: A multilevel analysis. *Educational Administration Quarterly, 45*(1), 4–33.

Adler, P. (1975). The transitional experience: An alternative view of culture shock. *Journal of Humanistic Psychology, 15*(4), 23–40.

Alexandrowicz, V. (1999, November). *Cultural democracy: Issues and conditions impacting K to higher education students.* Copresented with A. Ochoa, J. Kerper Mora. Association of Mexican American Educators (AMAE) Conference, San Diego, CA.

Anderson, R. E., & Dexter, S. (2005). School technology leadership: An empirical investigation of prevalence and effect. *Educational Administration Quarterly, 41*(1), 49–82.

Andrews, R., Biggs, M., & Seidel, M. (Eds.). (1996). *The Columbia world of quotations.* New York, NY: Columbia University Press. Quotation retrieved September 16, 2014, from http://www.bartleby.com/66

Arbinger Institute. (2002). *Leadership and self-deception: Getting out of the box* (New ed.). San Francisco, CA: Berrett-Koehler.

Ballmer, S. (2005). *AACIS unlimited potential grant announcement.* Retrieved from http://news.microsoft.com/2005/02/17/steve-ballmer-aacis-unlimited-potential-grant-announcement

Barth, R. (2001). *Learning by heart.* San Francisco, CA: Jossey-Bass.

Blumengarten, J. (2014). *Why should we use technology?* Retrieved from http://connect.learningtoday.com/use-technology

Boyd, V. (1992). *The school culture.* Retrieved from http://www.sedl.org/change/school/culture.html

Branson, C. M., & Gross, S. J. (2014). Introduction. In C. M. Branson & S. J. Gross (Eds.), *Handbook of ethical educational leadership* (pp. 1–3). New York, NY: Routledge.

Brockmeier, L. L., Sermon, J. M., & Hope, W. C. (2005). Principals' relationship with computer technology. *NASSP Bulletin, 89*, 45–63.

Bryk, A., & Schneider, B. (2002). *Trust in schools a core resource for improvement.* New York, NY: Russell Sage Foundation.

Bureau of Labor Statistics. (2012). Charts from the American Time Use Survey. Retrieved from http://www.bls.gov/tus/charts

Cairney, T. H. (2000). Beyond the classroom walls: The rediscovery of the family and community as partners in education. *Educational Review, 52*(2), 163–174.

Carr, C. (1989). *The new manager's survival manual* (2nd ed.). New York, NY: Wiley.

Chadwick, K. G. (2004). *Improving schools through community engagement: A practical guide for educators.* Thousand Oaks, CA: Corwin.

Chang, I-Hua. (2011). The effect of principals' technological leadership on teachers' technological literacy and teaching effectiveness in elementary schools. *Educational Technology & Society, 15*(2), 328–340.

Clark, F. (n.d.). Quotation retrieved December 15, 2015, from http://www.brainyquote.com/quotes/quotes/f/frankacla156704.html

ClickSoftware. (2013a). *How much time do smartphones save? 22 days a year.* Retrieved from http://ir.clicksoftware.com/phoenix.zhtml?c=122672&p=irol-newsArticle&ID=1822590

ClickSoftware. (2013b). *Your smartphone could be worth $12,000, new survey finds.* [Press release.] Retrieved from http://ir.clicksoftware.com/phoenix.zhtml?c=122672&p=irol-newsArticle&ID=1822590

Comer, J. P., & Haynes, N. M. (1991). Parent involvement in schools: An ecological approach. *The Elementary School Journal, 91*(3), 271–273.

Conzemius, A., & O'Neill, J. (2014). *The handbook for SMART school teams: Revitalizing best practices for collaboration* (2nd ed.). Bloomington, IN: Solution Tree Press.

Cookson, C. (2013). *3 tips on how to use technology to improve time management skills.* Retrieved from http://blog.grantham.edu/blog/bid/148078/3-Tips-on-How-to-Use-Technology-to-Improve-Time-Management-Skills

Copland, M. A. (2001). The myth of the superprincipal. *Phi Delta Kappan, 82*(7), 528–533.

Cordeiro, P. A., & Cunningham, W. G. (2012). *Educational leadership: A bridge to improved practice.* Boston, MA: Pearson Education.

Cover, D. R. (2014). *Exceptional leadership defined.* Unpublished interview. Department of Educational Leadership and Foundations, The University of Texas at El Paso, El Paso, TX.

Covey, S. (2004). *The 7 habits of highly effective people: Restoring the character ethic* (Rev. ed.). New York, NY: Free Press.

Crean, M. (2014). *10 sensational tips for managing your time as a teacher.* Retrieved from http://topnotchteaching.com/classroom-management-organisation/10-tips-managing-time-as-a-teacher

Cubberley, E. (1916). *Public school administration.* Boston, MA: Houghton Mifflin.

Cunningham, W. G., & Cordeiro, P. A. (2006). *Educational leadership: A problem-based approach.* Boston, MA: Pearson Education.

Daniels, L. (2014). *8 ways for teachers to save time in the classroom.* Retrieved on June 6, 2015, from http://www.teachthought.com/teaching/8-ways-teachers-save-time-classroom

DeMatthews, D. E. (2014a). How to improve curriculum leadership: Integrating leadership theory and management strategies. *The Clearing House: A Journal of Educational Strategies, Issues and Ideas, 87*(5), 1–5.

DeMatthews, D. E. (2014b). Principal and teacher collaboration. An exploration of distributed leadership in professional learning communities. *International Journal of Educational Leadership and Management*, 2(2), 176–206.

DeMatthews, D. E. (2015a). Making sense of social justice leadership. A case study of a principal's experiences to create a more inclusive school. *Leadership and Policy in Schools*, 14(2), 139–166.

DeMatthews, D. E. (2015b). Clearing a path for inclusion: Distributing leadership in a high performing elementary school. *Journal of School Leadership*, 25(6), 139–166.

DeMatthews, D. E. (2016). Competing priorities and challenges: Principal leadership for social justice along the US-Mexico border. *Teachers College Record*, 118(11), 1–35.

DeMatthews, D. E., Edwards, D. B., & Rincones, R. (in press). Social justice leadership and community engagement: A successful case from Ciudad Juárez, Mexico. *Educational Administration Quarterly*.

DeMatthews, D. E., & Mawhinney, H. B. (2014). Social justice and inclusion: Exploring challenges in an urban district struggling to address inequities. *Educational Administration Quarterly*, 50(5), 844–881.

Denhan, C., & Lieberman, A. (Eds.). 1980. *Time to learn.* Washington, DC: US Department of Education.

Dewey, J. (1916). *Democracy and education: An introduction to the philosophy of education.* New York, NY: Macmillan.

Dircks, H. (2012). *Perpetuum mobile: Or, a history of the search for self-motive power.* Ulan Press. (Original work published 1861)

Donohue, G. (2011, August 1). *Goal setting—Powerful written goals in 7 easy steps.* Retrieved from http://topachievement.com/goalsetting.html

Doran, G. (1981). There's a S.M.A.R.T way to write management's goals and objectives. *Management Review*, 70(11), 35–36.

Drago-Severson, E., Blum-DeStefano, J., & Asghar, A. (2013). *Learning for leadership: Developmental strategies for building capacity in our schools.* Thousand Oaks, CA: Corwin.

Drye, W. (n.d.). *Fountain of youth—Just wishful thinking?* Retrieved September 6, 2014, from http://science.nationalgeographic.com/science/archaeology/fountain-of-youth

EdTechReview Editorial Team. (2014). *Why should technology be used in education?* [Infographic]. Retrieved from http://edtechreview.in/trends-insights/insights/292-why-technology-in-education

Educational Research. (2015). *How principals manage their time is key to improving instruction in their schools.* Portland, ME: Author.

Emerson, R. W. (1841). *Spiritual laws: Essays, first series.* Quotation retrieved from http://www.csun.edu/~kjs26872/Teaching_Quotes.html

Epstein, J. L. (2001). *School, family, and community partnerships: Preparing educators and improving schools.* Boulder, CO: Westview Press.

Epstein, J. L. (2005). Attainable goals? The spirit and letter of the No Child Left Behind Act on parental involvement. *Sociology of Education*, 78, 179–182.

Epstein, J. L., Galindo, C. L., & Sheldon, S. B. (2011). Levels of leadership: Effects of district and school leaders on the quality of school programs of family and community involvement. *Educational Administration Quarterly*, 47(3), 462–495.

Feliciano, C. (2001). The benefits of biculturalism: Exposure to immigrant culture and dropping out of school among Asian and Latino youths. *Social Science Quarterly*, 82(4), 865–879.

Flaherty, J. (1999). *Coaching: Evoking excellence in others.* Boston, MA: Butterworth-Heinemann.

Flipped Classroom. (n.d.). Knewton infographic. Retrieved June 25, 2015, from http://www.knewton.com/flipped-classroom-2

Folkart, B. A. (1994*). Madeline Hunter: Revolutionary educator.* Retrieved from http://articles.latimes.com/1994–01–29/local/me-16521_1_madeline-hunter

Fullan, M. (2008). *The six secrets of change: What the best leaders do to help their organizations survive and thrive.* San Francisco, CA: Jossey-Bass.

Fullan, M. (2014). *The principal: Three keys to maximizing impact.* San Francisco, CA: Jossey-Bass.

Gibson, W. F. (2003). Books of the year 2003. *The Economist,* December 04, 11–27.

Goldberg, M. (1994). *Prisoners of time.* Report of the National Education Commission on Time and Learning. Retrieved from http://www2.ed.gov/pubs/PrisonersOfTime/index.html

Goodlad, J. (1990). *Teachers for our nation's schools.* San Francisco, CA: Jossey-Bass.

Graham, P., & Ferriter, W. (2010). *Building a professional learning community at work: A guide to the first year.* Bloomington, IN: Solution Tree Press.

Green, R. L. (2013). *Practicing the art of leadership: A problem-based approach to implementing the ISLLC standards.* Boston, MA: Pearson Education.

Gudenius, M. (2010). *Technology integration now: Why and how.* Retrieved from http://www.slideshare.net/kidelectric/technology-integration-now

Gustafson, K. L., & Branch, R. M. (1997). Revisioning models of instructional development. *Educational Technology Research and Development, 45*(3), 73–89.

Guthrie, J. W., & Schuermann, P. J. (2010). *Successful school leadership: Planning, politics, performance, and power.* Boston, MA: Pearson Education.

Haas, L. (2014). *Four reasons going all digital can improve the quality of education.* Retrieved from http://www.facultyfocus.com/articles/teaching-with-technology-articles/four-reasons-going-digital-can-improve-quality-higher-education

Hall, G., & Hord, S. (2001). *Implementing change: Patterns, principals, and potholes.* Boston, MA: Allyn & Bacon.

Hattie, J. (2012). *Visible learning for teachers: Maximizing impact on learning.* New York, NY: Routledge.

Heck, R. J., & Marcoulides, G. A. (1996). School culture and performance: Testing the invariance of an organizational model. *School Effectiveness and School Improvement, 7*(1), 76–96.

Heller, R. (1999). *Learning to lead.* New York: DK Publishing.

Hencley, S. P., McCleary, L. E., & McGrath, J. H. (1970). *The elementary school principalship.* New York, NY: Dodd, Mead.

Henderson, A. T., & Mapp, K. L. (2002). *A new wave of evidence: The impact of school, family, and community connections on student achievement.* Annual synthesis. Austin, TX: National Center for Family and Community Connections with Schools, Southwest Educational Development Laboratory.

Herman, J. L., & Yeh, J. P. (1983). *Some effects of parent involvement in schools. The Urban Review, 15*(1), 11–17.

Homer-Dixon, T. (2006). *The upside of down: Catastrophe, creativity, and the renewal of civilization.* Washington, DC: Island Press.

Hopkins, G. (2012). Principals offer practical, timely "time management" tips. Retrieved from http://www.educationworld.com/a_admin/admin/admin 436_a.shtml

Horng, E. L., Klasik, D., & Loeb, S. (2009). *Principal time-use and school effectiveness.* Stanford, CA: Institute for Research on Education Policy and Practice.

Horng, E. L., Klasik, D., & Loeb, S. (2010). Principal's time use and school effectiveness. American Journal of E*ducation, 116*(4), 491–523.

Hoy, W. K. (1990). Organizational climate and culture: A conceptual analysis of the school workplace. *Journal of Educational and Psychological Consultation, 1*(2), 149–168.

Hoy, W. K., & Miskel, C. G. (2012). *Educational administration: Theory, research, and practice.* Boston, MA: McGraw-Hill.

Ingersoll, R. (2003). *Who controls teachers' work? Power and accountability in America's schools.* Cambridge, MA: Harvard University Press.

Joplin, J. (n.d.). Quotation retrieved May 29, 2015, from http://quotepixel.com/picture/success/janis_joplin/now_that_im_here_where_am_i

Karlin, M. (April 25, 2013). *The importance of technology in education.* Retrieved from http://www.edtechroundup.org/editorials--press/my-personal-technology-vision-statement

Kemerer, F., & Walsh, J. (2000). *The educator's guide to Texas school law.* Austin: University of Texas Press.

Kist, W. (2013). New literacies and the Common Core. *Educational Leadership, 70*(6), 38–43.

Koestenbaum, P. (2002). *Leadership: The inner side of greatness, a philosophy for leaders* (New and rev. ed.). San Francisco, CA: Jossey-Bass.

Kohn, A. (2006). *Beyond discipline: From compliance to community.* Alexandria, VA: ASCD.

Kowalski, T. J. (2013). *The school superintendent: Theory, practice, and cases* (3rd ed.). Los Angeles, CA: Sage.

Kramer, D. A. II, Watson, M., & Hodges, J. (2013). *School climate and the CCRPI.* Atlanta, GA: Department of Education.

Lambert, L. (2003). *Leadership capacity for lasting school improvement.* Alexandria, VA: ASCD.

Lao-Tzu. (n.d.). Quotation retrieved December 14, 2015, from https://www.goodreads.com/author/quotes/262245.Lao_Tzu

Lazear, J. (1992). *Meditations for men who do too much.* New York, NY: Simon & Schuster.

Leachman, M., & Mai, C. (2014, May 20). *Most states funding schools less than before the recession.* Retrieved September 28, 2014, from http://www.cbpp.org/research/most-states-funding-schools-less-than-before-the-recession

Lee, J-S., & Bowen, N. K. (2006). Parent involvement, cultural capital, and the achievement gap among elementary school children. *American Educational Research Journal, 43*(193), 114–123.

Leithwood, K. (1992). The principal's role in teacher development. In M. Fullan & A. Hargreaves (Eds.), *Teacher development and educational change* (pp. 86–103). London, England: Falmer Press.

Leithwood, K., Harris, A., & Hopkins, D. (2008). Seven strong claims about successful school leadership. *School Leadership and Management, 28*(1), 27–42.

Leithwood, K., & Sun, J. (2012). The nature and effects of transformational school leadership: A meta-analytic review of unpublished research. *Educational Administration Quarterly, 48*(3), 387–423.

Lemov, D. (2015). *Teach like a champion 2.0.* San Francisco, CA: Jossey-Bass.

Lencioni, P. M. (2007). *Death by meeting.* San Francisco, CA: Jossey-Bass.

Lewis, D. J., & Weigert, A. (1985). Trust as a social reality. *Social Forces, 63*(4), 967–985.

Lick, D., Clauset, K., & Murphy, C. (2013). *Schools can change: A step-by-step change creation system for building innovative schools and increasing student learning.* Thousand Oaks, CA: Corwin.

Locke, E. A., & Latham, G. P. (1990). *A theory of goal setting and task performance.* Englewood Cliffs, NJ: Prentice-Hall.

Lohr, L. L. (2003). *Creating graphics for learning and performance.* Upper Saddle River, NJ: Prentice-Hall.

Lunenburg, F., & Irby, B. (2006). *The principalship: Vision to action.* Belmont, CA: Thomson/Wadsworth.

MacNeil, A. J., Prater, D. L., & Busch, S. (2009). The effects of school culture and climate on student achievement. *International Journal of Leadership in Education: Theory and Practice 12*(1), 73–84.

Marzano, R. J., Waters, T., & McNulty, B. A. (2005). *School leadership that works: From research to results.* Alexandria, VA: ASCD.

Maslowski, R. (2001). *School culture and school performance: An explorative study into the organizational culture of secondary schools and their effects.* Endschede, The Netherlands: Twente University Press.

Maxwell, K. & Bardwell, M. (2014). *Creating an effective learning environment.* Abilene, TX: Graduate Studies in Education, Abilene Christian University.

McNally, H. J., & Passow, A. H. (1960). *Improving the quality of public school programs. Approaches to curriculum development.* New York, NY: Bureau of Publications, Teachers College, Columbia University.

Metzger, C. (2008). Personal growth in the workplace: Spiritual practices you can use. In P. Houston, A. Blankstein, & R. Cole (Eds.), *Spirituality in educational leadership* (pp. 111–130). Thousand Oaks, CA: Corwin.

Mikoluk, K. (2013). *Time management strategies: 6 ways to stop wasting time.* Retrieved from http://www.udemy.com/blog/time-management-strategies

Millay, E. St. V. (1921). *A few figs from thistles.* New York, NY: Frank Shay.

Miller, S. (n.d.). *50 ways to use Twitter in the classroom.* Retrieved November 30, 2015, from http://www.teachhub.com/50-ways-use-twitter-classroom (Originally published on Samantha Miller's blog)

Mishra, A. K. (1996). Organizational responses to crisis: The centrality of trust. In R. M. Kramer & T. R. Tyler (Eds.), *Trust in organizations* (pp. 261–287). Thousand Oaks, CA: Sage.

MTN Universal. (2014). *Are you wasting your time?* Retrieved from http://www.mtnuniversal.com/are-you-wasting-your-time

Nachin, S. (2015). *Principal work in the digital age.* Unpublished interview, Department of Educational Leadership and Foundations, The University of Texas at El Paso, El Paso, TX.

National Center for Educational Statistics (NCES). (2013). *Characteristics of public and private elementary and secondary school principals in the United States: Results from the 2011–2012 schools and staffing survey.* Washington, DC: US Department of Education.

The National Center for Victims of Crime. (2014). Workplace violence. In *2014 NCVRW resource guide* (pp. 23–29).Washington, DC: Author.

National Policy Board for Educational Administration (NPBEA). (2015). *Professional standards for educational leaders 2015.* Reston, VA: Author.

Nettles, S. M., & Herrington, C. (2007). Revisiting the importance of the direct effects of school leadership on student achievement: The implications for school improvement policy. *Peabody Journal of Education, 82*(4), 724–736.

Noel, A., Stark, P., Redford, J., & Zukerberg, A. (2013). Table 2, *Parent and family involvement in education, from the National Household Education Surveys Program of 2012* (NCES 2008–050). Washington, DC: US Department of Education, National Center for Education Statistics. Retrieved from http://nces.ed.gov/nhes/ and http://www.childtrends.org/?indicators=parental-involvement-in-schools

O'Donovan, E. (2012, April). Technology solution resources. *District Administration.* Retrieved from http://www.districtadministration.com/author/eamonn-odonovan

Osborne, H. (2010). *Hearing, seeing, doing: Are you teaching in ways people learn?* Retrieved from http://www.healthliteracy.com/tips.asp?PageID=3649

Paine, L. S. (1994). Managing for organizational integrity. *Harvard Business Review* 72(2),106–117.

Paroby, D., & White, D. (2010). The role of shared vision and ethics in building an effective learning organization. *Southern Journal of Business and Ethics, 2,* 133–142.

Pascal, N., & Blankstein, A. (2008). Communities committed to learning. In A. M. Blankstein, P. D. Houston, & R. W. Cole (Eds.), *Sustaining professional learning communities* (pp. 168–171). Thousand Oaks, CA: Corwin.

PayScale. (2015a). *Average salary for all K–12 teachers (United States).* Retrieved from http://www.payscale.com/research/US/All_K-12_Teachers/Salary

PayScale. (2015b). *High school principal salary (United States).* Retrieved from http://www.payscale.com/research/US/Job=High_School_Principal/Salary

Perfect Order Professional Organizing. (2014). *Statistics.* Retrieved from http://www.perfectorderonline.com/stats.php

Peters, M. (n.d.). As quoted at quotationspage.com. Retrieved December 12, 2015, from http://www.quotationspage.com/quote/38969.html

Price, K. M., & Nelson, K. L. (2007). *Planning effective instruction.* Belmont, CA: Thomson Wadsworth.

Remen, R. N. (2001). *My grandfather's blessings: Stories of strength, refuge, and belonging.* New York, NY: Riverside Books.

Reven, P. W. (2014). *Sonofamogun: You said what? A principal's guide to techno lingo.* Unpublished interview, Department of Educational Leadership and Foundations, The University of Texas at El Paso, El Paso, TX.

Robertson, P. J. (2006). How principals manage their time. *Principal, 86*(2), 12.

Robinson, V., Lloyd, C., & Rowe, K. (2008). The impact of leadership on student learning outcomes: An analysis of the differential effects of leadership types. *Educational Administration Quarterly, 44*(5), 47–61.

Rogers, W. (n.d.). Quotation retrieved May 15, 2015 from http://www.brainyquote.com/quotes/ww/willrogers104938.html

Ross, D. (2009, July 13). *The role of ethics and integrity in organizations.* Retrieved from http://www.resultsthroughintegrity.com/restultsthroughintegrity/2009/07/the-role-of-ethics-and-integrity-in-organizations.html

Roy, P. (2007). *A tool kit for quality professional development in Arkansas.* Oxford, OH: National Staff Development Council.

Sanborn, M. (2006). *You don't need a title to be a leader: How anyone, anywhere, can make a positive difference.* New York, NY: Crown.

Sanders, M. G. (1999). Schools' programs and progress in the National Network of Partnership Schools. *Journal of Educational Research, 92*(4), 220–229.

Sanders, M. G. (2001). The role of "community" in comprehensive school, family, and community partnership programs. *The Elementary School Journal, 102,* 19–34.

Sanders, M. G., & Lewis, K. C. (2005). Building bridges toward excellence: Community involvement in high schools. *The High School Journal 88*(3), 1–9.

Saxena, S. (2015). *Using technology in education: Does it improve anything?* Retrieved from http://edtechreview.in/news/681-technology-in-education

Schlechty, P. (2005). *Creating great schools: Six critical systems at the heart of educational innovation.* San Francisco, CA: Jossey-Bass.

Schmidt, E., & Cohen, J. (2013). *The new digital age: Reshaping the future of people, nations, and business.* London, England: John Murray.

Schmoker, M. (2006). *Results now: How we can achieve unprecedented improvements in teaching and learning.* Alexandria, VA: ASCD.

Seckan, B. (2013). *Workplace violence in America: Frequency and effects.* Retrieved from http://journalistsresource.org/studies/government/criminal-justice/workplace-violence-america-frequency-effects

Seels, B., & Glasgow, Z. (1998). *Making instructional design decisions.* Upper Saddle River, NJ: Prentice-Hall.

Senge, P., Cambron-McCabe, N., Lucas, T., Smith, B., Dutton, J., & Kleiner, A. (2012). *Schools that learn: A fifth disciple fieldbook for educators, parents, and everyone who cares about education.* New York, NY: Doubleday.

Sergiovanni, T. J. (2007). *Rethinking leadership.* Thousand Oaks, CA: Corwin.

Sharp, W. L., & Walter, J. K. (2012). *The principal as school manager.* Lanham, MD: Rowman & Littlefield Education.

Sheldon, S. B. (2005, August). *Getting families involved with NCLB: Factors affecting schools' enactment of federal policy.* Paper presented to the Sociology of Education section of the No Child Left Behind Conference at the annual meeting of the American Sociological Association, Philadelphia, PA.

Sheldon, S. B., & Epstein, J. L. (2005). School programs of family and community involvement to support children's reading and literacy development across the grades. In J. Flood & P. Anders (Eds.), *Literacy development of students in urban schools: Research and policy* (pp. 107–138). Newark, DE: International Reading Association.

Silver, D., Berckemeyer, J., & Baenen, J. (2015). *Deliberate optimism: Reclaiming the joy in education.* Thousand Oaks, CA: Corwin.

Skiba, R. J., Horner, R. H., Karega Raush, M., May, S. L., & Tobin, T. (2011). Race is not neutral: A national investigation of African American and Latino disproportionality in school discipline. *School Psychology Review, 40*(1), 85–107.

Smith, G., & Smith, G. (2011). *Courage and calling: Embracing your God-given potential* (Rev. and expanded ed.). Downers Grove, IL: IVP Books.

Society for Human Resource Management. (2009). *Workplace flexibility in the 21st century: A survey report.* Retrieved from http://www.shrm.org/research/surveyfindings/articles/documents/09-0464_workplace_flexibility_survey_report_inside_finalonline.pdf

Sorenson, R. D., & Goldsmith, L. M. (2009). *The principal's guide to managing school personnel.* Thousand Oaks, CA: Corwin.

Sorenson, R. D., & Goldsmith, L. M. (2013). *The principal's guide to school budgeting*. Thousand Oaks, CA: Corwin.

Sorenson, R. D., Goldsmith, L. M., Méndez, Z. Y., & Maxwell, K. T. (2011). *The principal's guide to curriculum leadership*. Thousand Oaks, CA: Corwin.

Spillane, J. P., Halverson, R., & Diamond, J. B. (2001). Investigating school leadership practice: A distributed perspective. *Educational Researcher, 30*(3), 23–28.

Spiro, J. (2012). Winning strategy: Set benchmarks of early success. *Journal of Staff Development, 33*(2), 10–16.

Stuart, M. (Director). (1971). *Willy Wonka and the Chocolate Factory* [Motion picture]. United States: Paramount. Quotation retrieved June 18, 2015, from http://www.quotes.net/quote/37173

Sundell, K., Castellano, M., Overman, L. T., & Aliaga, O. A. (2012). The role of school culture in improving student achievement in POS. *Techniques: Connecting Education and Careers, 87*(1), 28–31.

Texas Education Agency. (2014, January 1). *2013–14 Texas academic performance report*. Retrieved from http://tea.texas.gov

Texas Education Agency. (n.d.). *2014–15 school report card.* Retrieved April 5, 2015, from https://rptsvr1.tea.texas.gov/perfreport/src/2015/static/campus/c061902001.pdf

Tolkien, J. (1993). *The fellowship of the ring: Being the first part of the lord of the rings* (2nd ed.). Boston, MA: Houghton Mifflin.

Tomlinson, C. A., & Imbeau, M. B. (2010). *Leading and managing a differentiated classroom*. Alexandria, VA: ASCD.

Tschannen-Moran, M. (2014). *Trust matters: Leadership for successful schools* (2nd ed.). San Francisco, CA: Jossey-Bass.

Tschannen-Moran, M. & Hoy, W. K. (2000). A multidisciplinary analysis of the nature, meaning, and measurement of trust. *Review of Educational Research, 71,* 547–593.

Turnbull, B. J., Haslam, M. B., Arcaira, E. R., Riley, D. L., Sinclair, B., & Coleman, S. (2009). *Evaluation of the school administration manager project*. Washington, DC: Policy Studies Associates for The Wallace Foundation.

Ubben, G. C., Hughes, L. W., & Norris, C. J. (2015). *The principal: Creative leadership for excellence in schools* (8th ed.) Upper Saddle River, NJ: Pearson.

University of New South Wales (UNSW) Sydney. (2014). *Time management and technology*. Retrieved from https://student.unsw.edu.au/time-managment-and-technology

University of Wisconsin–Madison Teaching Academy. (2014). *Asynchronous vs. synchronous communication*. Retrieved October 16, 2014, from https://tle.wisc.edu/blend/facilitate/communicate

US Census Bureau. (2014). *Annual estimates of the resident population by sex, race, and Hispanic origin for the United States, States, and Counties, April 1, 2010 to July 1, 2013*. Retrieved from http://factfinder2.census.gov/faces/tableservices/jsf/pages/productview.xhtml?src=bkmk

Van Voorhis, F. L., & Sheldon, S. B. (2004). Principal's roles in the development of U.S. programs of school, family, and community partnerships. *International Journal of Educational Research, 41*(1), 55–70.

Von Bergen, J. M. (2006). *So many reasons to neaten up, but it's too imposing*. Retrieved from http://www.boston.com/jobs/news/articles/2006/03/12/so_many_reasons_to_neaten_up_but_its_too_imposing

Wang, C.-H. . (2010). Technology leadership among school principals: A technology-coordinator's perspective. *Asian Social Science, 6*(1), 51–54.

West, D. M. (2012). *Digital schools: How technology can transform education.* Washington, DC: Brookings Institution Press.

Whitehead, B. M., Jensen, D. F. N., & Boschee, F. (2013). *Planning for technology.* Thousand Oaks, CA: Corwin.

Wilson, A. (2015). *4 tips to become a better, more effective teacher.* Retrieved from http://www.dailyteachingtools.com/4-tips-to-become-a-better-more-effective-teacher.html

Wincer, S. (Director). (1985). *D.A.R.Y.L.* [Motion picture]. Paramount Pictures.

Wooden, J. (n.d.). As quoted at brainyquote.com. Retrieved May 22, 2015, from http://www.brainyquote.com/quotes/quotes/j/johnwooden384653

Workplace Violence Research Institute. (2012). *Workplace violence: An employer's guide.* Retrieved from http://www.noworkviolence.com/articles/employers_guide.htm

Ybarra, S., & Hollingsworth, J. (2001). Increasing classroom productivity. *Leadership, 31*(1), 34–35.

Yukl, G. A. (2012). *Leaders in organizations.* Upper Saddle River, NJ: Prentice-Hall.

Zarbo, B. (2014). *Time vs. completion: Principals at work.* Unpublished interview, Department of Educational Leadership and Foundations, The University of Texas at El Paso, El Paso, TX.

Zirkel, P. (2015). Ethical codes for school leaders. *UCEA Review, 26*(5).

Index

A SAGE Publishing Company

Helping educators make the greatest impact

CORWIN HAS ONE MISSION: to enhance education through intentional professional learning.

We build long-term relationships with our authors, educators, clients, and associations who partner with us to develop and continuously improve the best evidence-based practices that establish and support lifelong learning.

Solutions you want. Experts you trust. Results you need.

AUTHOR CONSULTING

Author Consulting

On-site professional learning with sustainable results! Let us help you design a professional learning plan to meet the unique needs of your school or district. www.corwin.com/pd

INSTITUTES

Institutes

Corwin Institutes provide collaborative learning experiences that equip your team with tools and action plans ready for immediate implementation. www.corwin.com/institutes

ECOURSES

eCourses

Practical, flexible online professional learning designed to let you go at your own pace. www.corwin.com/ecourses

READ2EARN

Read2Earn

Did you know you can earn graduate credit for reading this book? Find out how: www.corwin.com/read2earn

Contact an account manager at (800) 831-6640 or visit **www.corwin.com** for more information.